M000104882

American Politics
on the
Rocks

The Bizarre Side of American Politics

By
Rich Rubino

Copyright © 2018 by Rich Rubino
All Rights Reserved
Including the right of reproduction in whole and in part in any form without written permission from the author

Library of Congress Control Number: 2018912065

ISBN 978-0-692-15600-1

Dedication

I dedicate this book to two proud political operatives and junkies who are no longer with us.

Thomas J. D'Amore Jr. of Winsted, CT (1941-2014)

Brian Miller of Marblehead, MA (1981-2017)

·

Table of Contents

Introduction

Grab your hat and fasten your safety belt. You are about to embark on a ride which will take you on a whirlwind tour through the bizarre back streets of American politics. If you think politicians are just suit-wearing stiffs, think again. This book of politically humorous and obscure political information will enable you to dazzle your friends at cocktail parties, at the office water cooler, or at the coffee shop. Politics does not have to be a blood sport where people remain entrenched in their views and fight it out like they are on The Jerry Springer Show. As outrageous as it may sound, this book will provide you with ammunition to make a political conversation fun, and allow you to sound smart at the same time. Major topics in this book include the following: unusual presidential facts, feisty first ladies, family feuds, debate debacles, White House rats, diabolical dirty tricks, embarrassing hot microphone moments, inflammatory insults, White House ghosts, and humiliating bloopers.

When political conversations get ugly, my advice is to insert some peculiar political minutia and then divert -- divert--divert. Instead of focusing on the divisive side of politics, why not lighten up the conversation by mentioning the battle with rats (the furry ones, not the corrupt ones) at the White House, or haunted happenings in the White House, or mentioning some of the more famous insults politicians have made to harm their opponents, or the dirty tricks politicians play on one another, or the hilarious bloopers politicians have made. Politicians can be witty, nasty, callous, and just plain nutty. As Mark McKinnon, the executive producer of the hit "Showtime" series "The Circus" opines about this book: "It is terrifically entertaining and fun. And it's non-partisan so you can break it out at parties and not offend anyone." Like the cover of this book, we are all in the same leaky boat together. So why not lighten up?

The information contained in this book was collected from various sources. As I discovered interesting quotations and related stories, I verified them as much as reasonably possible. If something doesn't seem probable, and I can't corroborate it, I discard the story.

In the pages that follow, quotations are in bold font to help the reader differentiate the quotation from the context. When reading the book, please note that the House occupied by the President was originally known as the "Executive Mansion." It wasn't until 1902, that President Theodore Roosevelt officially changed the name to "The White House." Accordingly, I refer to the building as The White House throughout this publication.

Below are some examples of interesting stories contained in this book.

⇒ A losing Presidential candidate who endorsed his party's Presidential nominee by averring: "I'm voting for him and I think you should suffer with me." (Page 71)

⇒ A Presidential nominee who said to a heckler: "Listen, you son of a bitch, why don't you kiss my ass." (Page 149)

⇒ A future President who, while serving as a law professor, lost the completed final exams of his students, gave all students a B+. (Page 31)

⇒ A Presidential candidate who snapped at a critic: "Check back into your cave." (Page 73)

⇒ The President who said of the New Hampshire Presidential Primary: "I think New Hampshire is the only place where a candidate can claim 20 percent is a landslide, 40 percent is a mandate and 60 percent is unanimous." (Page 85)

⇒ A member of the Congressional leadership who pledged to fellow caucus members to be "a nicer son-of-a-bitch." (Page 232)

⇒ A Chicago Cubs Pitcher who got inundated with vitriol by Twitter users who confused him for Presidential debate moderator Lester Holt. (Page 82)

⇒ A Presidential nominee who responded to a voter who told him "Every thinking man will vote for you" with the rejoinder: "Madam, that is not enough. I need a majority." (Page 86)

⇒ The man with the Green Hat who became the U.S. Congress' resident bootlegger during Prohibition. (Page 226)

⇒ A former Presidential nominee who after his third loss in the Presidential sweepstakes conceded: "I'm beginning to think those fellows don't want me in there." (Page 75)

⇒ A Presidential candidate who told a reporter: "There is too much dignity in government now. What we need is some meanness." (Page 85)

⇒ A Presidential nominee who deadpanned: "Wherever I have gone in this country, I have found Americans." (Page 69)

⇒ The President who said of his administration: "Not Since Harry Truman has anybody done so much. That's a long time ago." (Page 25)

⇒ A Governor who introduced President George H.W. Bush as follows: "My friends, it's with a great deal of pride that I present to you a President who wants to cut jobs, who wants to cut taxes and cut jobs, who wants to stop the regulations and cut the jobs." (Page 190)

⇒ The President who "while in office," had to borrow a horse and buggy because he was broke. (Page 7)

⇒ A President who threatened to fire, on the spot, any staff members who referenced the White House ghost, which they referred to as "the thing." (Page 92)

⇒ Two brothers who ran against each other for Governor of Tennessee. (Page 99)

⇒ A former U.S. Secretary of State who averred: "People say, if the Congress were more representative of the people, it would be better. I say the Congress is too damn representative. It's just as stupid as the people are; just as uneducated, just as dumb, just as selfish." (Page 149)

⇒ A former President who called his successor: "A barbarian who could not write a sentence of grammar, and hardly could spell his name." (Page 108)

⇒ A U.S. Senator who called the President: "The coldest blooded, and most selfish ruler beneath the stars today" (Page 133)

⇒ A former President who seconds before an important interview asked the journalist the burning question: "Well did you do any fornicating this weekend?" (Page 5)

⇒ A U.S. Senator who called his opponent "a document-shredding, Constitution-trashing, Commander in Chief-bashing, Congress-thrashing, uniform-shaming, Ayatollah-loving, arms-dealing, criminal-protecting, résumé-enhancing, Noriega-coddling, Social Security-threatening, public school-denigrating, Swiss-banking-law-breaking, letter-faking, self-serving, election-losing, snake-oil salesman who can't tell the difference between the truth and a lie." (Page 135)

⇒ A future Democratic Speaker of the U.S. House of Representatives who said: "I believe in Academic Freedom, but not as it is expounded by kooks, commies and egghead professors." (Page 116)

⇒ The President who exclaimed: "If I don't have a woman for three days I get terrible headaches." (Page 8)

⇒ An incumbent President who asked for "a 'splash' more of coffee" at a New Hampshire truck stop. (Page 165)

⇒ The instance where a single vote literally decided the winner of a Massachusetts Gubernatorial election. (Page 175)

⇒ How the Kennedy's persuaded a man with the same name as an opponent to enter their race for a U.S. House seat, (Page 192)

⇒ How American politics popularized the word "OK." (Page 211)

⇒ A military governor who when asked in Court what his neighbors would think if they knew that he requisitioned $8000 from a local bank without accounting for where the money went, responded; "The people would think I was a fool for not having taken twice as much." (Page 227)

⇒ A politician who turned an insult comparing him to a coon into an indelible trademark. (Page 240)

⇒ A modern politician who prided himself on having "the values of the 17th century, and was "proud of it." (Page 242)

⇒ A porn star that ran for Governor of Nevada pledging to deal with gang violence "so they don't do it anymore." Page 242)

⇒ The fact that some people consider that George Washington should be referred to as the "Eighth President of the United States." (Page 23)

⇒ The President who owned an amphicar: a car that could travel on land and water. (Page 24)

⇒ The President who whacked a swimming rabbit with a canoe paddle to keep it away from his boat. (Page 32)

⇒ The only President who did not get a state funeral after his death. (Page 12)

⇒ The only President who was baptized while in office. (Page 46)

⇒ A failed U.S. Senate candidate who averred: "It was not my first defeat. There was the Rhodes scholarship, the Marshall scholarship, the Harvard Law Review. My life is a tangled wreck of failures." (Page 163)

⇒ The Gillette Stockroom supervisor named John Kennedy who won a race for Treasurer and Receiver General of Massachusetts in part because voters thought he was U.S. Senator John F. Kennedy (D-MA). (Page 180)

⇒ The Presidential candidate who could not remember her college major. (Page 191)

⇒ The time Bill Clinton was roundly booed at a Democratic National Convention (Page 198)

⇒ The cab driver who was stiffed by John F. Kennedy (Page 231)

⇒ The Republican U.S. Senator who loves Gangsta Rap (Page 241)

⇒ The Arkansas Gubernatorial candidate, who was expecting to debate Bill Clinton, but landed up debating Hillary Clinton instead. (Page 225)

Chapter I

The Presidents

The Presidents

Successful Presidential Cover-up: Grover Cleveland suffered from a cancerous tumor at the top of his mouth. Doctors told him that it must be removed to save his life. Cleveland agreed to have it removed only if news of the operation did not get leaked to the press. The nation was enveloped in an economic depression and the President was trepidatious about the potential effect his condition would have on the stock market. Cleveland and the doctors formulated a scheme wherein the President would tell the media that he was taking a four-day fishing excursion on a friend's yacht from New York City to his summer home in Buzzards Bay, Massachusetts. Six doctors performed the surgery on the boat.

Two months after the surgery, E.J. Edwards of *The Philadelphia Press* wrote a story about the operation, telling readers that one of the doctors had leaked the information about the operation to him. Cleveland vociferously denied the story, and it soon died. However, the scheme was revealed in 1917 (24 years later) when one of the doctors, William Keen, admitted the entire story.

Grover Cleveland
Library of Congress

The Beltway is an Island Unto itself: Believing that the Nation's Capital is set apart form the rest of the nation, Andrew Johnson said: **"Washington, D.C. is 12 square miles bordered by reality."**

Andrew Johnson
Library of Congress

Elaborate Practical Joke: Position is Everything: Harry S. Truman enjoyed practical jokes. On one occasion, the President was visiting South America, and the press corps came along. He had heard that one of the reporters had a phobia of getting medical needle shots. The reporter was quite relieved that on this trip yellow fever shots were optional. As a joke, Truman had the White House doctor contact this needle-phobic reporter to tell him that yellow fever shots were now mandatory. The reporter was determined to do the right thing, and upon entering the clinic, noticed the biggest hypodermic needle he had ever seen. Reluctantly, he had pulled down his trousers, and bent over in preparation for the shot. When the doctor came into the examining room, the doctor said: **"This won't hurt a bit."** The reporter immediately realized that the voice on the other end was in fact Truman's. The reporter allegedly replied: **"Mr. President, I do not usually greet Presidents of the United States from this position. "**

Harry S. Truman
Harry S. Truman Library and Museum

A Liquid Breakfast: Part of John Adams' morning ritual was to down a huge glass of hard cider.

John Adams
Library of Congress

The Presidents

Da Bears: In 1925, Calvin Coolidge met Chicago Bears football player Harold Edward "Red" Grange. Coolidge joked: **"I'm glad to know you. I always did like animals."**

Harold Edward "Red" Grange
Library of Congress

Losing his Marbles: Vice President John Tyler was playing a game of marbles with his friends when he found out that President William Henry Harrison had died and he was now the President.

John Tyler
Library of Congress

He Just Had to Go: When Lyndon B. Johnson was in the military during **WWII**, he got on an airplane called the "**Wabash Cannonball**." Before the plane departed, he got off it to make a mad dash for the closest bathroom. His bathroom visit took longer than he had planned. While in the bathroom, the Wabash Cannonball had taken off.

Lyndon B. Johnson
Library of Congress

Recording the President: Benjamin Harrison was the first President to have his voice recorded and saved. It was recorded onto a wax phonograph cylinder in 1889 and lasted just 36 seconds. The President said: **"As President of the United States, I was present at the first Pan-American Congress in Washington D.C. I believe that with God's help, our two countries shall continue to live side-by side in peace and prosperity. Benjamin Harrison."** Interestingly, in 1878, Rutherford B. Hayes made recordings on tinfoil sheets when Thomas Edison, the inventor of the phonograph, visited him at the White House. However, the recordings have been lost.

Benjamin Harrison
Library of Congress

The Presidents

How Long Did it Take LBJ to think of that? Lyndon B. Johnson named his dogs: "Him" and "Her."

Him and Her
Lyndon Baines Johnson Library and Museum

Also Might be a Member of the Flat Earth Society: John Quincy Adams became obsessed with articles published by Captain John Symmes Jr., who was convinced that the earth is hollow and that mole people actually inhabit the middle of the Earth. Adams raised funds for an Arctic Circle expedition whose goal was to drill a whole into the Earth's interior to prove that the Earth was in fact hollow. Luckily for Adams, the expedition never came to fruition. Therefore he was able to keep his reputation in tact.

Captain John Symmes Jr.
Library of Congress

Financially Naïve: William McKinley was naïve about who to trust financially. McKinley had gone bankrupt during the panic of 1893 (a financial depression). He had naively co-signed a $100,000 loan to a friend whose factory went under. McKinley, Governor of Ohio at the time, was convinced that his political career was over due to the fact that it had become common knowledge that he was broke. Surprisingly, his Ohio constituents re-elected him, understanding that the panic of 1893 had financially devastated many Americans. His financial problems did not hinder his Presidential dreams, as he was elected President in 1896.

William McKinley
Library of Congress

Snakes Couldn't Save Presidents Life: William Henry Harrison died of pneumonia. His contemporaries believed that the fact that he chose not to wear a coat during his two-hour plus inaugural address was the reason for the President's death. At the time, they were not aware that pneumonia is a bacterial infection, and is not the result of getting chilled. Medical experts were brought in and used bleeding techniques to rid him of the disease. As he became sicker and sicker, Native American medical techniques were tried. One such technique utilized live snakes. Within a month of taking the Oath of Office, the President was dead.

William Henry Harrison
Library of Congress

The Presidents

Bush Calls Himself a Media Creation: In a 1989 interview with *The Midland Reporter Telegram* (five years before his successful run for Governor of Texas), George W. Bush said: **"You know, I could run for governor and all this but I'm basically a media creation. I've never really done anything. I've worked for my dad. I worked in the oil industry. But that's not the kind of profile you have to have to get elected to public office."**

George W, Bush
Official Photograph as Governor of Texas

Lincoln's Opponent Bursts Into Tears: During a political event, future President Abraham Lincoln made fun of Jesse Thomas, an Illinois politician. Lincoln was ruthless in mocking his opponent's voice, physical characteristics, and gestures, to the point that Thomas burst into tears and ran off. Lincoln later apologized to Thomas.

Abraham Lincoln
Library of Congress

No Truth to the Rumor: When Vice President Gerald R. Ford assumed the Presidency in 1974, after the resignation of Richard M. Nixon, he chose former New York Governor Nelson Rockefeller to assume the Vice Presidency. However, an allegation was gaining traction that Rockefeller had hired henchmen to disrupt the Democratic National Convention. Hamilton Long, a crusader against Communism, leaked the allegations to the Press. This prompted Ford to instruct the FBI to investigate the charges.

Rockefeller was cleared when the accusations against him proved mendacious. Long had claimed that there was a safe deposit box which contained documents proving the accusations. However, the safe deposit box housed no such documents. Ford subsequently announced Rockefeller as his choice for Vice President.

Gerald R. Ford and Nelson Rockefeller Button

Fair Deal: Andrew Jackson was not a heavy drinker. During a physical he told his physician: **"Doctor, I can do anything you think proper, except give up coffee and tobacco."**

Andrew Jackson
Library of Congress

The Presidents

White House an Adult Day Care Center: After President Donald Trump unleashed a series of tweets, U.S. Senator Bob Corker (R-TN) responded: **"It's a shame the White House has become an adult day care center. Someone obviously missed their shift this morning."** Interestingly, Donald Trump seriously considered Corker as a Vice Presidential running mate during the 2016 Presidential Election.

Bob Corker
Official Photograph

Bizarre Small Talk: In 1977, British Journalist David Frost secured the first set of interviews with former President Richard M. Nixon since his resignation in 1974. Literally seconds before the interview started, Nixon asked Frost: **"Well did you do any fornicating this weekend?"** Frost did not answer the question, instead began the program.

TV Guide **Cover From 1977 on the Nixon-Frost Interviews**

President Welcomes Baseball Teams to the White House in the 1860's: The first President to welcome a sports team to the White House was Andrew Johnson. In 1865, he played host to the Brooklyn Atlantics and the Washington Nationals (amateur baseball clubs). In 1869, Johnson's successor, Ulysses S. Grant, welcomed the Cincinnati Red Stockings to the White House. They were the first professional baseball team in the U.S.

Cincinnati Red Stockings
Baseball Hall of Fame

Young Bill Clinton and the Bible: Bill Clinton's parents did not attend Church. As a young boy, Bill Clinton would walk to Church by himself with the Holy Bible in hand.

Bill Clinton as a Boy
William J. Clinton Presidential Museum

The Presidents

Medical Ignorance Costs President His Life: James Garfield was the victim of an assassination attempt. In an effort to locate and remove the bullet, the doctors decided to use the most modern technology, a metal detector invented by Alexander Graham Bell. The doctors had little experience using this new technology and failed to take into consideration that the metal bedsprings would render the results inaccurate. By following the medal-detector's lead, the doctors repeatedly cut in the wrong places. During that time period, sterilization techniques were unheard of. As the doctors poked and prodded into the President's wound, they introduced deadly bacteria that killed him.

Alexander Graham Bell
Library of Congress

That's Big: Theodore Roosevelt drank a gallon of coffee per day. His son, Theodore Roosevelt Jr., joked that the President's Coffee mug was **"more in the nature of a bathtub."**

Theodore Roosevelt Jr.
Official Photograph

Presidential Duel to the Death: Andrew Jackson is the only President known to have killed someone. In 1806, Jackson killed attorney Charles Dickenson in a duel after Dickinson insulted his wife, Rachel Jackson.

Andrew Jackson Shoots Charles Dickenson
Library of Congress

"Give me a 'W:'" During his senior year at Philips Academy in Andover, Massachusetts, George W. Bush was the **"Head Cheerleader."**

George W. Bush as Head Cheerleader
Philips Academy Yearbook, 1964

The Presidents

Humble Millard Fillmore: Millard Fillmore was contacted by the University of Oxford in England to discuss giving him an honorary degree. Fillmore humbly declined. Feeling unworthy of the honor, Fillmore wrote: **"I have neither literary nor scientific attainment."**

Millard Fillmore
Library of Congress

Presidential Pranks: Calvin Coolidge, a.k.a. Silent Cal, had a very childlike sense of humor in that he liked to play hide-and-seek. One of his more childish pranks was when he buzzed the Secret Service and then hid behind the drapes. His goal was to make the Secret Service believe that he had been kidnapped. His prank proved to be a failure as his feet were sticking out from the bottom of the curtain.

Calvin Coolidge
Library of Congress

Predecessor has Garfield's Back: Unlike most Presidents, James Garfield was not a wealthy man. At the time, the President was expected to pay out of his own pocket the operating costs of the White House and for lavish dinner parties. Since so much of the President's salary went to this, the President could not afford to purchase a horse and buggy. Luckily for Garfield, his predecessor, Rutherford B. Hayes, was able to lend him a carriage so he could get around town.

James Garfield
Library of Congress

No Job is too Small for this Former President: John Quincy Adams was the only former President to win a seat in the U.S. House of Representatives. He served the Twelfth Congressional District of Massachusetts from 1831-1848. Unfortunately, Adams suffered a cerebral hemorrhage on the House Floor during a debate honoring veterans of the Mexican-American War. He died two days later.

John Quincy Adams on his Death Bed
Library of Congress

The Presidents

Bad Way to say Goodbye: George Washington died at 67, likely due to the unusual medical treatment he received rather than from the throat infection that he was suffering from. His death in 1799 was well before the discovery of antibiotics. In an effort to cure him, doctors used a breathing technique and removed 32 ounces of his blood, made him gargle with vinegar and forced him to drink a gooey concoction made of cider vinegar, molasses's, and butter. It appears that the cure was a lot worse than the disease.

George Washington
Library of Congress

Truman Gets Testy: At the end of a 1948 press conference, a reporter asked Harry S. Truman: **"Is there anything we have overlooked, Mr. President?"** Truman responded: **"I don't believe there is. If I could think of any, why would I give it to you."**

Harry S. Truman at a Press Conference
Harry S. Truman Library and Museum

Andrew Johnson Dodged the Bullet: The plot to assassinate Abraham Lincoln also included a plot to kill Vice President Andrew Johnson. However, his would-be assassin, George Atzerotz, changed his mind. Consequently, Instead of being buried, Johnson was sworn in as President in 1865.

Andrew Johnson
Photograph by Vannerson

Girls, Girls, Girls: John F. Kennedy, known for his sexual prowess, once confided to British Prime Minister Harold Macmillan: **"If I don't have a woman for three days, I get terrible headaches."**

John F. Kennedy (L), Harold Macmillan (R)
John F. Kennedy Presidential Library and Museum

The Presidents

Guerilla Tactics and Presidential Nudity: John Quincy Adams was a tough man to pin down for an interview. Ann Royall, a journalist, became cognizant of the fact that the President swam nude every morning in the Potomac River promptly at 5:00 A.M. Royall hid in the bushes before at that time and then came out after Adams was in the water. She grabbed Adam's clothes off of a rock near the Potomac River and made it clear to him that the only way he would win his clothing back was if she would be allowed to interview him. Adams had few options and granted Royall an interview. She has the distinction of being the first female in history to interview a U.S. President.

Ann Royall
Library of Congress

"Ike" Will Do: Dwight D. Eisenhower earned three nicknames. The first was **"Duckpin."** That nickname came from the fact that he loved duckpin bowling, a version of 10-pin bowling. The second was **"The Kansas Cyclone"** because of his skills as a running back on the West Point football team. The third was **"Ike"** for Eisenhower.

Dwight D. Eisenhower
Harry S. Truman Presidential Library and Museum

Keeping it On the Down-low: Franklin D. Roosevelt, who suffered from polio, was determined to keep the fact that he was wheelchair-bound from his constituents. The media was discreet, and rarely mentioned his condition. The Secret Service would rip the film out of any photographer's camera who was attempting to snap a picture of the President while in his wheelchair.

Rare Photograph of Franklin D. Roosevelt in a Wheelchair, with Daughter Ruthie and Dog Falla.
Franklin D. Roosevelt Presidential Library and Museum

Fooling People: During an address to the Gridiron Club in 2001, George W. Bush revealed advice given to him by former Democratic National Committee Chairman Robert Strauss: **"You can fool some of the people all of the time, and those are the ones you need to concentrate on."**

Robert Strauss
U.S. Government Photograph

The Presidents

Waterworks: As a master politician, Lyndon B. Johnson, knew that a President must be an ally of FBI Director J. Edgar Hoover because of his potential to destroy adversaries. Johnson said: **"I would rather have him inside the tent pissing out than outside the tent pissing in."**

J. Edgar Hoover
Lyndon Baines Johnson Library and Museum

Control Freak: Thomas Jefferson was such a control freak that he left exact instructions as to what should be written on his tombstone: **"Here was buried Thomas Jefferson, author of the Declaration of Independence, of the statute of Virginia for Religious Freedom and Father of the University of Virginia."** Shockingly, it appears that he was not proud of the fact that he served for two terms as President.

Thomas Jefferson's Grave at Monticello
Library of Congress

Did Somebody Say Beer? Grover Cleveland had a beer belly. On a typical day he ingested 4-8 tankards, definitely not good for his waistline.

Grover Cleveland
Library of Congress

Strange Gift: The President of Azerbaijan, Heyder Aliyev, wanted to give a great gift to Bill and Hilary Clinton, so he employed a popular carpet-portrait artist to have his and her images made into a beautiful rug. Twelve female carpet weavers worked for ten weeks making the carpet. The President of Azerbaijan proudly presented this handmade carpet to the Clintons' in 1997.

Hayder Aliyev (L), Bill Clinton (R)
International Online Library

The Presidents

Consummate Campaigner: Lyndon B. Johnson was fond of telling a story he heard in his childhood about a man who was about to suffer a public hanging. **"The sheriff told the condemned man that under the state law he would be allowed five minutes to choose whatever words he cared to speak as his last act. The prisoner promptly responded and said, 'Mr. Sheriff, I haven't got anything to say, so just get on and get it over with.' But a man way back in the audience jumped up and said, 'Well, if he doesn't want those five minutes, Sheriff, I'd like to have them. I'm a candidate for Congress.'"**

Lyndon B. Johnson
Lyndon Baines Johnson Library and Museum

Divine Intervention? When George Washington took the Oath of Office in 1789, he put his hand on the Holy Bible. By chance, it opened to Genesis. Presidents Warren G. Harding, Dwight D. Eisenhower, Jimmy Carter, and George H.W. Bush swore on the same Bible at their Inaugurations.

First Inauguration of George Washington
Encyclopedia Britannica

True Wisdom: Martin Van Buren believed in the value of hard work, and once averred: **"It is easier to do a job right, than to explain why you didn't."**

Martin Van Buren
Library of Congress

The First Case of Presidential Telephobia? Calvin Coolidge refused to use the telephone as President. He said: **"If you don't say anything, you won't be called on to repeat it."**

Calvin Coolidge Reluctantly Tries Using the Telephone
Library of Congress

11

The Presidents

Leaking is Not New: In 1870, U.S. Attorney General Ebenezer R. Hoar of Massachusetts was asked by President Ulysses S. Grant to resign his Cabinet position. Grant told Hoar that Southern Senators were lobbying him to put a Southerner in the Cabinet and also protested that he had too many Massachusetts' natives in his Cabinet. However, before Grant could publically announce the resignation, Grant's personal secretary leaked the information to the media, and in the process blindsided Grant's staff and Cabinet.

Ebenezer R. Hoar
Library of Congress

Not a Dramatic Ending: Millard Fillmore died after suffering a stroke in his beloved Buffalo, New York in 1874. These last words were spoken to his physician and were about the soup he was eating: **"The nourishment is palatable."**

Millard Fillmore
Beinecke Rare Books and Manuscripts Library Yale University

Ambidextrous President: James Garfield amused friends by writing with both hands. He could write in Greek with one hand while writing in Latin with the other hand.

James Garfield
Library of Congress

Former President Actively Supported the Confederacy: Former President John Tyler, a steadfast Confederate supporter, was elected to the House of Representatives of the Confederate Congress during the Civil War, but died before he could assume the office. Because of his fidelity to the Confederacy, he was the only President not to be officially mourned in the U.S.

John Tyler
Library of Congress

The Presidents

Close Quarters: While serving as a Civil War General, Ulysses S. Grant was extremely shy about showering with his troops. There was no privacy at the camps during the war and all of the men bathed in public. They dumped buckets of water on one another to rinse off the soap. Grant was sensitive about being overweight, and would hide in his tent so that he could bath in seclusion.

Ulysses S. Grant
Library of Congress

Conquering Reading Problems: Woodrow Wilson had a tough time learning to read, and didn't conquer the art of reading until he was 11 years old. He then went on to earn a Ph.D. in Political Science from Johns Hopkins University.

Woodrow Wilson
Official Photograph as Governor of New Jersey

A Bright Idea: Chester A. Arthur would often doze off in the middle of meetings or conversations. Those close to him described him as being lazy. In reality, he was hiding the fact that he suffered from Bight's Disease. Its symptoms are high blood pressure and extreme tiredness.

Chester A. Arthur
Library of Congress

Grasshoppers in His Ears: Harry S. Truman said of one of his successors, John F. Kennedy: **"He had his ear so close to the ground that it was full of grasshoppers."**

John F. Kennedy (L), Harry S. Truman (R)
Harry S. Truman Library and Museum

13

The Presidents

A Great Gift: Benjamin Franklin and George Washington had become close friends while working on the Declaration of Independence and the U.S. Constitution. When Franklin was writing out his will, he left a cherished walking stick to George Washington. In the will he wrote: **"My fine crab tree walking stick, with a gold head curiously wrought in the form of the cap of liberty, I give to my friend, and the friend of mankind, George Washington."**

Benjamin Franklin
Library of Congress

Big Wheel: Andrew Jackson was given a gift of a 1,400-pound wheel of cheddar cheese. As the cheese aged, the smell became more than anyone could bear. Jackson, along with his family and staff, nibbled on a bit of it, but were perplexed on what to do with the rest of it. As a man who advertised himself as a **"tribune of the people,"** Jackson let the public into the White House so they could chat with him and eat from the block of cheese. The public attacked the wheel of cheese like locust, the cheese and its stench finally left the White House.

Andrew Jackson
Library of Congress

Acing Yale Without even Showing Up: In 1972, Bill Clinton and his girlfriend Hillary Rodham, both law students at Yale University, spent a semester in Texas working on George McGovern's failed Presidential campaign. The couple never attended class, came in to take the final exams, and both aced them.

Bill and Hillary Clinton as Yale Students
Clinton Family Collection

The Presidential Alligator: John Quincy Adams was the proud owner of a full-grown alligator. The French military officer Marquis de Lafayette gave Adams this unusual pet. The alligator took up residence in a claw-footed bathtub in the White House. Adams enjoyed introducing his guests to the unusual occupant living in the bathtub.

Alligator
Photograph by Tatarus

14

The Presidents

Poker Face: Richard M. Nixon donated the $6,000 he won playing poker with his Navy buddies to his first Congressional campaign in 1946. As a Navy Ensign, Nixon was invited to a small dinner gathering with acclaimed aviator Charles Lindbergh. Instead, Nixon attended a poker game. Nixon regretting the move saying in 1983: **"Believe it or not, I turned it down because I was the host of a poker game that night. I think back to turning down a chance to sit down with Lindbergh to have a poker game. I can't imagine it happening. Years later, I was glad that he could be the guest at the White House when I was President."**

Punchcard for Richard M. Nixon for Congress in 1946

President Suffers from Fear of Insanity: Rutherford B. Hayes suffered from lyssophobia, the fear of going insane.

Rutherford B. Hayes
Library of Congress

A President who Actually Reads: Millard Fillmore, an avid reader, risked his life battling a fire that engulfed the Library of Congress. He subsequently signed legislation to appropriate money to supplant all the books that had vanished in the fire.

Millard Fillmore
Library of Congress

Weird Hobby Horse: Thomas Jefferson had a weird hobby. He spent hundreds of hours at the White House attempting to assemble the bones of a mastodon (woolly mammoth) into a complete skeleton.

Thomas Jefferson
Library of Congress

The Presidents

Only Fresca: Lyndon B. Johnson enjoyed drinking Fresca so much that he actually had a Fresca-only soda fountain installed in the Oval Office. The beverage was introduced in 1966 during his Presidency.

Lyndon B. Johnson
Lyndon Baines Johnson Library and Museum

Bid to Get Former President Back in Office: Ulysses S. Grant was the first former two-term President who sought to serve a third term. Though he never declared himself a candidate, he pushed his surrogates to advance his name as a candidate in 1880 for the Republican Presidential nomination. Grant lost the nomination to U.S. Representative James Garfield (R-OH).

Ulysses S, Grant
Library of Congress

Burying the Hatchet, Big Time: As an Ex-President, Bill Clinton struck up an unlikely friendship with Christopher S. Ruddy, a former vociferous critic of Mr. Clinton. Ruddy is now CEO of conservative *NewsMax Media*. In 1994, Ruddy published *The Strange Death of Vincent Foster: An Investigation* where he linked Mr. Clinton to the death of Deputy White House Counsel and lifetime Clinton friend, Vincent Foster. Despite the publication of this book, Clinton and Ruddy became allies in the fight against poverty. Mr. Ruddy now says: **"I am a great admirer of President Clinton. He has not only redefined the post-presidency, but has served as an exemplary goodwill ambassador for our country throughout the whole world. His efforts transcend politics and deserve support."**

Bill Clinton
William J. Clinton Presidential Library and Museum

Grammar Ain't Everything: After the 1923 death of Warren G. Harding, the esteemed poet Edward Estlin Cummings commented: **"The only man, woman, or child who ever wrote a simple declarative sentence with seven grammatical errors is dead."**

Edward Estlin Cummings
Library of Congress

The Presidents

Betting the White House China: Inveterate poker player Warren G. Harding once bet the White House China on a game and lost it. He often gambled with his Cabinet, earning them the moniker: **"The Poker Cabinet."**

Warren G. Harding
Library of Congress

Did Someone Say 'Beer'": In his 1932 Presidential campaign, Franklin D. Roosevelt supported ending the Prohibition of Alcohol. In 1933, the House had still not acted, though it had popular support, which prompted members to chant: **"Vote Vote, We Want Beer."** Soon enough the House, then the Senate, passed legislation allowing for the sale of alcohol. The 21st amendment to the U.S. Constitution came later, which officially ended prohibition. This occurred during Roosevelt's presidency.

Franklin D. Roosevelt
Franklin D. Roosevelt Presidential
Library and Museum

When Ruth Met Bush: In 1948, George H.W. Bush was captain of the Yale University Baseball team. As captain, he officially accepted a donation from Baseball Hall of Famer Babe Ruth. Ruth donated the manuscript of his autobiography, *The Babe Ruth Story*, to the Yale University Library.

Babe Ruth with George H. W. Bush
National Archives and Records Administration

Getting Stoned in The White House: Musician Willie Nelson was invited by Jimmy Carter to spend the night after a concert at the White House. As written in *Willie: An Autobiography*, to mellow out, Nelson went up onto the White House roof and lit up a marijuana joint. Carter, who became a close friend of Nelson, later opined to *Rolling Stone*: **"all the good things I did as President, all the mistakes I made - you can blame half of that on Willie."**

Willie Nelson
Photograph by Robbie Work

The Presidents

Putting it Mildly: U.S. Senator Orrin Hatch (R-UT) observed that the Democrats are **"crazy to not try and deal with President Donald Trump directly. He was a Dem. It doesn't take brains to realize that he'd be open."**

Orrin Hatch
Official Photograph

Sleep Apnea: William Howard Taft suffered from obesity and is believed to also have suffered from sleep apnea. His sleep disturbances at night made it difficult for him to stay awake during the day. At times he actually fell asleep during meetings. He found that he was able to get a few z's if he went to a screen porch on the top of the White House where he could sleep in a chair.

William Howard Taft
Library of Congress

The Pinnacle of Pomposity: Pope Paul VI was the first Pope to visit America while serving as the Pontiff. He visited New York City and met with President Lyndon B. Johnson at the Waldorf Astoria Hotel, addressed the United Nations, and visited Yankee Stadium. Johnson and the Pontiff exchanged gifts. The Pope gave Johnson a Renaissance era painting of the nativity scene. Johnson gave the Pope a five-inch bust of himself.

Lyndon B. Johnson With Pope Paul VI
Lyndon Baines Johnson Library and Museum

It's Blue Whiskey Van: Martin Van Buren earned the nickname **"Blue Whisky Van."** His diet was comprised of rich fatty foods, washed down with glasses of whiskey. His unhealthy diet resulted in the President suffering from heart problems and gout in later life.

Martin Van Buren
Harvard University Library

The Presidents

President Still Bashing Vanquished Opponent: In 2017, President Donald Trump tweeted: **"I was recently asked if Crooked Hillary (Clinton) is going to run in 2020? My answer was 'I hope so.'"**

Donald Trump
Official Photograph

Dodging the Draft: Grover Cleveland hired a substitute to serve for him after being drafted for the Civil War. This practice was legal at the time.

Grover Cleveland
Portrait by Andres Zorn

Can't Balance His Own Budget: Thomas Jefferson came from a patrician pedigree, but was a horrible money manager. He took out huge loans on his Monticello estate, as his tobacco farming was not always lucrative. In an effort to pay off his debts, he formulated a plot to raffle off Monticello in a huge lottery. The scheme never came to fruition, and he died deeply in debt.

Monticello
Photograph by Martin Falbisoner

Champaign Taste on a Beer Budget: Chester A. Arthur, a.k.a. "Elegant Arthur" was determined to redecorate the White House, making it the most fashionable building in the land. His goal was to purchase new furniture. His problem was that he did not have the money. In order to raise cash, he sold twenty-four wagonloads full of historical items, which included a hat worn by John Quincy Adams.

Chester A. Arthur
Library of Congress

The Presidents

Coach Eisenhower: After graduating from West Point, Dwight D. Eisenhower coached the Peacock Military Academy team. He made $150 for the job. A year later, he coached the St. Louis University team. (The school is now called St. Mary's.)

Dwight D. Eisenhower on the Football Field
National Archives

The Slugger and the President: In 1930, New York Yankees Right Fielder Babe Ruth saw his salary increased from $70,000 to $75,000. This was during the Great Depression. Ruth now made more money than President Herbert Hoover. Many Americans were blaming the President for the Great Depression. When asked about the situation, Ruth deadpanned: **"What the hell has Hoover got to do with it. Besides, I had a better year than he did."**

Babe Ruth (L), Herbert Hoover (R)
Herbert Hoover Presidential
Library and Museum

LBJ, Jesus Christ, and the Press: Lyndon B. Johnson often mused: **"If one morning I walked on top of the water across the Potomac River, the headline that afternoon would read 'President Can't Swim.'"**

Lyndon B. Johnson
Lyndon Baines Johnson Library and Museum

The Silent Man Dies: When the news was reported that former President Calvin Coolidge ("Silent Cal") had died, satirist Dorothy Parker, noting Coolidge's silent nature, quipped: **"How do they know?"**

Dorothy Parker
Library of Congress

20

The Presidents

Embargoed Christmas Tree: Theodore Roosevelt did not believe that trees should be cut down for Christmas decorations and then discarded. Roosevelt would hold a children's party at the White House each year, including Santa Claus-shaped ice-cream cones, but no tree. Archie Roosevelt, one of the President's sons somehow managed to sneak a small Christmas tree into the White House, hiding it in an upstairs room.

Theodore Roosevelt
Library of Congress

No Butter, No Sugar, No Sweets: Harry S. Truman was determined to shed pounds while he was in the White House. He kept a diet diary and wrote down everything he ate. In a 1952 diary entry, he wrote of one particular day: **"No butter, no sugar, no sweets."**

Harry S. Truman Eating Cake
Harry S. Truman Presidential Library and Museum

Presidential Stamps Collector: Franklin D. Roosevelt must have been a very patient man. He was a stamp collector his entire life, and managed to collect about 1.2 million stamps. He enjoyed looking at stamps with historical themes. However, his collection was extremely disorganized. He did manage to find time to organize the collection when he was wheelchair-bound from polio later on in his life. After Roosevelt died in 1945, the stamp collection was sold for $228,000.

Franklin D. Roosevelt with his Stamps
FDR Presidential Library and Museum

Cowboy Cal: Strangely, Calvin Coolidge grew up in Vermont, not on the frontier, but had a strange fascination with cowboys. While in the White House, he had a mechanical horse installed so that he could use it to entertain his friends.

Calvin Coolidge
Library of Congress

21

The Presidents

Weird living Gift: In 1990, George H.W. Bush received a flesh-eating Komodo Dragon as a gift of friendship from the Indonesian government. He donated this soft cuddly man-eating pet to the Cincinnati Zoo, where it grew to 9 feet and weighed 300 pounds. The Komodo Dragon is a fierce predator that can bring prey down twice its size, including animals as big as a water buffalo.

Komodo Dragon
Photograph by Dezidor

Where Did The Idea Come From: Barack Obama got one of the oddest house warming presents from Mahmud Abbas, the President of the Palestinian Authority. According to the Federal Registry, he received a $75 bottle of olive oil. Perhaps he should have sprung for an entire case.

Mahmud Abbas
Kremlin Photograph

Remembering Lincoln: Following the assassination of Abraham Lincoln, an historic two-week train procession covering over 1,600 miles followed as a way to honor the President. The train that carried his remains visited a hundred and eighty cities, making its last stop in Springfield, IL. It is estimated that 1/3 of the U.S population was involved in commemorating the former President. In order to keep the body fresh, considering that the casket was unsealed, the body had to be re-embalmed before each train stop, to slow down the decaying process. With the exception of New York City, the funeral was segregated. Two hundred African-Americans participated at the end of the procession. The following day the *New York Times* reported that the crowd was moved by the African-Americans participation and: **"was the only portion of the procession which was received with any demonstration of applause."**

Train Procession for Abraham Lincoln
Library of Congress

The Nickname Game: Benjamin Harrison had two nicknames: **"The Human Iceberg"** because his personality was cold and unapproachable, and **"Kid Gloves Harrison"** because he wore gloves to cover up a skin condition on his hands.

Benjamin Harrison
Library of Congress

The Presidents

Fake News? After a series of Editorials critical of his administration, John F. Kennedy canceled the White House subscription to *The New York Herald Tribune*. However, an embargoed copy slipped into the White House and was used in a puppy box. The President joked: **"It's finally found its proper use."**

John F. Kennedy
Harry S. Truman Presidential Library and Museum

Truman Never Said It: Although conventional belief is that the quote: **"If you want a friend in Washington, get a dog"** was first said by Harry S. Truman, in reality there is no record of him making such a statement. Instead, the quote comes from the play: **"Give 'em Hell, Harry!"** (a play about Truman.)

Harry S. Truman
Harry S. Truman Presidential Library and Museum

The Real First President? President George Washington is credited with being the First President of the United States. However, prior to his inauguration in 1781, when the U.S. was governed by the *Articles of Confederation and Perpetual Union*, John Hanson Jr. was elected by the Continental Congress as: "First President of the United States in Congress Assembled." He resigned after one year and had seven successors. George Washington wrote to President Hanson congratulating him on winning "the most important seat in the United States." Some argue that Washington should be referred to the "Eighth" President of the United States.

John Hanson Jr.
Library of Congress

John Hanson Jr.'s Lasting Legacy: John Hanson Jr., the first President of the Congress Assembled, approved the Great Seal of the United States in 1782.

Official Presidential Seal

The Presidents

Oh My God! Lyndon B. Johnson had a twisted sense of humor. He would often retreat to his Texas ranch for rest and relaxation during his Presidency. He had purchased an amphicar that was a regular blue convertible that could travel on land and in the water. While he was on vacation, he loved to invite friends for a ride around his property in his blue convertible. He would then head toward the lake from a steep hill, and would scream: **"the breaks don't work!"** The passenger would scream as the car went faster, believing that they would die as the car plunged into the lake. The President would have a serious look as the car would splash into the water. Then he would laugh hysterically as the car began operating as a boat and cruising across the lake. Few people even knew these cars existed.

Lyndon B. Johnson Driving Visitors in his amphicar
Lyndon Baines Johnson Library and Museum

You can only Wear One at a Time: Ronald Reagan received 372 belt buckles as gifts while he was in office.

Belt Buckle with Ronald Reagan Picture

Wicked Overachiever: Andrew Johnson was a wicked overachiever. He never attended school, taught himself how to read, escaped being an indentured servant to a tailor, owned his own tailor shop by the time he was 19, and was the Mayor of Greenville, TN when he was just 22. He went on to serve in the Tennessee House of Representative, then in the State Senate, before serving in the U.S. House, then serving in the U.S. Senate, then serving as Vice President, then serving as President of the United States.

Andrew Johnson
Library of Congress

Arresting the President: While serving as President, Franklin Pierce was arrested. He was accused of running over a woman with his horse. Luckily for him, the charges were dropped because of lack of evidence and witnesses to incident.

Franklin Pierce on his Horse
Waterman Lilly Ormsby

The Presidents

Say What? During a 2007 statement at the White House, George W. Bush exclaimed: **"Our enemies are innovative and resourceful, and so are we. They never stop thinking about new ways to harm our country and our people, and neither do we."**

George W. Bush
Photograph by Eric Draper

Lights, Camera, Action: Outgoing President Grover Cleveland and incoming President William McKinley were the first Presidents to be filmed. They were filmed at McKinley's inauguration in 1897.

William McKinley (C) Takes 1896 Oath of Office and Grover Cleveland (R) Looks on
The Life of William McKinley by Oscar King Dacis
(1901)

Braggadocios: During an interview recapping his first 100 days in office, Donald Trump told *The Washington Examine*r: **"Not Since Harry Truman has anybody done so much. That's a long time ago."**

Donald Trump
Official Photograph

The President as a Glorified PR Man: In a 1947 letter written to his sister Mary Jane Truman, Harry S. Truman wrote: **"The President is a glorified public relations man who spends his time flattering, kissing, and kicking people to get them to do what they are suppose to do anyway."**

Harry S. Truman with Sister Mary Jane Truman
Harry S. Truman Presidential Library and Museum

The Presidents

No "W:" As a prank, in 2001, staffers of the outgoing administration of Bill Clinton removed the W's from the computer keyboards in an effort to confound and frustrate the incoming George W. Administration. It cost the White House almost $5,000 to replace the keyboards with keyboards that contained all the letters.

George W. Bush on Inauguration Day, 2001
Photograph by TSgt. Lou Briscese, USAF

Goldman Government: At the 2017 Gridiron Dinner, U.S. House Minority Leader Nancy Pelosi (D-CA) quipped about Donald Trump: **"The President has appointed so many people from Goldman Sachs to high positions that there's nobody left there to listen to Hillary's speeches."**

Donald Trump and Nancy Pelosi
Photograph by U.S. Air force Staff Sgt. Martinique Santos

I'll Buy One of Everything: After serving two terms in the White House, Ulysses S. Grant and his wife went on a wild spending spree, traveling throughout the globe. When they got back, they were looking for a "get rich scheme. They invested one hundred thousand dollars in an investment-banking firm called "Grant and Ward." It turned out Grant was swindled out of his money, as were many veterans and other investors. Grant was out of money. Luckily for Grant, his best friend was Mark Twain, and together they wrote the former President's memoirs. The book became a huge success, bringing in $450,000 in royalties. He died shortly after publication, leaving his wife financially well off.

Ulysses S. Grant Writing his Memoirs
Library of Congress

Holding his Liquor: James Buchanan was a man who could definitely hold his liquor. He could drink several bottles of alcohol while socializing at the White House and would remain sober and congenial. It did not appear that he was an alcoholic, but just somebody who liked to drink.

James Buchanan
Library of Congress

The Presidents

Home-Schooled President: When Theodore Roosevelt was a child, he suffered from severe Asthma, a condition that could have cost him his life. He was subjected to medical cures that range from breathing crisp coastal air to inhaling the smoke from cigars. Due to the severity of his Asthma, he spent much of his time secluded inside his family home with no friends to play with. His family hired private tutors so that Theodore could receive a quality home school education. As his health improved, his family took him to Europe and the Middle East.

Theodore Roosevelt at age 11
U.S. Office of Personnel Management

Lyndon on Jack: Assessing his presidency and that of his predecessor, John F. Kennedy, Lyndon B. Johnson observed: **"Jack was out kissing babies, while I was out passing bills, someone had to tend the store."**

Lyndon B. Johnson (L), John F. Kennedy (R)
Lyndon Baines Presidential Library and Museum

Just Let Him Rest in Piece: Zackary Taylor died from a stomach-related illness. His wife Margaret demanded that his body not be embalmed. This was a very strange request and soon rumors were circulating around Washington D.C. Many people believed that Margaret had poisoned her husband, and that she believed that if he was not embalmed and entered into the ground quickly, that she would get away with his murder because his body would decompose quickly. Taylor's body was finally exhumed in 1991 and a small amount of genetic material was removed. The DNA evidence proved that Margaret was not a murderer and that Taylor had not been poisoned.

Zackary Taylor
Library of Congress

Richard the Lionheart: Richard M. Nixon was named for King Richard I, a.k.a. Richard the Lionheart, the King of England from 1189 to 1199. Three of his four brothers were also named after English Kings.

Effigy of Richard the Lionheart
Photograph by Adam Bishop

The Presidents

A Big Appetite: William Howard Taft, who weighed in at 335 pounds during his Presidency, eat enormous meals. He enjoyed eating a large steak with every meal with large amounts of melted butter on top.

William Howard Taft
Library of Congress

Ouch: George Washington suffered from chronic pain. His teeth and gums were constantly infected and he took the opiate Laudanum so that he could function. This narcotic was legal at the time and was considered an effective treatment.

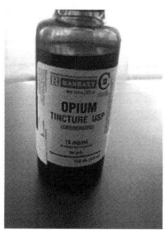

Opiate Laudanum
Photograph by Djm55

Oh Nuts: In a 1964 Presidential tape-recording of Lyndon B. Johnson talking to his tailor, The President said: **"The crotch, down where your nuts hang, is always a little too tight."**

Lyndon B. Johnson
Lyndon Baines Johnson Library and Museum

Rodents at White House: While other Presidents tried to rid the White House of rodents, Andrew Johnson enjoyed the critters so much that he kept white mice as pets.

Andrew Johnson
Library of Congress

The Presidents

The Limits of Presidential Power: Questioning those who believed Lyndon B. Johnson was nearly omnipotent, Lyndon B. Johnson shot back: **"Power, the only power I've got is nuclear, and I can't even use that."**

Lyndon B. Johnson with Dog Yuki
Lyndon Baines Johnson Library and Museum

Killer Trees? In 1981, President Ronald Reagan said: **"Trees cause more pollution than automobiles do."** He was referring to the fact that in hot weather, trees release organic hydrocarbons, which are linked to smog. After this statement, Presidential Press Secretary James Brady joked to Reporters: **"Watch out for the killer trees."**

Ronald Reagan
Official Portrait

Hey! What's That You're Smoking? In 1978, President Jimmy Carter visited the battleground state of North Carolina. His Secretary of Health, Education, and Welfare, Joe Califano, was an outspoken critic of tobacco, a major cash crop in that state. Carter told his audience: **"I had planned today to bring Joseph Califano with me, but he decided not to come. He discovered that not only is North Carolina the number-one tobacco-producing state, but that you produce more bricks in the nation as well. Joe did encourage me to come though. He said it was time for the White House staff to start smoking something regular."**

Joseph Califano
Lyndon Baines Library and Museum

Calvin Coolidge: A Man of Few Words: When Vice President Calvin Coolidge ("Silent Cal") visited Channing Cox (his successor as Governor of Massachusetts), Cox asked for advice. Cox complained that people talked to him all day and that he could not get out of his office until late at night. Coolidge gave the following reason for Cox's time management problem when people speak to him: **"You talk back."**

Channing Cox
Official Photograph

The Presidents

A Most Unusual Gift from the Sultan: Martin Van Buren received a gift of two tiger cubs from the Sultan of Oman. They were sent to a zoo.

Martin Van Buren
Gubernatorial Portrait by Daniel Huntington

Rutherford B. Hayes, National Hero in Paraguay: Rutherford B. Hayes is a national hero in Paraguay for his role in arbitrating a land dispute between Paraguay and Argentina. Hayes allowed Paraguay to keep a large swath of the cattle-farming Chaco territory. February 16th is a national holiday in Paraguay to honor Hayes.

Rutherford B. Hayes
Rutherford B. Hayes Presidential Center

The Importance of Bloviating: The term "bloviating" was popularized by Warren G. Harding, who called it: **"The art of speaking for as long as the occasion warrants without saying anything."**

Warren G. Harding
Library of Congress

The Wrong Wilson: Richard M. Nixon, an admirer of President Woodrow Wilson, requested "the Wilson desk" to be used in the Oval Office. By mistake, he received the desk used by the obscure Vice President Henry Wilson (1873-1875). Nixon did not find this out until well into his Presidency. He even referenced the desk as belonging to Woodrow Wilson during his famous **"Silent Majority"** speech in 1969.

Henry Wilson
Library of Congress

The Presidents

Absent Minded Professor: In 1973, Bill Clinton, teaching as an adjunct professor of Admiralty Law at the University of Arkansas Fayetteville, lost the final exams. As a remedy, Clinton offered to give all students a 'B+.' One student, Susan Webber Wright, believing she deserved an 'A,' challenged the grade and spoke with the Professor's girl friend Hillary Rodham. Wright was able to convince Rodham that a grade change was in order and she received the 'A.' Interestingly, later in life, Wright became a judge in Arkansas. In that capacity, she dismissed a sexual harassment suit brought by Arkansas resident Paula Jones against now President Bill Clinton.

Susan Webber Wright
Official Photograph

Smoking Can be Harmful to Your Health: John Adams began smoking a pipe at eight years of age. His teeth denigrated to a horrible condition, and he eventually lost all of his teeth. Unwilling to wear dentures, he instead preferred to speak with a lisp.

John Adams
Portrait by Benjamin Blith

Reagan Lampoons Protestor Where it Hurts: While Governor of California, Ronald Reagan saw a protestor with a sign that read: **"Make love not war."** Reagan yelled: **"By the looks of you, you don't look like you can do much of either."**

Ronald Reagan
Official Photograph as Governor of California

Self-Dentistry: Abraham Lincoln was terrified of dental work. He preformed dentistry on himself. However, he was a bit too zealous. As he was extracting his own tooth, he managed to remove a small piece of his jawbone. Dentistry during this time period was rather ghoulish. Anesthesia did not exist.

Abraham Lincoln
Library of Congress

The Presidents

Obama's Peculiar Entry into Elective Politics: In 1996, Barack Obama won a Democratic Primary for a State Senate seat representing Chicago's South Side. This was Obama's first foray into elective politics. A campaign volunteer successfully challenged the legitimacy of the other four Democratic candidates, including the popular incumbent State Senator Alice Palmer. Chicago election officials ruled in favor of Obama, determining that he was the only candidate with enough **"valid"** signatures to make the Primary ballot. Obama subsequently went on to win the General Election, garnering 82% of the vote.

Barack Obama
Official Photograph as a State Senator

Carter whacks Swimming Rabbit: In 1979, while fishing in his hometown of Plains, Georgia, a swamp rabbit swam toward the President's small boat. Carter swatted at the rabbit with his canoe paddle, scaring it away.

Jimmy Carter with the Swamp Rabbit (Right)
Jimmy Carter Library and Museum

The Devil Made me do it: When Richard M. Nixon was asked by Journalist David Frost why he did not burn the tape implicating him in the Watergate cover-up, Nixon answered: **"I was under medication when I made the decision not to burn the tapes."**

Book by David Frost about his Interviews with Richard M. Nixon

Cynicism Toward Media: Thomas Jefferson wrote: **"The man who reads nothing at all is better educated than the man who reads nothing but newspapers."**

Thomas Jefferson
Portrait by Mather Brown

32

The Presidents

White House Goes Solar: During the energy crisis, President Jimmy Carter ordered 32 solar heating panels to be installed on the White House roof. His successor, Ronald Reagan, ordered them removed when maintenance was being performed. They were never put back up on the White House roof. Most of these original solar panels are now owned by Unity College in Unity, Maine.

Jimmy Carter with the White House Solar Panels
White House Museum

Move Over Columbus Day: In 1964 President Lyndon B. Johnson signed a proclamation declaring October 9th **"Leif Ericson Day"** in commemoration of the Norse explorer being the first European to discover America. The U.S. Congress approved the proclamation unanimously. October 9 was the day chosen to commemorate this event because October 9, 1825 represents the start of organized immigration from Scandinavia to the United States.

Leif Ericson
Library of Congress

Ghoulish Criminals: In 1876 grave robbers attempted to steal Abraham Lincoln's carcass from his tomb at Oak Ridge Cemetery in Springfield, Illinois. Their plan was to hold the cadaver for a $200,000 ransom and to convince authorities to free their friend, Benjamin Boyd, from prison. Their ransom plot failed when the police and the media were alerted to the plot. The perpetrators were apprehended before they could remove the body from the sarcophagus. Instead of freeing their friend Benjamin Boyd from jail, the perpetrators were sentenced to one year behind bars.

Abraham Lincoln
Library of Congress

New Digs for Taft: In 1909, William Howard Taft became the first President to work from an Oval Office. This Oval Office burned down in a 1929 fire. Herbert Hoover ordered the Oval Office re-built in 1930.

Postcard of the Original Oval Office in 1909
Library of Congress

33

The Presidents

Number Please: Not wanting to use "go betweens," Grover Cleveland answered his own telephone at the White House.

Grover Cleveland
Library of Congress

How Low Can You Go? In 2013, burglars broke into the James A. Garfield memorial in Cleveland and stole 13 commemorative collectors spoons from his Presidential inauguration. The robbers left the remains of a couple of cigarettes. a shattered stained-glass window, some soiled clothing and an empty liquor bottle.

James A. Garfield Memorial
zzzuucx

Ouch: Jimmy Carter made his fortune as a Georgia peanut farmer. While working on the farm, he became injured, leaving one of his fingers permanently bent.

Jimmy Carter
Library of Congress

If You Fight for the Flag, You Should Not Be Killed by It: In 2012, former President Bill Clinton spoke at a memorial dedication to former Vice President Hubert Humphrey in St. Paul, Minnesota. An American Flag fell behind him. Clinton picked it up and recounted: **"I once saw a State Senator of mine get hit by the American Flag and he said 'you know I risked my life in WWII and I don't think I should get killed by it.'"**

Bill Clinton
Official Photograph

The Presidents

A Gambling Man: George Washington loved lotteries, raffles, card playing, and cock fighting.

George Washington
Portrait by Gilbert Stuart

First Plot to Assassinate JFK: On December 11, 1960, President-elect John F. Kennedy's life was threatened in Florida by a postal worker who had loaded his car with dynamite and who was planning to crash into Kennedy's car. However, moments before the planned assassination, 73-year old Richard Pavlick backed off when he saw Kennedy saying goodbye to his wife and daughter. Pavlick was arrested just three days later when, after a traffic stop, it was discovered that his car was filled with dynamite. Pavlick was sent to prison for six years.

John F. Kennedy
Executive Office of the President

President Mummified by Mistake: Anarchist Leon Czolgosh assassinated William McKinley in 1901. Following his assassination, anyone who criticized the late president was threatened, fired from their job, and sometimes beaten by a crowd. Czolgosh was executed. Officials feared that grave robbers would steal McKinley's body and sell parts of it as relics. In response, McKinley was placed in a pine box and barrels of Quick Lime and sulphuric acid were poured onto the body before the top was sealed. It is now believed that instead of making the body decompose faster, the chemical reaction resulting from amalgamating these two substances actually preserved the body much like the mummification process.

Artists Rendition of William McKinley Assassination
T. Dart Walker

Some Move Up the Ladder Faster Than Others: In 2005, when he assumed his seat in the U.S. Senate, Barack Obama (D-IL) was ninety-ninth in seniority. Four years later he was President of the United States.

Barack Obama
White House Photograph by Pete Souza

35

The Presidents

Elegant Arthur: Chester A. Arthur earned the moniker "Elegant Arthur" for his fancy clothes and sense of fashion.

Chester A. Arthur
Library of Congress

No Pearly Whites: Woodrow Wilson suffered from extreme tooth decay. When he smiled, people were horrified with the condition of his teeth.

Woodrow Wilson Smiling
Library of Congress

Another Fish Story? Calvin Coolidge was a recreational angler. As President, he vacationed at the Cedar Island Lodge in Wisconsin. After a failed fishing excursion, Coolidge was asked how many trout there were in the river. His response was: **"About forty-five thousand. I haven't caught them all yet, but I've intimidated them."**

Calvin Coolidge Fishing in Wisconsin
Wisconsin Historical Society

FDR Defines Conservatism the Way he Sees It: During a radio address to *The New York Herald Tribune* forum in 1939, Franklin D. Roosevelt observed: **"A conservative is a man with two perfectly good legs who, however, has never learned to walk forward."**

Franklin D. Roosevelt
Franklin D. Roosevelt Presidential
Library and Museum

The Presidents

Hoover Not Impressed With White House Staff: Herbert Hoover had some strange rules around the White House. He wanted the White House staff to quietly move through the White House unseen. The White House cooks and house-keeping staff were told to hide if they heard him coming. The President threatened to fire them if he could see them.

Herbert Hoover
Library of Congress

Missed Me: Ronald Reagan was shot in 1981 and survived. In 1987, while giving a speech at a U.S. Airbase in West Berlin celebrating the city's 750th birthday, he quipped: **"Its not often you get to go to a birthday party for something older than I am."** A balloon suddenly popped sounding like a gunshot, and the President joked: "**Missed me.**"

Ronald Reagan
Official Photograph

The Big Guy: William Howard Taft was a large man weighing in at over 300 pounds. Not taking his weight into account, nor the theory of water displacement in a bathtub, he hopped into a hotel bathtub. His body displaced the bath water, which moved like a title wave across the floor. The water could not be contained, and dripped on the peoples heads one floor below. In order to cover up his embarrassment, he told this joke as he looked out his window overlooking the Atlantic Ocean: **"I'll get a piece of that fenced in someday, and then I venture to say there won't be any overflow."**

William Howard Taft
Library of Congress

Master of the Obvious: During the Great Depression, former President Calvin Coolidge noted the dire circumstances of the American economy. In a 1930 Newspaper column, he stated: **"The final solution for unemployment is work."**

Calvin Coolidge
Library of Congress

The Presidents

"I Plead Guilty Only to Being Drunk:" Jimmy Carter enjoyed telling audiences the story about: **"an old man who was arrested and taken before the judge for being drunk and setting a bed on fire. And he said, 'Judge, I plead guilty to being drunk, but the bed was on fire when I got in it.'"**

Jimmy Carter
Jimmy Carter Library and Museum

Fake News: In 1975, Gerald R. Ford delivered a speech where he denied requests from New York City for federal help to avoid bankruptcy. *The Daily News* printed the banner headline the next day: **"FORD TO CITY: DROP DEAD."** Ford never used that phrase, but many New Yorkers took the headline to be a quote by Ford. Ford later blamed his razor-thin loss in the pivotal showdown state of New York in the 1976 Presidential election to that false headline.

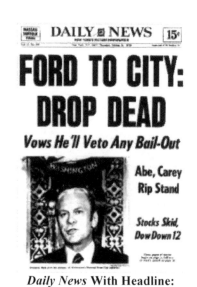

Daily News **With Headline:
"FORD TO CITY: DROP DEAD"**

The President and the Mummy: At a Democratic Fundraiser, U.S. Senator Joe Lieberman (D-CT) joked about Bill Clinton's appearance at the Washington National Geographic Society. At that event, Clinton viewed the preserved Incan mummy Princess of Ampato. She was killed in the fifteenth century. Lieberman joked, **"She dated Bob Dole"** (former U.S. Senator and Republican Presidential nominee). When Bill Clinton took to the podium he told the crowd: **"I don't know if you've seen that mummy. But you know, if I were a single man, I might ask that mummy out. That's a good-looking mummy. That mummy looks better than I do on my worst days."**

Bill Clinton
Official Photograph

Controversial Period: Some contend that there should not be a '.' After the 'S' in Harry S. Truman. The S does not stand for a name. Rather, it is there to symbolize the "S" in the name of his two grandfathers, Anderson Shipp Truman and Solomon Young. However, Truman always used the period. According to *The Chicago Manuel of Style*, the '.' should be there even if the S does not stand for a name. Truman himself used the '. ' after the 'S.' in his signature.

Harry S. Truman
Harry S. Truman Presidential Library and Museum

The Presidents

Into Animal Heads: Theodore Roosevelt was not only obsessed with hunting, he was obsessed with having the heads of the animals on his walls to show off. Roosevelt, who had been on many African safaris, had somehow amassed 11,000 mounted animal heads. He was so surrounded by animal heads that he donated all but 24 of them to the Smithsonian Institute.

Theodore Roosevelt with his Gun
Library of Congress

Presidential Maxim For a Happy Marriage: When Princess Margaret of Great Britain (accompanied by her husband Lord Snowdon, Antony Armstrong-Jones) visited the White House in 1965; Lyndon B. Johnson gave Lord Jones some unsolicited advice for a happy marriage. Johnson told him: **"I've learned that there are only two things necessary to keep your wife happy. First, let her think she's having her way. And second, let her have it."**

Lyndon B. Johnson and Wife Lady Bird entertain Princess Margaret Rose and her Husband Lord Armstrong Jones of Snowden
Lyndon Baines Johnson Library and Museum

Help a President Out: Harry S. Truman inherited money from his family and invested it in a zinc mining company that went bankrupt. He went on to be the co-owner of a haberdashery that went under. Instead of filing bankruptcy, he paid off that debt slowly over a multi-year period. He had been saddled with debt for so long that when he became President, he had accumulated few assets. In 1949, while Truman was President, the U.S. Congress increased the annual Presidential salary to $100,000 per year, plus an additional $50,000 that could be used for expenses.

Harry S. Truman
Harry S. Presidential Library and Museum

He Gets No Respect: Speaking of his Vice President Hubert Humphrey and the little power he garnered, Lyndon B. Johnson exclaimed: **"All that Hubert needs over there is a gal to answer the phone, and a pencil with an eraser on it."**

Lyndon B. Johnson (L), with Hubert Humphrey (R)
Lyndon Baines Johnson Library and Museum

The Presidents

He Wanted it all: Theodore Roosevelt loved when the attention was on him. His daughter Alice opined: **"My father always wanted to be the corpse at every funeral, the bride at every wedding and the baby at every christening."**

Theodore Roosevelt
Library of Congress

How is that Possible: John Tyler was born in 1790. His plantation, Sherwood Forest, located in Charles City, VA, was formerly owned by President William Henry Harrison. Harrison Ruffin Tyler, a grandson born in 1929, now owns the property.

Sherwood Forest
Library of Congress

Rating His Teacher: In a 1838 diary entry, future President Rutherford B. Hayes, at the time a student at a preparatory school in Middletown, Connecticut, said of his teacher: **"The French tutor is a passionate old fellow. He looks more like a plump feather bed than anything else I know of!"**

Rutherford B. Hayes
Library of Congress

Hillary and Dubya in Unison: In her book, *What Happened*, Hillary Clinton writes that after hearing President Donald Trump's Inauguration speech, George W. Bush uttered: **"That was some weird Shit."** Clinton wrote: **"I couldn't agree more."**

Donald Trump Delivering Inauguration Address
Photograph by U.S. Marine Corps Lance Corporal Cristian L. Ricardo

The Presidents

Television: In 1927, future President Herbert Hoover, then U.S. Commerce Secretary, was involved in the first exhibition of television in American history. In the broadcast, Hoover spoke from Washington DC to members of the media in New York. He said: **"Human genius has now destroyed the impediment of distance."**

Herbert Hoover
Library of Congress

Fast George: In 1993, future President George W. Bush completed the Houston Marathon in 3 hours, 44 minutes, and 52 seconds.

George W. Bush
Photograph by Shawn Clark of Lazyeights Photography

Formal Attire: When Richard M. Nixon walked on the beach, he wore dress shoes and pants.

Richard M. Nixon walking the Beach
National Archives

Meet me at High Noon: Bill Clinton was enamored with the movie "High Noon," so much so that he ordered it played 17 times in the White House Movie Theater.

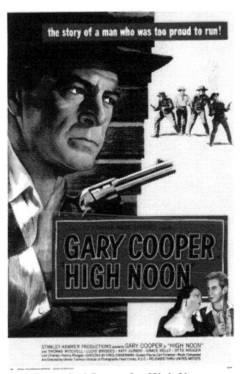

Theatrical Poster for High Noon

The Presidents

President wants College Basketball Players Back in Jail: In 2017, President Donald Trump arranged for the release of three UCLA basketball players from China who were arrested for shoplifting. A few days later, Trump tweeted: **"Now that the three basketball players are out of China and saved from years in jail, LaVar Ball, the father of LiAngelom, is unaccepting of what I did for his son and that shoplifting is no big deal. I should have left them in jail!"**

Donald Trump
Photograph by Gage Skidmore

FBI Agent Nixon: Before entering elective politics, Richard M. Nixon was accepted for a position with the Federal Bureau of Investigation. However, federal budget cuts eliminated what would have been his position.

Flag for the Federal Bureau of Investigation

Bill Clinton on the Saxophone: Bill Clinton played tenor saxophone in the High School band at Hot Springs High School. His music prowess earned him music scholarships that Clinton considered. Ultimately however he enrolled at Georgetown University and earned a Bachelor of Science Degree in Foreign Services.

Bill Clinton in his High School Band Uniform
Herbert Hoover Museum

Obama and Spear fishing: As a young man in Hawaii, Barack Obama spearfished off of Kailua Bay.

Barack Obama
Punahou High School Year Book Photograph

The Presidents

His Real Ambition: John Tyler played the violin and wanted to become a concert violinist.

John Tyler
Library of Congress

Obama's Favorite Television Program: In 2014, Barack Obama was asked by a Minneapolis resident to name his favorite television show. After thinking about it, Obama answered with the comedy **"MASH,"** which originally aired from 1973-1983.

The Cast of MASH in 1974
CBS Television

The Bush-Nixon Date, Not Exactly a Match: The first time George W. Bush ever visited the White House was to go on a date with First Daughter Tricia Nixon. George H.W, Bush, a Texas Congressman at the time, arraigned the date. The date occurred at a gala held for the Apollo 8 spaceflight team. In his book, 43 on 41, Bush describes the disastrous date. **"I fired up a cigarette, prompting a polite suggestion from Tricia that I not smoke."** After the dinner, Tricia told Bush to drive back to the White House. No further dates followed.

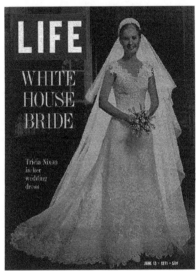

Tricia Nixon on the Cover of *Life Magazine* before Marrying Ed Cox

Yikes: Theodore Roosevelt was no fan of U.S. Supreme Court Justice Oliver Wendell Holmes Jr. He felt that Holmes needed to be tougher. Roosevelt said of Holmes: **"I could carve out of a banana a justice with more backbone than that."**

Oliver Wendell Holmes Jr.
Library of Congress

The Presidents

Not the Smartest Group: In 1940, U.S. Senator and future President Harry S. Truman (D-MO) while discussing his job cracked: **"When I first came to Washington, for the first six months I wondered how the hell I ever got here. For the next six months, I wondered how the hell the rest of them ever got here."**

Harry S. Truman in 1940
Harry S. Truman Presidential Library and Museum

How About Them Apples? U.S. Representative Benjamin Butterworth (R-OH) was a critic of his fellow Ohio Representative and future President William McKinley. He once observed: **"Why, if McKinley and I were walking through the orchard which had only one bearing tree, and that tree had two apples, he would pick both, put one in his pocket, take a bite out of the other, and then calmly turn to me and ask 'Ben, do you like apples.'"**

Benjamin Butterworth
Official Photograph

The Preaching President: In 1977, President Jimmy Carter used a speech to employees of the U.S. Department of Housing and Urban Development to preach about workers' personal lives. He said: **"We need better family life to make us better servants of the people. So those of you living in sin, I hope you get married. And those of you who have left your spouses, go back home. And those of you who don't remember your children's names, get reacquainted."**

Jimmy Carter
Official Portrait by Robert Templeton

Trump and CNN: Donald Trump tweeted in 2017, **"While in the Philippines I was forced to watch @CNN, which I have not done in months, and again realized how bad, and FAKE it is. Loser!"**

CNN Logo

The Presidents

Atwater Saw Clinton Threat Early On: Lee Atwater, the Chairman of the Republican Party, feared Arkansas Governor Bill Clinton would be the 1992 Presidential nominee. In response, he recruited former U.S. Representative Tommy Robinson, a former Democrat, to run in the 1990 Republican Gubernatorial primary. Robinson's Press Secretary, Rex Nelson, remembers Atwater telling the campaign staff: **"The media's full of talk about Mario Cuomo or Bill Bradley. We know how to paint them up as northeastern liberals like Dukakis. That's easy! What scares me is a southern moderate or conservative Democrat, and the scariest of all, because he's the most talented of the bunch, is Bill Clinton."**

Robinson was merely a pawn for Atwater, who continued: **"We're going to take Tommy Robinson and use him to throw everything we can think of at Clinton—drugs, women, whatever works. We may or may not win, but we'll bust him up so bad he won't be able to run again for years."**

Ultimately, Robinson lost the Republican primary race to Sheffield Nelson, who in turn lost to Bill Clinton.

Lee Atwater
Executive Office of the President

Private Information: Lyndon B. Johnson ordered the White House staff to make it so that the shower nozzle would point directly at the Presidents penis. The staff argued that that would take a great deal of plumbing. Johnson was unsympathetic, telling them: **"If I can move 10,000 troops in a day, you can certainly fix the bathroom any way I want it."** The obsequious staff fixed the shower to meet the President's needs.

Lyndon B. Johnson
Lyndon Baines Johnson Library and Museum

College President Learns on the Job: In 1947, future President Dwight D. Eisenhower took a position as President of Columbia University. He was picked for the position based on his leadership in the military. He had little knowledge of the interworkings of a university. Upon accepting the incumbency, Eisenhower told *The New York Times*: **"I hope to talk to various officials . . . and possibly get some advance inkling of what a college president is up against. I know nothing about it."**

Columbia University Shield

The Presidents

The Excitement of a President eating Pancakes: Calvin Coolidge came off to some as non-emotional. To make the President appear more human, Edward Bernays, a public relations guru, arranged for Coolidge and his wife Grace to eat a pancake breakfast with actors. *The New York Times* wrote an article on the event under the rubric: **"Actors eat cake with the Coolidge's. President Nearly Laughs."**

Calvin and Grace Coolidge
Library of Congress

President Baptized: Dwight D. Eisenhower was the only President to be baptized while in office. He always called himself a Christian, but had never been baptized. In 1953, just 11 days after assuming office, Eisenhower was baptized at the National Presbyterian Church in Washington, D.C.

Dwight D. Eisenhower
Library of Congress

A Tad too Personal: During a 1994 MTV townhall meeting, Bill Clinton was asked by a teenager: **"Mr. President, the world is dying to know. Is it boxers or briefs?"** Rather than laugh off the question, Clinton answered: **"usually briefs."**

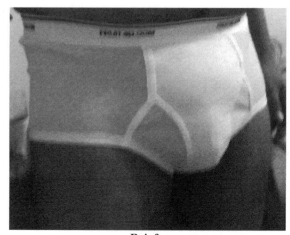

Briefs
Mjoseoc

Gerald R. Ford Graffiti: In 2012, a graffiti artist painted portraits of Gerald R. Ford on public property of Ford's hometown of Grand Rapids, MI. One likeness included the phrase Ford popularized in his 1974 Inauguration speech: **"I am indebted to no man."** Another featured Ford on the ski slopes. The graffiti was soon removed.

Gerald R. Ford
Lyndon Baines Johnson Library and Museum

The Presidents

Ike v. Harry: John Eisenhower, the son of incoming President Dwight D. Eisenhower, was used as a political football. During the traditional ride from the White House to the Presidential Inauguration, President-Elect Eisenhower asked outgoing President Harry S. Truman (who had ordered Eisenhower's son John to return from active duty in the Korean War), to attend his father's inauguration. Eisenhower feared that the public would view this as his son receiving preferential treatment. Truman testily retorted in the third person: **"The President of the United States ordered your son to attend your inauguration. The President thought it was right and proper for your son to witness the swearing-in of his father to the Presidency. If you think somebody was trying to embarrass you by this order, then the President assumes full responsibility."** The two men had a rapprochement later in life, becoming good friends.

As for John Eisenhower, he was the last son of a President to serve his father in the White House. John served as the Assistant White House Staff Secretary and as an assistant to General Andrew Goodpaster.

Harry S. Truman (L), and Dwight D. Eisenhower (R) in Car Driving to Presidential Inauguration
Library of Congress

Nixon Turns Down Job Working in the White House Mailroom: During the 1968 Presidential campaign, Republican nominee Richard M. Nixon hired his brother Ed to superintend the mail operations during his Presidential campaign. Pleased with Ed's work, President-Elect Nixon offered his brother the job of running the White House mailroom. Ed declined the offer, later telling *The Times Union*: **"It was a nice gesture, but I knew it was not the job for me."**

Richard M. Nixon
Library of Congress

Calling Play-by-Play Without Seeing the Game: In the 1930's, Ronald Reagan delivered play-by-play for Chicago Cubs baseball games on radio station WHO, the Des Moines, IA NBC affiliate. He did this from the radio studio, through the telegraph. Although he never saw the games he would broadcast, his description of the plays was flawless.

Ronald Reagan on WHO Radio
Reagan Foundation

The Garfield Theorem: While a member of the U.S. House of Representatives, future President James Garfield developed his own mathematical proof to the Pythagorean Theorem $(a^2 + b^2 = c^2)$. Garfield's Proof was published in the *Journal of Education* in 1876.

James Garfield
Library of Congress

Chapter II

First Ladies

First Ladies

First Lady Takes Flight: Warren G. Harding's wife Florence was the first First Lady to fly in an airplane. In 1920, after her husband won the Presidency, Mrs. Harding was a passenger in a seaplane while visiting a Naval air station in Panama.

Florence Harding
Library of Congress

A Sad State of Affairs: Ida McKinley was devastated by the death of her two daughters and her mother. Soon after their deaths she began having epileptic seizures and fainting spells. Her husband, President William McKinley, insisted that she sit next to him at family dinners. When Ida had a seizure, the President would calmly and kindly hold a linen napkin in front of her face until the seizure ended. He did not want her to be embarrassed in front of the assembled guests. The dinner party would then resume as if nothing had happened

Ida McKinley
Library of Congress

Not Salubrious: John Quincy Adams' wife Louisa suffered from many illnesses, some real and some probably psychosomatic. It is now believed that some of her illnesses were a direct result of breathing the air through the heater grates from a coal-fired furnace. She spent her afternoons resting in her bedroom, eating chocolate, and inhaling the fumes.

Louisa Adams
Library of Congress

Betty Ford Makes it On Her Own: First Lady Betty Ford played a cameo role as herself in a 1975 episode of *The Mary Tyler Moore Show*.

Betty Ford (C), with Mary Tyler Moore (R), and co-producer Ed Weinberger (L)
Gerald R. Ford Library & Museum

First Ladies

Tying the Knot Again: Two First ladies got re-married. They were Frances Cleveland and Jacqueline Kennedy. Frances married Thomas Preston, a Princeton University Professor, and signed her name "Frances F. Cleveland Preston." Until her death in 1947, she took full advantage of a free government perk called **"the free frank privilege."** This enabled her to send all of her mail for free, as long as she wrote her signature in the upper right hand corner where a stamp is usually placed. Kennedy married Aristotle Onassis, a wealthy Greek shipping magnet. She signed her name "Jacqueline Kennedy Onassis."

The Humor of Mrs. Bush: Barbara Bush championed the fight against illiteracy while her predecessor Nancy Reagan fought the war against drugs. An example of Bush's self-deprecating humor was when she once compared what she and Mrs. Reagan had in common: **"She adores her husband; I adore mine. She fights drugs; I fight illiteracy. She wears a size three . . . so is my leg."**

Aristotle Onassis
National Archief

Barbara Bush
White House Photograph by David Valdez

Teetotaler: Sarah Polk, wife of James K. Polk, had the weird nickname of **"Sahara Sarah"** because she banned hard liquor in the White House. Visitors thought that visiting the White House was like visiting the Sahara Desert, a location where no one could get a drink.

Those were the Days of Her Life: Dwight D. Eisenhower's wife Mamie spent many afternoons watching television soap operas in the White House.

Sarah Poke (L), James K. Polk (R)
Public Domain

Mamie Eisenhower
White House Photograph

First Ladies

Un Lady-Like: Jacqueline Kennedy believed that smoking cigarettes was not lady-like. However, she was a chain smoker who smoked in private whenever she could. She asked photographers not to photograph her while she was smoking. However, some pictures of her smoking do exist.

Jacqueline Kennedy
Photograph by Robert Knudsen

Kowtowing: Andrew Johnson's wife Eliza brought cows to the White House and enjoyed milking them every morning.

Eliza Johnson
Library of Congress

All in the Family: President Martin Van Buren and his wife Hannah were first Cousins once removed.

Hannah Van Buren
Library of Congress

Breaker - - Breaker, Do You Copy? As First Lady, Betty Ford enjoyed conversing with Americans via her CB radio. Her handle was: **"First Mama."**

Betty Ford
Gerald R. Ford Presidential Library and Museum

First Ladies

All in the Family: Harry S. Truman's wife Bess was employed by her husband as a clerk while her husband served in the U.S. Senate.

Harry S. Truman (L), Bess Truman (R)
Harry S. Truman Presidential Library and Museum

Shop Until You Drop: Mary Todd Lincoln was a shopaholic. She spent a fortune refurnishing the White House and was trepidatious to tell her husband. Instead, she sold the manure that was supposed to fertilize the White House grounds and then fired most of the White House servants to save money.

Mary Todd Lincoln
Library of Congress

Going Above and Beyond: Chester A. Arthur's sister, Mary Arthur McElroy, served as White House hostess due to the fact that Ellen Arthur, Chester's wife, died of pneumonia twenty months before he assumed the Presidency in 1881.

Mary Arthur McElroy
Library of Congress

She Wore the Pants in the Family: Richard M. Nixon's wife Pat made a fashion statement. She was the first First Lady to go out in public wearing pants.

Pat Nixon
Richard Nixon Presidential Library and Museum

First Ladies

Shunning Ceremonial Duties: Zackary Taylor's wife Margaret was one tough woman. She and her husband had once lived on the Western frontier, where she learned how to shoot and hunt. She hated social obligations and refused to serve as the White House hostess. Her daughter, Betty Taylor Bliss, became the White House hostess.

Margaret Taylor
Public Domain

Size Doesn't Matter: Abraham Lincoln was 6'4 while his wife Mary was only 5'2.

Abraham Lincoln (L) with Mary Todd Lincoln (R)
Public Domain

Social Outcast: James Monroe's wife Elizabeth made a huge social blunder. It was considered good etiquette for the First Lady to make the first social call to the wives of the important government officials in Washington DC. She decided it was a waste of time. This in turn insulted the government officials' wives who in turn refused to attend any of the White House receptions.

Elizabeth Monroe
Portrait by John Vanderlyn

First Lady Tradition: It is a tradition that every First Lady serves as the Honorary Chairwoman of the Girl Scouts of America. This tradition began in 1917 with First Lady Edith B. Wilson.

Girl Scouts Meet First Lady Bess Truman
Harry S. Truman Library and Museum

First Ladies

A Real Family Man: John Tyler was married twice and had 15 children and 44 grandchildren. His first wife, Letitia, died in 1842 after suffering a stroke. John then married Julia Gardner who was only 24 years old. This caused family problems, because Tyler's new wife was younger than his eldest daughter, and Tyler's son had once dated Julia.

Julia Gardner
Library of Congress

No Will: Abraham Lincoln left no will. His wife, Mary Todd, asked U.S. Supreme Court Justice David Davis, who was nominated by Lincoln, to administer the estate. The Justice did this, pro bono. When the estate closed in 1867, there was $110,296.80.

Justice David Davis
Library of Congress

She was Right, Bold, But Right: In 1889, after Grover Cleveland had been defeated for the Presidency, First Lady Francis Cleveland told the White House Staff that the family would be back in the White House in four years. Sure enough, after beating Harrison in 1893, the Cleveland's were back in the White House for a non-consecutive four-year term.

Frances Folsom Cleveland
Library of Congress

Fashionistas: Martha and George Washington loved expensive clothing. George wore a wig that was the style of the time. He only felt comfortable going wigless around close friends and his family.

Martha Washington (L), George Washington (R)
Library of Congress

First Ladies

Cross-Eyed: Julia Dent Grant, Ulysses S. Grant's wife, suffered from Strabismus (cross-eyed). She never had this problem corrected. In order to appear more beautiful in portraits, her portraits were painted so that her eye condition would not show. Many of her portraits were done in profile. As a First Lady, she had to host many fancy White House parties. Her eyesight was so bad that she would usually stand by herself in a corner. She would try to move as little as possible so she would not bump into people that she could not see. Many of her guests thought that she was strange because when she did move, she would move along the wall sideways. She was aware of the fact that she had become a laughing-stock and that people called her a crab because she walked sideways, just like a crab in the ocean. Her husband was deeply in love with her and said: **"Did I not see you and fall in love with you with these same eyes? I like them just as they are now, and now remember; you are not to interfere with them. They are mine, and let me tell you, Mrs. Grant, you had better not make any experiments, as I might not like you half so well with any other eyes."**

Julia Grant
Library of Congress

Hopeless Anyway, Let a Republican Deal With It: In an interview with Arthur M. Schlesinger (a former advisor to her husband John F. Kennedy), Jacqueline Kennedy reveals why she believes her husband nominated erstwhile Republican rival Henry Cabot Lodge Jr. to become U.S. Ambassador to Vietnam, **"I think he probably did it . . . rather thinking it might be such a brilliant thing to do because Vietnam was rather hopeless anyway, and put a Republican there."**

Henry Cabot Lodge Jr.
Eric Koch/National Archief

The Genesis of Lady Bird: Lady Bird Johnson's real name was Claudia. The nickname Lady Bird was coined by a nurse who said she was as pretty as a **"Lady Bird."**

Lady Bird Johnson
Lyndon Baines Johnson Library and Museum

First Ladies

Free Clothes: Abraham Lincoln received many gifts while in the White House, and he kept them all. A company in Chicago made his Inaugural suit and it was reported that the President told his wife Mary Todd about one of the benefits of being President: "there is one thing to come out of this scrape. We are going to have some new clothes."

Abraham Lincoln
Library of Congress

Morose: Rutherford B. Hayes missed his wife Lucy terribly, and often visited her gravesite. Nine days before dying of a heart attack, he visited his late wife's grave, and wrote a journal entry, which read: **"My feeling was one of longing to be quietly resting in a grave, by her side."**

Lucy Hayes (L), Rutherford B. Hayes (R)
Library of Congress

Former First Lady Pitches Margarine: In 1959, former First Lady Eleanor Roosevelt (1933-1945) starred in a commercial for "Good Luck Margarine." In the commercial, Roosevelt asserts: **"Years ago, most people never dreamed of eating margarine, but times have changed. Nowadays, you can get margarine like the new Good Luck, which really tastes delicious. That's what I've spread on my toast, Good Luck. I thoroughly enjoy it."** Eleanor Roosevelt donated the money earned from her appearance to UNICEF.

Eleanor Roosevelt
Franklin D. Roosevelt Presidential Library and Museum

Robber: A White House lawyer claimed that Mary Todd Lincoln had a stealing problem stating: **"Stealing was a sort of insanity in her."** One of the methods that she employed was to bill the Federal Government for materials that she never purchased and also billed them for employees at the White House that never existed. She kept the money and her husband never found out.

Mary Todd Lincoln
Library of Congress

Chapter III

Presidential Family Members

Presidential Family Members

He was Fired: Donald Trump has been married three times and has five children. The eldest son, Donald Trump Jr., got in a controversy in 2012. He attended a legal hunting safari in Africa. Photographs of him posing with an endangered leopard that he had shot came to light. At the time, Donald Trump and his son Donald Trump Jr. were both appearing on Celebrity Apprentice. The photographs became such a huge public spectacle that one sponsor was forced to drop their sponsorship of the program.

Donald Trump Jr.
Photograph by Greg Skidmore

Betting the Farm: Martin Van Buren's son John was a drunk and a gambler. He enjoyed attending horse races, and usually had to be carried home because he was so drunk. At one point, when his gambling was out of control, it was said that he bet his mistress on a card game when he ran out of money.

John Van Buren
Library of Congress

Senior Prom Like You Have Never Seen Before: Susan Ford, the daughter of President Gerald R. Ford was lucky enough to have her Senior Prom at the White House.

Susan Ford with Cat Shan
Gerald R. Ford Presidential Library

Wild Child: Theodore Roosevelt's daughter Alice was more than a handful. She loved to stay out late unsupervised and enjoyed gambling. A newspaper cameraman once photographed her as she was collecting her winnings from the local bookie. She married U.S. Representative Nicolas Longworth (R-OH). Gossip columnists were kept busy following both of their extramarital affairs. Alice even went so far as to admit that her daughter's father was U.S. Senator William Borah (R-ID) and not her husband. On the couch, next to where she was always sitting was a needle point pillow that read: **"If you haven't got anything good to say about anybody, come sit next to me."** Considering her wild lifestyle, it is amazing that she lived until the age of 86.

Alice Roosevelt (L), Nicolas Longworth (R)
Library of Congress

Presidential Family Members

Rebelling Against Society: Ronald Reagan's daughter, Patti Davis, from her first marriage was anything but conservative. She was a non-conformist, participated in anti-nuclear protests, posed nude for *Playboy Magazine*, and wrote a candid book gossiping about her family. She had no relationship with her family for years, but later reconciled with them.

Patti Davis
National Archives and Records

Born To Be Wild: Abraham Lincoln's oldest son Tad had a propensity for wild behavior. In an effort to raise money, he held a yard sale on the front lawn of the White House. He is also credited with tying goats to a sled that pulled him like a chariot through an official White House reception.

Abraham Lincoln (L), with Tad Lincoln (R)
Library of Congress

He Had to Go: Robert Todd Lincoln was the only surviving child of Abraham Lincoln. In order to keep him out of the Civil War, Robert was sent to a University. Both the President and his son were excoriated for Todd's dodging military service. Robert Todd could not stand the pressure and joined the Union Army. Luckily, he survived.

Robert Todd Lincoln
Library of Congress

I want to be Captain Too: Franklin D. Roosevelt's son Elliot, a member of the U.S. Army Air Corp., was promoted so often that there was a public outcry of nepotism. The political slogan **"I want to be captain, too"** haunted President Roosevelt's 1940 re-election bid. Elliot eventually became a brigadier general, and the Press had a field day. He later went on to fabricate war stories, one of which he claimed that he almost died in the same mid-air crash that killed John F. Kennedy's older brother, Joseph. In reality, not only did Elliot not almost die, but he was on the ground at the time of the crash.

Elliot Roosevelt
Official Photograph

Presidential Family Members

A Real Problem: James Madison had a problem stepchild named John from Dolly Madison's first marriage. He had an uncontrollable urge to gamble, was an alcoholic, and was addicted to spending money. No matter what the Madison's did to change his behavior, nothing worked. He was an embarrassment to the President. After leaving the Presidency, the Madison's retirement was very humble. Unfortunately, problem stepchild John continued to beg for money. When James Madison died, Dolly continued to give her son money, and she was facing bankruptcy. In order to save her future, she sold her husband's papers to the U.S. Congress in exchange for a monthly annuity payment. This prevented her son from extorting any more money from her.

John Madison
Met Museum

I'm the Only Sane One in the Family: In the Book, *Redneck Power: The Wit and Wisdom of Billy Carter* by Jeremy Rifin and Ted Howard, Billy Carter, a gas station owner and the brother of President Jimmy Carter, is quoted as saying in 1976, **"I got a mama who joined the Peace Corps when she was 68. I got one sister who's a Holy Roller preacher. Another wears a helmet and drives a motorcycle. And my brother thinks he's going to be President, so that makes me the only sane one in the family."**

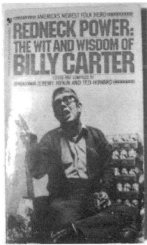

Redneck Power:
The Wit and Wisdom of Billy Carter
By James Rifkin and Ted Howard

Twilight Zone: Robert Todd Lincoln, son of Abraham Lincoln, was slated to attend the play *My American Cousin* with his father in 1865. Feeling fatigued, he canceled. He would have been seated behind his father, making it hard for actor John Wilkes Booth to assassinate his father. In 1881, Todd Lincoln, now Secretary of War, was with President James Garfield when the President was shot in Washington, D.C. In 1901, Lincoln was on his way to visit President William McKinley when McKinley was shot. Quite ironically, in 1864, Todd Lincoln fell off a train platform and onto the tracks as a train was approaching. In a twist of fate, Lincoln was saved by Edwin Booth, the brother of John Wilkes Booth.

Robert Todd Lincoln
Library of Congress

Watching Election Returns with Mom: Franklin D. Roosevelt spent election days with his mother, Sarah Ann Delano Roosevelt, at her residence in Hyde Park, New York.

Franklin D. Roosevelt with his Mother Sarah Ann Delano Roosevelt
Franklin D. Roosevelt Presidential Library and Museum

Presidential Family Members

Brother Billy: Jimmy Carter's brother Billy was a piece of work. Billy was considered a beer-drinking redneck who was always anxious to talk to the press. A brewer named his beer **"Billy Beer"** in an effort to improve sales. Sadly, the brewer soon went bankrupt. However, Billy was not done embarrassing his brother. He opened an unofficial diplomatic relationship with Libya, and would entertain Libyan government officials when they came for official visits to Washington D.C. The Justice Department later figured out that Billy was the proud recipient of a quarter million dollars as a paid lobbyist for Libyan President Muammar Kaddafi.

Jimmy Carter (L), Billy Carter (R)
Library of Congress

Being Stiffed by a Future President: During future President John F. Kennedy's first Congressional bid in 1946, Kennedy's mother, Rose, was riding in a cab. Mrs. Kennedy asked the driver his view on Kennedy and his congressional bid. The driver responded: **"It looks very good. He seems like a nice kid – a war hero."** Rose then boasted that John was her son. The driver looked at her and averred: **"I'm glad to run into you. Jack owes me two dollars and eighty-five cents from the last time he was in my cab."**

Rose Kennedy (L), John F. Kennedy (R)
John F. Kennedy Presidential Library and Museum

Remember the Alamo: Samuel Early Johnson Jr., the father of Lyndon B. Johnson, was a member of the Texas State Legislature. In that capacity, he was the chief sponsor of a bill for that state of Texas to purchase the Alamo.

Samuel Early Johnson Jr.
Lyndon Baines Johnson Presidential Library and Museum

Even a President is not good enough for her daughter: Madge Gates Wallace, the mother-in-law of Harry S. Truman, thought her daughter, Bess Wallace Truman, married beneath her social class. She referred to Harry as Mr. Truman throughout her life, including when he was President.

Madge Gates Wallace
Harry S. Truman Library and Museum

Chapter IV

Presidential Nepotism

Presidential Nepotism

Brother Shadowing: Lyndon B. Johnson employed his brother, Sam Houston Johnson, as an administrative aide. After the President left office, Sam wrote a book about his experience working for his brother entitled: *My Brother Lyndon*. While the book is mostly complimentary of the President, it criticizes some of his methods as a boss.

My Brother Lyndon **by Sam Houston Johnson**

"The Adams Family" In 1797, President John Adams appointed his son John Quincy Adams as Minister to Prussia. In addition, President Adams appointed his son-in-law, William Stephens Smith, as a Customs Agent, and appointed John Quincy Adams' Father-in-law, Joshua Johnson, to the position of Superintendent of Stamps.

John Adams
Painting by Gilbert Stuart

Working the System: In order to avoid charges of nepotism, President Andrew Jackson manipulated the situation so that his nephew, Andrew Jackson Donelson, would be hired as a general land office clerk. Jackson then requested he be assigned to work with Jackson in the White House.

Andrew Jackson Donelson
Library of Congress

Making Light of Nepotism: The issue of nepotism took center stage in the political arena in 1960. President-Elect John F. Kennedy nominated his younger brother, Robert F. Kennedy, to the esteemed position of U.S. Attorney General. It was crystal clear to most political observers that the younger Kennedy was under-qualified for the position. Kennedy was just 35 years old and sported no courtroom experience. John F. Kennedy made light of his brother's lack of experience and the nepotism charges, telling the Alfalfa Club that he nominated his brother: **"to give him a little experience before he goes out to practice law."**

Actually, Kennedy was very apprehensive about nominating his brother, but did so at the beseeching of his father Joseph P. Kennedy. The U.S. Senate on a voice vote confirmed Kennedy expeditiously. Had there been a roll call vote, it is unlikely that Robert F. Kennedy would have been confirmed. *Nation Magazine* called the nomination: **"the greatest example of nepotism this land has ever seen."**

John F. Kennedy (L), Robert F. Kennedy (R)
John F. Kennedy Presidential Library and Museum

Presidential Nepotism

Roundabout: Martin Van Buren circumvented the system the same way as Andrew Jackson did this by hiring his son Martin Jr. as a general land clerk and his other son Abraham as Second Auditor at the U.S. Treasury Department. He then had them transferred to the White House, and like Jackson, Van Buren utilized his sons as private secretaries. Presidents John Tyler and Millard Fillmore used these same methods to get their sons employed at the White House.

Martin Van Buren
Daguerreotype by Mathew Brady

Honorable: James K. Polk did not approve of the practice of making taxpayers pay for Presidential relatives on the federal payroll. However, he wanted his nephew James Knox Walker to work at the White House. Accordingly, Polk paid his salary out of his personal account.

James K. Polk
Library of Congress

No Age Limit Here: President Rutherford B. Hayes employed his son, Webb Hayes, as his confidential secretary, personal assistant, and bodyguard. At the time of his hiring, the younger Hayes was just 21 years old. Webb also served as the official greeter at White House functions.

Webb Hayes
Library of Congress

A lot of Responsibilities: Franklin D. Roosevelt appointed his son James as an administrative aide, coordinating the activity of 17 federal agencies. The younger Roosevelt came under assault by *The Saturday Evening Post* for allegedly using his title as the President's son to win contracts for his insurance firm. James vehemently denied these insinuations.

James Roosevelt
Harris & Ewing

Chapter V

Presidential Campaigns

Presidential Campaigns

Man of the People: During his campaign for the 1976 Democratic Presidential nomination, former U.S. Senator Fred Harris (D-OK) campaigned in a Winnebago and stayed at voter's houses rather than hotels. Harris promised those who hosted him would be invited to stay in the White House should he win. Harris lost, so he could not fulfill that pledge.

Fred Harris
University of Oklahoma

A Man who Stands by his Words, No Matter What they were: In May 2012, Republican Presidential candidate Mitt Romney was asked at a press conference in Jacksonville, FL, about comments he made in a February interview with FOX News talk show host Sean Hannity. Romney answered: **"I'm not familiar precisely with what I said, but I'll stand by what I said, whatever it was."**

Mitt Romney
Photograph by Greg Skidmore

Trigger-Happy? In 1964, President Lyndon B. Johnson campaigned for a full Presidential term in office in part by trying to tether his Republican opponent, Barry Goldwater, to extremists. When the Goldwater campaign used the slogan: **"In your heart you know he's right,"** the Johnson campaign cleverly retorted: **"In your gut you know he's nuts."**

Goldwater denied charges that he was **"trigger-happy."** He argued that Johnson's Secretary of Defense, Robert McNamara, had authorized the use of nuclear weapons in Vietnam. Actually, McNamara had ordered the Seventh Fleet to the Gulf of Tonkin, authorizing them to use **"whatever force is necessary,"** but had categorically discounted the use of nuclear weapons.

In order to combat Goldwater's line of attack that Johnson was actually more bellicose than him, either Johnson or a subordinate leaked to Chalmers Roberts of *The Washington Post* that Johnson had ordered the usage of **"conventional ordinances only."** This was proved by listening to Johnson directly giving that order. The President recorded his telephone conversations.

Barry Goldwater (L) and Lyndon B. Johnson (R)
Lyndon Baines Johnson Library and Museum

Americans are All Over America: In 1936, Republican Presidential nominee Alfred Landon said in a campaign speech: **"Wherever I have gone in this country, I have found Americans."**

Alfred Landon
Official Photograph

Presidential Campaigns

Cleveland Supporters Have Last Laugh: During the 1884 Presidential election, the Republicans alleged that Democrat Grover Cleveland had fathered an illegitimate child while a Buffalo attorney with Maria Crofts Halpin. When he found out about this illegitimate child, he had the child taken from the mother and placed in the Buffalo Orphan Asylum. The mother was institutionalized at the Providence Lunatic Asylum. Luckily for Maria Halpin, it did not take much time for her to pass psychiatric evaluation; she was clearly not insane and was let go. A smear campaign was then launched, making Maria Halpin appear that she had been a promiscuous woman. In reality, she was a religious widow who was raising two young children. Cleveland did not pay child support to Halpin, leading Republican opponents to chant: **"Ma, Ma, Where's my pa?"** After Cleveland won the election, his supporters returned fire, leading to chants of **"Gone to the White House Ha Ha Ha!"**

A Political Cartoon making light of the allegations that Cleveland had fathered Oscar Folsom Cleveland out of wedlock printed in *Judges Magazine*
Library of Congress

Jack Daniels is Ok with Pat Buchanan: When asked if he had ever used cocaine, 2000 Reform Party Presidential Candidate Pat Buchanan answered: **"No to marijuana, no to cocaine, and a question mark over Jack Daniels."**

Campaign Bumper Sticker for Pat Buchanan's 2000 Presidential campaign

Great Slogan: In 1972, former Massachusetts Governor Endicott Peabody ran unsuccessfully for the Democratic Vice Presidential nomination. His memorable slogan was: **"The number one man for the number two job."**

Endicott "Chub" Peabody
Library of Congress

Hoosierism: At the 1988 Republican National Convention, Republican Vice Presidential nominee Dan Quayle told California delegates: **"Let me just tell you how thrilling it really is, and how what a challenge it is, because in 1988 the question is whether we're going forward to tomorrow or whether we're going to go past to the back! ... That's Hoosierism. You've got to get used to that!"**

Dan Quayle
Official Photograph

Presidential Campaigns

Truman Does Not Want to be Vice President: In 1944, incoming Democratic National Committee Chairman Robert Hannigan told U.S. Senator Harry S. Truman (D-MO) that President Franklin D. Roosevelt wanted him to be his Vice Presidential runningmate. Harry S. Truman responded: **"Tell him to go to Hell! I'm for Jimmy Brynes."** Brynes was the Director of the Office of War Mobilization and a former South Carolina Governor, and U.S. Supreme Court Justice. Truman eventually relented and accepted Roosevelt's request. Roosevelt won re-election and died just 83 days into his fourth term, making Truman President.

Harry S. Truman (L),
Franklin D. Roosevelt (R)
Harry S. Truman Presidential Library and Museum

Luke Worm Endorsement: In 1968, U.S. Senator Eugene McCarthy (D-MN), who had unsuccessfully challenged Vice President Hubert Humphrey for the Democratic Presidential nomination, did not endorse Humphrey until the later days of the General Election. McCarthy's endorsement was tepid at best. He said: **"I'm voting for Humphrey, and I think you should suffer with me."** Many Humphrey supporters blame McCarthy's late luke warm endorsement for costing Humphrey the General Election to Republican nominee Richard M. Nixon.

Hubert Humphrey (L), Eugene McCarthy (R)
Library of Congress

Party Unity My Ass: In 1904, the Democratic Party nominated conservative New York Appeals Court Judge Alton B. Parker for President. William Jennings Bryan, the populist firebrand who had won the nomination in 1896 and 1900 declared: **"No self-respecting man would vote for him."**

Alton B. Parker
Library of Congress

One and Done? During a 1992 television interview, Democratic Presidential candidate Bill Clinton was asked if there is anything in his life he regrets. Clinton responded: **"When I was in England, I experimented with Marijuana a time or two and I didn't like it and didn't inhale and never tried it again."**

Bill Clinton 1992 Campaign Button

Presidential Campaigns

Tepid Endorsement: In 1972, former President Lyndon B. Johnson, who had escalated the U.S. role in the Vietnam War, was less than enthusiastic that his Democratic Party nominated vociferous Vietnam War critic George McGovern for President. Johnson offered this luke warm endorsement, without even mentioning McGovern's name: **"I believe the Democratic Party best represents the people. Therefore I intend to support the 1972 Democratic nominee."**

Lyndon B. Johnson
Lyndon Baines Johnson Library and Museum

Tree Hugger: In 2012, while campaigning in Michigan for the Republican Presidential nomination, Mitt Romney told the Detroit Economic Club: **"I love this state. The trees are the right height."**

Mitt Romney
Photograph by Greg Skidmore

Lampooning the Opposition: During the 1948 Presidential Election, Democratic President Harry S. Truman said that the strategy of his Republican opponents was: **"If you can't beat them, confuse them."**

Harry S. Truman
Harry S. Truman Presidential Library & Museum

Vote for the Wife: In 1976, Gerald R. Ford's wife Betty became so popular, that is was not unusual to see bumper-stickers and campaign buttons reading: **"I'm voting for Betty's Husband."**

Gerald R. For President Pin 1976

Presidential Campaigns

Dole Gives It Right Back: Before the New Hampshire Primary in 1988, Republican Presidential candidate Bob Dole was confronted by a heckler who said: **"You've voted for tax increases 600 times in your career. How can you defend that?"** Dole responded: **"Check back into your cave."**

Bob Dole Campaigning for President in 1988
Robert J. Dole Archives and Special Collections

The Trifecta: When speculating about a possible bid for the 1960 Democratic Presidential nomination, U.S. Senator Eugene McCarthy (D-MN) jokingly compared himself to the three declared candidates for the nomination: **"I'm twice as liberal as Hubert Humphrey, twice as intelligent as Stuart Symington, and twice as Catholic as Jack Kennedy."**

Eugene McCarthy
Library of Congress

The Adams v. Jefferson Slugfest: During the 1800 Presidential election, John Adams and Thomas Jefferson were embroiled in an intense and dirty Presidential election. During the campaign, Adams branded Jefferson **"a mean-spirited, low-lived fellow, the son of a half-breed Indian squaw, sired by a Virginia mulatto father."** The Adams campaign warned that a Jefferson Presidency would usher in an era of: **"murder, robbery, rape, adultery, and incest will be openly taught and practiced, the air will be rent with cries of the distressed, the soil will be soaked with blood and the nation black with crimes."** Despite these attacks and admonishments against him, Jefferson won the election.

Thomas Jefferson (L), John Adams (R)
Library of Congress

Hog Days of Summer: At a 1992 luncheon at the Democratic National Convention in New York, Texas Governor Ann Richards drew laughter by commenting: **"Well, you can put lipstick on a hog and call it Monique, but it's still a pig."** She was referring to feckless government programs.

Ann Richards
Texas State Libraries and Archives Commission

Presidential Campaigns

Why Bring Leonard Wood Into This? In 2012, Republican Presidential candidate Newt Gingrich called opponent Mitt Romney **"the weakest Republican frontrunner since Leonard Wood in 1920."** Americans who looked up the reference found that the now obscure figure was the early front-runner in 1920. He led in Republican delegates, but lost the nomination to U.S. Senator Warren G. Harding (R-OH.)

Leonard Wood
U.S. Army Employee

Name Recognition: In a 2015 address in Fort Dodge, Iowa, Republican Presidential candidate Donald Trump referred to opponent Carly Fiorina as: **"Carly-whatever-the-hell-her-name-is."**

Cary Fiorina
Photograph by Gage Skidmore

The Unhappy Warrior: In 1936, the Democratic Party's 1928 Presidential nominee Al Smith endorsed the Republican Presidential nominee Alf Landon over Democratic nominee President Franklin D. Roosevelt. Smith, a conservative Democrat, became a critic of the more liberal Roosevelt, saying his domestic New Deal Programs pit: **"class against class."** That prompted U.S. Senator Joseph Robinson (D-AR), Smith's former runningmate, to brand Smith derisively as **"The Unhappy Warrior."** Roosevelt had given Smith the moniker: **"Happy Warrior"** in 1924 when the two were allies. It was meant as a term of endearment.

Campaign Poster for the Al Smith/Joseph Robinson Ticket in 1934

Eating One's Words: During the 2016 Presidential election, U.S. House Minority Leader Nancy Pelosi (D-CA) told Kara Swisher, host of Recode Decode: **"Donald Trump is not going to be President of the United States. Take it to the bank, I guarantee it."**

Nancy Pelosi
Official Photograph

76

Presidential Campaigns

Humphrey Plays "Tonto:" During the 1968 Presidential campaign, Republican Vice President Spiro Agnew compared Democratic Vice Presidential nominee Hubert Humphrey to Tonto (the Native American sidekick of The Loan Ranger in the 1950s television series by the same name) for his role as loyal Vice President to President Lyndon B. Johnson. Agnew told a rally in Las Vegas: **"After playing Tonto for so long, apparently Mr. Humphrey isn't comfortable playing the Loan Ranger. In fact, with all of Humphrey's efforts to break away from the administration, perhaps Dick Nixon and I should keep quiet and let Mr. Humphrey and Mr. Johnson fight it out."**

Lyndon B. Johnson (L), and Hubert Humphrey (R)
Lyndon Baines Johnson Presidential Library

A Dose of Reality Finally Sets In: William Jennings Bryan was the Democratic Presidential nominee in 1896, 1900, and 1908. He lost all three Presidential elections. After losing for the third time, Bryan opined: **"I'm beginning to think those fellows don't want me in there."**

William Jennings Bryan
Library of Congress

When Republicans Were Democrats: In 1888, Republican Presidential nominee Benjamin Harrison defeated incumbent Democratic President Grover Cleveland by advocating what are now considered Democratic proposals. He pledged to expand the money supply, expand the protective tariff, and to increase federal funding for social services.

Benjamin Harrison
Library of Congress

Frustration with New Fangled Invention: With the advent of the teleprompter, Presidential candidates were expected to use the device so they would not have to look down during their speeches. In a 1952 speech in Indianapolis, Indiana, Republican Presidential nominee Dwight D. Eisenhower became impatient with the devise. He yelled to the operator of the devise: **"Go ahead! Go ahead! Go ahead! Yah, damn it, I want him to move up."**

Dwight D. Eisenhower
Library of Congress

77

Rage Against Paul Ryan: When Mitt Romney selected Paul Ryan as his Vice Presidential running mate in 2012, it was publicized that his favorite band was the rap metal band "Rage Against the Machine." The band's guitarist Tom Morrello did not return the love and blasted Ryan, exclaiming **"Ryan is the embodiment of the machine that our music has been raging against for two decades."**

Paul Ryan
Official Photograph

The 103rd Ballot: In 1924, John W. Davis, the former U.S. Solicitor General and past U.S. Ambassador to the United Kingdom, won the Democratic Presidential Nomination on a record 103rd ballot. But all was for not, as Davis lost the general election to Republican President Calvin Coolidge.

John W. Davis
Library of Congress

Unpack: In 1928, Democrat Al Smith became the first major party Presidential nominee to be Catholic. Rumors swirled that Pope Pious XI would come to the United States and become a puppeteer pulling Smith's strings. The day after Smith lost the election in an electoral landslide, a joke disseminated that Smith telegrammed the Pope with the statement: **"Unpack."**

Al Smith
Photograph by Harris and Ewing

Not so Sober Advice: In 1856, President Franklin Pierce lost his own Party's nomination for reelection to James Buchanan who was serving as Ambassador to the United Kingdom. When he found out that he had lost, Pierce deadpanned: **"There's nothing left to do but get drunk."**

Franklin Pierce
Library of Congress

Presidential Campaigns

Oh, so that is how that Works: In 2015, Republican Presidential aspirant Ben Carson said in an exchange with CNN that Homosexuality is a choice and that this is proved **"Because a lot of people who go into prison, go into prison straight. And when they come out, they're gay. So did something happen while they were in there? Ask yourself that question."**

Ben Carson
Official Photograph

Presidential Nominee Gets Cut Off for Talking too Much: On the last night before the 1952 Presidential election, Democratic Presidential nominee Adlai Stevenson addressed the nation. His campaign paid for the allotted time. However, Stevenson droned on and the networks cut off the broadcast with Stevenson in mid-sentence. This embarrassing moment proved a harbinger of things to come, as Stevenson lost the election the next day in an electoral landslide to Republican Dwight D. Eisenhower.

Adlai Stevenson 1956 Campaign Poster

President of What? In 1974, Jimmy Carter told his mother, Lillian Carter, that he would seek the Presidency. She responded: **"President of What?"**

Jimmy Carter (L), Lillian Carter (R)
National Archives and Records Administration

Trump is in the Wrong State: In 2016, Republican Presidential nominee Donald Trump became the third person elected President despite losing his home state of New York. The other two were James K. Polk of Tennessee in 1844 and Woodrow Wilson of New Jersey in 1916. Trump lost his home state of New York, a Democratic citadel and the adopted home state of Democratic nominee Hillary Clinton, by 22.49% of the popular vote. Clinton won Queens, the borough where Trump was born, with 75% of the vote, and Manhattan, where Trump resided, with 87% of the vote.

Trump Tower in Manhattan
Photograph by Jorge Lascar

Presidential Campaigns

Less Intelligent? In 1968, after losing the Democratic Presidential primary in Indiana, Eugene McCarthy told a crowd in Oregon, the next contest, that supporters of Rival Robert F. Kennedy **"were among the less intelligent and less educated people in America."**

Robert F. Kennedy Addresses His Supporters
English Wikpedia

Getting the Money out of Politics: After dropping out of the 2016 Republican Presidential sweepstakes, U.S. Senator Lindsey Graham (R-SC) endorsed his former rival Jeb Bush for the nomination. About his own effort, Graham opined: **"I got out because I ran out of money. If you want to get money out of politics, you should have joined my campaign."**

Lindsey Graham
Official Photograph

Obama Promoted by a Republican in Advertisement: In an advertisement run during the 2008 Democratic Presidential Primaries, Obama did not present himself as an unadulterated progressive. He held himself out as a post partisan figure that would work toward bipartisan solutions to the nation's problems. Obama featured Kirk Dillard, a Republican who worked with Obama when both served in the Illinois State Senate, in a campaign advertisement wherein Dillard explained: **"Senator Obama worked on some of the deepest issues we had, and he was successful in a bipartisan way. Republican legislators respected Senator Obama. His negotiation skills and an ability to understand both sides would serve the country very well."**

Kirk Dillard
Official Photograph

The Babe Makes an Endorsement: After the New York Yankees won the 1928 World Series, slugger Babe Ruth gave speeches for Democratic Presidential nominee Al Smith from the back of the train, which was carrying the championship team home to New York. He was not gracious to hecklers. At one stop, Ruth bellowed: **"If that's the way you feel, the hell with you."**

Babe Ruth (L), Al Smith (R)
Library of Congress

Presidential Campaigns

Heckler Puts Presidential Nominee in His Place: In 1896, Democratic Presidential nominee William Jennings Bryan broke precedent and barnstormed the country, campaigning for himself. He delivered over 600 speeches in 27 states. Prior to this, candidates used surrogates to campaign for them, and only spoke to voters who came to their hometowns to visit them. At one stop, Bryan told the audience: **"After the election, I will be sleeping in the White House."** A heckler who supported the campaign of Republican Presidential nominee William McKinley bellowed: **"If you do, you'll be sleeping with Mrs. McKinney."**

Ida McKinley
Library of Congress

If only Reagan had Campaigned Harder for Me: During the summer of 1976, Democratic Presidential nominee Jimmy Carter held a 34-point lead over Republican President Gerald R. Ford. Ford almost closed the gap, just losing the election by two percentage points. Ford believed that had former California Governor Ronald Reagan campaigned for him with conservative Democrats in the South that he would have won the election. Reagan had challenged Ford in the Republican Primary and was popular with the conservative base. To Ford's dismay, Reagan had other commitments and spent limited time on the campaign trail.

Ronald Reagan (L) and Gerald R. Ford (R) at the 1976 Republican National Convention
Gerald R. Ford Presidential Library and Museum

Premarital Affair: In 1975, Democratic Presidential candidate Jimmy Carter was asked by a reporter how he would feel if his daughter Amy participated in a premarital affair. Carter responded: **"I would be deeply shocked and disappointed --- because our daughter is only seven years old."**

Amy Carter with her Cat
Executive Office of The President
of the United States

Cry Babies: After Donald Trump was elected President in 2016, some universities held **"cry-ins"** for students and staff members to bewail his election. This prompted Trump supporter and former New York City Mayor Rudy Giuliani to label the participants **"a bunch of spoiled crybabies."**

Rudy Giuliani
Photograph by Jason Bedrick

Presidential Campaigns

Define Restrained: In 2016, after being elected President, Donald Trump was asked by reporter Leslie Stahl on *60 Minutes*: **"Are you going to be tweeting?"** Trump answered: **"I'm going to be very restrained, if I use it at all."**

Lesley Stahl
Photograph by Charles Bogel

Early Microtargeting: In 1896, the campaign of Republican Presidential Nominee William McKinley put out the first publication promoting a Presidential campaign in Yiddish.

William McKinley
Library of Congress

Playing the Invalid Card: In 1988, the Democratic Presidential nominee did not release his medical records. President Ronald Reagan remarked as he was leaving a press conference: **"I'm not going to pick on an invalid."** A contrite Reagan later remarked that day: **"I was kidding . . . I was just trying to be funny and it didn't work."** The remarks prompted speculation by some that Dukakis may have had mental health problem.

Michael Dukakis for President Pin, 1988

Just the Facts: During his 1988 speech at the Republican National Convention, where Vice President George H.W. Bush was nominated for President, Ronald Reagan attempted to quote John Adams, who said: **"Facts are stubborn things."** Reagan mistakenly said: **"Facts are stupid things."**

Ronald Reagan
National Archives and Records Administration

Presidential Campaigns

Mortician-in-Chief: In 1952, after Dwight D. Eisenhower announced his candidacy for the Republican Presidential nomination, the campaign manager for an opponent, Robert A. Taft, reacted: **"We don't want to turn the party over to a good looking mortician."**

Dwight D. Eisenhower
Library of Congress

The Panacea, Cut Capital Gains: At the 1991 New Hampshire Democratic Party Convention, Presidential candidate Tom Harkin (D-IA) made fun of Republican President George H.W. Bush's emphasis on cutting Capital Gains Taxes. Harkin Said: **"Bush's recovery program can be summed up in three words: Cut Capital Gains. That's his answer to everything. Give more tax cuts to the rich. You've got eight million unemployed, cut Capital Gains. Stagnant economy, cut capital gains, trade deficit, cut Capital Gains. Got a tooth ache, cut Capital Gains."**

Tom Harkin for President Bumper Sticker

Friends and Opponents: The grandmother of future Vice President Alben Barkley was a childhood friend of Vice President Adlai Stevenson. In 1952, Alben Barkley sought but did not garner the Democratic Presidential nomination. He lost to Illinois Governor Adlai Stevenson III, Stevenson's Grandson.

Adlai Stevenson III
Library of Congress

"Wild Man" Tim Kaine: In 2016, *New York Times* reporter Yamiche Alcindor received a fraudulent email allegedly from Democratic National Committee Chairwoman Donna Brazile, with an article allegedly written by Democratic Vice Presidential Nominee Tim Kaine. The piece was about the responsibilities of the Vice President. It read: **"It's like when you go to a club, and you see those hot girls next to their boring ugly friends. I'm the one that doesn't get drugged at the bar, because no one wants to touch me with a fifty-foot pole."**

Tim Kaine
Official Photograph

83

Presidential Campaigns

"Ladies and Gentlemen, Moderating Tonight's Debate, John Lester:" A 2016 Presidential debate between Hillary Clinton and Donald Trump was moderated by NBC News Anchor Lester Holt. Trump supporters were irate that Holt asked tough questions of Trump. Accordingly, they went to Twitter and excoriated him. The problem is that they typed **"Lester"** and Chicago Cubs pitcher John Lester usually came up. John Lester received many angry tweets when he told the tweeters that they have the wrong person. One Trump supporter suggested John Lester might be trying to get an appointment in a Hillary Clinton administration, to which Lester responded: **"I'll be pretty busy doing my own thing so I think I'll be okay. Perhaps you should send this to Lester Holt."**

John Lester
Photograph by Arturo Pardavila 1lll

Inadvertent Gaffe Corrected: During a 2007 Iowa debate, Democratic Presidential aspirant John Edwards said: **"I want every caucus-goer to know I've been fighting these people and winning my entire life. And if we do this together, rise up together, we can actually make absolutely certain, starting here in Iowa, that we make this country better than we left it."** After an uproarious laughter by the audience, Edwards corrected himself and said: **"Leave it better than we started."**

John Edwards
Official Photograph

Spreading Partisan Manure: In 1896, Democratic Presidential nominee William Jennings Bryan noticed at a campaign stop in Missouri that there was no platform from which to deliver his stump speech. A supporter found a manure spreader and rolled it out for Bryan to stand on. Bryan stood on the spreader and said: **"This is the first time I have ever spoken from a Republican Platform."**

William Jennings Bryan
Library of Congress

Vice President? No Way: In 1980 there was speculation that Independent Presidential candidate John Anderson would ask former U.S. Health, Education, and Welfare Secretary Joseph Califano to be his Vice Presidential running mate. Califano told Civil Liberties Attorney Mitchell Rogovin: **"Vice Presidents are candidates for castration."**

Joseph Califano
Lyndon Baines Johnson
Presidential Library and Museum

Presidential Campaigns

Shark Attack: In a 2012 interview with Ben Howe of the Iowa Republican TV Channel, 2008 Republican Presidential candidate Tom Tancredo shared a story from his campaign. **"We were at the University of New Hampshire and we were all going to a debate and there are all Ron Paul people and they're very excited and there's a guy standing there in a shark suit and one of my staff goes up and says 'Oh hi, are you with the Ron Paul people?' and the guy goes, Oh No! They're all nuts. I just wear a shark suit."**

Tom Tancredo
Official Photograph

Going the Distance: In 1964, many down ballot Republican candidates tried to distance themselves from their party's Presidential nominee Barry Goldwater, who was unpopular in much of the country. In Michigan, Governor George Romney's re-election campaign mailed out about 200,000 mock ballots showing voters how to mark their ballots for Democratic President Lyndon B. Johnson for President and Romney for Governor. Romney won re-election, while Goldwater handily lost Michigan.

George Romney
Library of Congress

Straight Whiskey and Politics: At the 1904 Republican National Convention, the Chairman, U.S. House Speaker Joe Cannon (R-IL), introduced former Kentucky Governor William O'Connell Bradley who seconded the nomination of President Theodore Roosevelt, as coming from a state **"where Republicans take politics, like whisky, straight."**

William O'Connell Bradley
Sketch by M.H. Thatcher

Likability Factor: 2008 Democratic Presidential candidate Hillary Clinton was asked in a debate why some voters like her opponent Barack Obama more than her. Clinton replied: **"Well that hurts my feelings but I'll try to go on." He's very likable. I don't think I'm that bad."** Obama interjected: **"Your likable enough Hillary, don't worry about it."**

Hillary Clinton
William J. Clinton Presidential
Library and Museum

Presidential Campaigns

No Love for the Job: When Republican Calvin Coolidge garnered the GOP Vice Presidential nomination in 1920, incumbent Vice President Thomas Riley Marshall telegraphed Coolidge: **"Please accept my sincere sympathy."**

Thomas Riley Marshall
Library of Congress

Putting the Cart Before The Horse: In 1940, after the Republicans nominated Wendell Willkie as their Presidential nominee, a reporter asked him if he would meet with Democrat Franklin D. Roosevelt should he win re-nomination by the Democrats for a third Presidential term. Willkie responded: **"Certainly, if I am invited. One should always be courteous to one's predecessor."**

Wendell Willkie
Library of Congress

From George W. to George W: In his speech accepting the Republican Party's Presidential nomination in Philadelphia in 2000, George W. Bush paid homage to the city for hosting the Constitutional Convention in 1787. He exclaimed: **"Ben Franklin was here. Thomas Jefferson. And, of course, George Washington -- or, as his friends called him, George W."**

George W. Bush
White House Photograph by Eric Draper

That is All I am Going to Say: In 1940, Republican Presidential candidate Robert A. Taft was meeting with Republican luminaries. His cousin, David Ingalls, was listening to the conversation and heard radio silence. He saw Taft reading a newspaper while his confused guests were waiting for Taft to say more. He told Ingalls he was reading the newspaper because: **"I had learned all that I could."**

Robert A. Taft
Ohio History Central

86

Presidential Campaigns

A Message of Inclusion and Hope: While exploring a Presidential candidacy in 1968, George Wallace told a reporter: **"There is too much dignity in government now. What we need is some meanness."**

George Wallace for President Campaign Banner

The Simple way of Doing Things: In 1927, while on vacation at his vacation home in the Black Hills of South Dakota, President Calvin Coolidge personally handed a piece of paper to reporters with the words: **"I do not choose to run for President in nineteen-twenty-eight."** He then walked back into the house, without answering any questions.

Calvin Coolidge
Library of Congress

Going to Korea and the White House: 1952 Republican Presidential nominee Dwight D. Eisenhower announced that if elected he would **"go to Korea"** to negotiate an end to the Korean War. His Democratic opponent, Adlai Stevenson retorted: **"If elected, I shall go to the White House."** Eisenhower won the election and did go to Korea and the White House.

Dwight D. Eisenhower
Library of Congress

Showdown State: In the 2012 Presidential campaign, President Barack Obama made no effort to hide his focus on Ohio above the non-battleground states. This is evidenced by a statement he made on *The Tonight Show with Jay Leno* on October 25, 2012. Six days prior to Halloween, the President joked that trick or treaters should come to the White House. He added: **"If anybody comes from Ohio, they can expect a Hershey bar 'This' big [moving his hands outward]."**

Barack Obama
White House Photograph

Presidential Campaigns

A Definitive Plan? In 1980, Democratic Presidential aspirant Ted Kennedy was asked how he would handle the Iranian Hostage Crisis differently than President Jimmy Carter. He responded that he **"would have explored every foreign policy initiative, encouraged every member of the House and Senate to speak out with their ideas, and sought creative, imaginary ideas from other leaders."** Carter defeated Kennedy for the nomination.

Ted Kennedy (L), Jimmy Carter (R)
National Archives and Records Administration

Fat v. Skinny Cats: In the 2000 race for the Republican Presidential nomination, George W. Bush raised record amounts of money, many from well-heeled benefactors, often derisively referred to as "fat cats." An opponent, Orrin Hatch, quipped: **"George Bush has fat cats. I want skinny cats."** After Bush raised $36 million, Hatch asked and received donations of just $36 dollars. In the end, Bush won the nomination, and Hatch dropped out of the race in January.

Orrin Hatch
Official Photograph

Only in New Hampshire Politics: In the 1968 New Hampshire Democratic Primary, there was speculation that challenger Eugene McCarthy might garner more votes than expected. This would be seen in many political circles as a victory for McCarthy. The night of the primary, incumbent President Lyndon B. Johnson joked at a Veterans of Foreign Wars dinner: **"I think New Hampshire is the only place where a candidate can claim 20 percent is a landslide, 40 percent is a mandate and 60 percent is unanimous."** Johnson won the state, with 49.2 percent of the vote. However, the media covered McCarthy's 42.2 percent like it was a victory.

Eugene McCarthy Campaign Poster

The Thinking Person's Vote Will Not Cut It: During the 1952 Presidential election, an enthusiastic supporter approached the Democratic Presidential nominee, Adlai Stevenson, and said: **"Governor, every thinking person will be voting for you."** Stevenson replied: **"Madam that is not enough. I need a majority."**

Adlai Stevenson
Library of Congress

Chapter VI

Haunted White House Happenings

Just Give the Ghost His Land Back: David Burns was forced to sell his land to the Federal Government in 1790 so that the Executive Mansion (Now Known as the White House) could be built. He did not want to sell his land. One day during the Presidency of Harry S. Truman, a White House Security Guard heard a ghostly voice repeating: **"I am Mr. Burns"** and **"I am David Burns."** Burns evidently never let go of his grievances even after his death about being forced to sell his land to the Federal Government.

Plan for Construction of Washington D.C.
Library of Congress

Honest Abe Still Making Waves: Queen Wilhelmina of the Netherlands occasionally was a Houseguest at the White House. On one visit, she heard a knock at the door and went to answer it. She was horrified to see the Ghost of Abraham Lincoln standing in front of her in full physical form. She screamed and passed out. She was later found on the floor by White House staff.

Queen Wilhelmina of the Netherlands
Library of Congress

Trying The Supernatural: Mary Todd Lincoln was devastated by the assassination of her husband Abraham. Believing that Spiritualists who had helped her communicate with her dead son in the past could be a way to communicate with her late husband, she took a trip to New England and stayed at a Spiritualist commune. While she was there, she met William Mumler was a photographer who claimed that he had a special power to photograph the spirit of the departed. The photograph that he took of her became one of her most valued possessions. It is now known that the sleight of hand this photographer used was to superimpose images to make it look like the dead had returned. It showed Abraham Lincoln in a wispy cloudlike specter with his hands grasping Mary's shoulders. Mrs. Lincoln wrote to a friend: **"A very slight veil separates us from the loved and lost."** During this time period the Spiritualist Church had over two million members. Many members wanted to have one last word with those loved ones lost in the Civil War.

Mary Todd Lincoln
Library of Congress

Ghostly Proposal: John Tyler must have been quite the romantic. On numerous occasions he has been spotted in the Blue Room as he proposes to his beloved second wife, Julia Gardner.

Julia Gardner Tyler
Library of Congress

Laughing Andy: Andrew Jackson was known for enjoying a good joke. In fact, since the 1860's, he has been spotted lying in his old bed, which is now the Rose Room, letting out bursts of hysterical laughter.

Andrew Jackson
Library of Congress

He Was Only There for 31 Days, Let him Stay: It appears that President William Henry Harrison continues to walk through the halls of the White House attic, apparently looking for something. Those who allege to have seen him have seen him rummaging around through old boxes hunting for a lost item. Later Presidents have complained that they have heard weird noises directly above the Oval Office, in the attic. Hopefully, at some point, William Henry Harrison will find what he is looking for and can finally rest in peace, and allow others to rest as well.

William Henry Harrison
Portrait by Otis Bass

She Just Won't Leave: It is rumored that Abigail Adams, the wife of President John Adams, never moved out of the 1600 Pennsylvania Avenue. When Abigail lived there, the White House was cold and damp. Surprisingly, she did her own laundry and hung it in the East Room, which was the only room that was warm enough and dry enough that her laundry would dry. President William Howard Taft told friends that he had seen Abigail floating down the second floor and walking directly through a door. She allegedly continues to haunt the East Room. She can be seen gliding into the room carrying a basket of wet laundry that is scented with lavender. There have been reports that tourists visiting the White House in 2002 saw Abigail dressed in a lace shawl.

Abigail Adams
Library of Congress

Dog Sense: Ronald Reagan was convinced that the reason his dog Rex would back up and refuse to go into the Lincoln bedroom was because he was able to see Lincoln's ghost.

Rex
Ronald Reagan Presidential Library & Museum

White House Haunted Happenings

Bring in the Mediums: Abraham Lincoln's son William "Willie" Lincoln fell victim to Typhoid Fever while living in the White House. In the 1870's staffers to President Ulysses S. Grant claimed to have witnessed seeing Willie's ghost. In the 1960's, Willie's ghost reappeared to President Lyndon B. Johnson's daughter, Linda Bird. The room that Linda Bird was staying in was the same room where Willie Lincoln died. She claims to have seen him on numerous occasions and even had a conversation with him. The public had very little sympathy for Mrs. Lincoln, believing that she was lucky to be at her son's side at his death, whereas many other mothers lost their sons on the battlefield of the Civil War. Desperate to speak to her dead son, Mary Lincoln brought in a series of mediums in an attempt to contact him. A famous medium nicknamed Colchester of Georgetown came to the White House to conduct a séance he termed **"Calls to the dead."** Mrs. Lincoln was convinced that all of the spiritualists that she had brought to the White House actually brought her son back to her. She claimed that her dead son took physical form and stood at the foot of her bed.

Willie Lincoln
Library of Congress

Crazy Ghost: Mary Todd Lincoln claims to have seen the Ghost of Andrew Jackson multiple times in the White House. She complained that he would be crashing around the long corridors yelling curse words at absolutely no one.

Andrew Jackson
Library of Congress

Ghost Dolly: Dolly Madison, the wife of President James Madison, loved gardening and spent much of her free time in the White House Rose Garden. Over a hundred years later, President Woodrow Wilson's wife Ellen told the White House gardeners that she wanted the Rose Garden removed. To the gardeners' horror, Dolly Madison's ghost appeared before them and stopped them from destroying the garden. The garden continues to bloom in its splendor, and often times the smell of roses can unexpectedly fill the rooms on that side of the White House, even when there are no roses present. Many people believe this is Dolly Madison checking in.

Dolly Madison
Library of Congress

Jefferson Still Playing Tunes: Thomas Jefferson was a music aficionado, and would play the violin to unwind. It is believed that Jefferson continues to give concerts for everyone who would like to hear him in the Yellow Oval Room.

Thomas Jefferson
Library of Congress

White House Haunted Happenings

Sad Ghost: Mary Surratt was hanged for her involvement in the assassination of Abraham Lincoln in 1865. It is believed that the ghost of Surratt's daughter sometimes violently bangs on the White House door pleading her mother's innocence, and demanding that she be released. Supposedly, the Ghost reappears every June 7th, which is the anniversary of her mother's hanging. The Ghost sits on the White House steps weeping.

Mary Surratt
Library of Congress

Abe Will Just Not Leave: First Lady Grace Coolidge reportedly saw Abraham Lincoln in the White House in the mid-1920's. Coolidge walked into the Oval Office and to her surprise, Lincoln was looking out the window beyond the Potomac River to land that was formally Civil War battlefields.

Grace Coolidge
Library of Congress

"The Thing." During the William Howard Taft Presidency, domestic staff members became aware of an eerie presence in the White House. The spirit became visible and was that of a teenage boy. The White House staff was terrified and named the ghost "The thing." They claimed that they could feel him leaning against them or looking over their shoulder. Even Major Archibald Butt, The President's military aide, wrote to his sister about the ghostly encounters. It reached the point where Taft had to intervene. He lectured Butt about how this "ghost talk" was agitating the staff. He told Butt to make it perfectly clear to all staff members that the next person referencing **"the thing"** would be fired on the spot.

William Howard Taft
Library of Congress

Oh, Hello Mr. Lincoln: Lady Bird Johnson was an Abraham Lincoln aficionado. While watching a television show about Lincoln's death, she claims she ran into Lincoln face-to-face. Her husband, Lyndon's' Presidency was embroiled in controversy over Civil Rights legislation, racial rioting, and protests over the war in Vietnam. It is believed that Abraham Lincoln's ghost appears in the White House during a time of extreme crisis. Perhaps it is possible that his ghost had returned from the grave in an effort to stabilize the nation.

Lady Bird Johnson
Lyndon Baines Johnson Library and Museum

Chapter VII

White House Rats

Chasing Rats: Andrew Jackson had a problem with rats in the White House during his Presidency from 1829-1837. He could hear the rats in the basement chewing on wood and making strange noises. He was at his wits end and finally hired an exterminator. The rats were poisoned, but rather than running outside to die, they went back into their dens in the basement. Instead of hearing horrible sounds in the basement, he had to put up with the stench of rotting rat flesh that permeated the entire White House.

Andrew Jackson
Portrait by Ralph W. Earl

You Filthy Rats: When Benjamin Harrison moved into the White House in 1889 his wife Carolyn was appalled at the filthy living conditions. She gave the mansion a good scrubbing and soon realized that the White House was totally infested with rats. Mrs. Harrison wrote in her diary: **"The rats have nearly taken the building so it has become necessary to hire a man with ferrets. They [rats] have become so numerous and bold they get up on the table in the Upper Hall and one got up on Mr. Halford's bed."** Halford was Mr. Harrison's Secretary who was living in the White House following surgery.

Benjamin Harrison
Portrait by Eastman Johnson

White House Safari: Theodore Roosevelt was annoyed by the rodent infestation in the White House. He and his children would pretend to go on safari, and would actually hunt rats throughout the White House.

Theodore Roosevelt (C), with His Offspring
Library of Congress

Mystery Solved: When Harry S. Truman and his family moved into the White House residence, he was disgusted by the smell. Workers at the White House assured him that he had nothing to worry about because the smell was coming from outside. He was not so sure. Upon investigation, he was positive that the putrid odor was in fact coming from the White House. Finally, White House repairmen crashed through the wall and the stench became greater. Upon closer observation, they found a decomposing rat next to a moldy hambone. The mystery smell was solved.

Harry S. Truman
Harry S. Truman Presidential Library and Museum

This is a Job For Kennedy: John F. Kennedy was horrified when he heard that rats have been seen swimming in the White House swimming pool. When rats finally invaded the Oval Office, he had reached his breaking point. He quickly removed his shoe and lobbed it directly at one of the little scoundrels.

John F. Kennedy
Harry S. Truman Presidential Library and Museum

The Rodent War: Jimmy Carter was disgusted because the Oval Office was infested with mice. He was embarrassed because when the Prime Minister from Italy was in his office it was obvious that something had died in the walls and that the stench was something more than they could stand. Carter complained to the maintenance staff who suggested it was not politically correct to use mousetraps. The number of mice seemed to be increasing daily, and Carter's patience had worn thin. He finally got the National Park Service, the General Service Administration, and the Interior Department involved in getting rid of the mice. Within days, hundreds of spring traps and fifty bate boxes were put in place. With this superior power, Carter had won the Rodent War.

Jimmy Carter
Official Photograph

A Tail of a Ginormous Rat: Barbara Bush has her own "rat tail" to tell. Mrs. Bush enjoyed swimming laps in the White House pool every day. On one such occasion, she noticed a fury black creature swimming in her direction. She was awe struck by this ginormous rat doing laps beside her. Her trusted k-9 companion Millie jumped into the water to save her from the giant rat. Ultimately, her husband, George H.W. Bush, saved the day. He held the rat below the surface of the water until he drowned the rude rodent. Mrs. Bush later reflected on the incident with reporters, and explained why she thought the rat was in the pool. It was her opinion that the groundskeepers had recently put rat poison around the White House grounds. When rats ate the rat poison, they got an insatiable thirst for water and the pool offered a place to quench their thirst.

Barbara and George H.W. Bush
National Archives and Records Administration

A Chubby Rat Takes the Bully Pulpit: In 2010, with the White House press corps assembled, President Barack Obama was delivering a speech on financial reforms when a chubby rat came out of the bushes and ran directly in front of the President's podium.

Barack Obama
Official Photograph

Chapter VIII

Political Family Feuds

Political Family Feuds

Brother Against Brother: In 1888, the two major party Gubernatorial nominees in Tennessee were brothers. The Democrats nominated former U.S. Representative Robert Taylor (D-TN). The Republicans nominated Robert's older brother, attorney Alfred "Alf" Taylor. The two brothers remained on good terms and traveled together throughout the campaign. Bob said at one of their debates that the two brothers were "roses from the same garden." Accordingly, the race earned the moniker: **"The War of the Roses."** Robert later recalled of this peculiar race: **"There were lots of old fellows who didn't vote for either of us because they were friends of both, but I do not know of a single Republican vote that I got nor a single Democrat vote that he got."** Robert won the election by about 16,000 votes. The election was uncommonly civil. Robert went on to serve for four years as the Governor of the Volunteer state. Alfred eventually captured the Tennessee Governorship in 1920.

Robert Taylor
Library of Congress

Alfred "Alf" Taylor
Library of Congress

Roosevelt Dynasty Crumbles: This family has not always been in electoral unison. In 1912, former President Theodore Roosevelt defected from the Republican Party and ran for President as the nominee of the Progressive Party (a.k.a. Bull Mouse Party). Roosevelt's son-in-law, Nicholas Longworth, was married to Roosevelt's daughter Alice. Longworth was a Republican member of the U.S. House of Representatives from Ohio. Ironically, Longworth did not support his father-in-law for political office, but instead, supported the Republican nominee, President William Howard Taft. Longworth styled himself as **"a Taft man through-and-through."** Roosevelt's populist insurgent campaign enjoyed a groundswell of support in Longworth's Ohio Congressional District. Unlike her husband, Alice supported her father's campaign for President. In fact, she made an appearance with California Governor Hiram Johnson, (Roosevelt's Vice Presidential runningmate) in her husband's Congressional District. This surreal event galvanized Progressive voters to turn out at the polls to support Roosevelt. Most of these voters also voted for the Progressive Party House Candidate Millard F. Andrew, who siphoned votes from Longworth, allowing Democrat Stanley Eyre Bowdle to upset Longworth by just 101 votes. It can be reasonably argued that Alice's campaign appearance with her father's runningmate cost her own husband the Congressional race. The election was so close that a six-day recount was performed, with Bowdle declared the winner. Ironically, both Roosevelt and Taft lost the Presidential election to Democrat Woodrow Wilson. The election was an electoral disaster for the Roosevelt family.

In 1924, the Democrats nominated New York Governor Al Smith for re-election. The Republicans countered by nominating Assistant U.S. Navy Secretary Theodore Roosevelt Jr., the son of the former President. Franklin D. Roosevelt (Theodore Jr.'s cousin) and his wife Eleanor Roosevelt (always faithful to the Democratic Party) were foursquare for Smith. In fact, they went full throttle, attacking cousin Theodore. Franklin publically categorized Theodore Jr.'s record as: **"wretched."**

Al Smith
Library of Congress

Political Family Feuds

Not Really a Unified Family: In Massachusetts, State Representative Mark Roosevelt, the grandson of Theodore Roosevelt Jr., was the Democratic nominee for Governor of Massachusetts, running against Republican Governor William F. Weld. Weld was married to Susan Roosevelt Weld, a cousin of Mark Roosevelt. This family feud was a nasty slugfest. Despite Weld's commanding lead, Weld ran up the electoral score in part by approving advertisements attacking Roosevelt. Roosevelt in turn said of Weld: **"He's indifferent, apathetic, feckless, aloof, passive and lazy. Did I say uncaring? He's uncaring."** Weld won the race with a record 71% of the vote.

Mark Roosevelt
Photograph by Mark Rauterkus

Like Father, Not Like Son: In 2004, while U.S. Senator Edward M. Kennedy (D-MA) was stumping for Massachusetts Senate colleague John Kerry, his son, U.S. Representative Patrick Kennedy (D-RI), threw his support for President behind former U.S. House Minority Leader Richard Gephardt (D-MO).

Patrick Kennedy
Official Photograph

Bay State Family Affair: In 1962, the two candidates for a U.S. Senate Seat in Massachusetts were Ted Kennedy (the brother of President John F. Kennedy) and Edward McCormack, (the nephew of U.S. House Speaker John McCormack (D-MA). While McCormack had risen to the level of Massachusetts Attorney General, Kennedy had just reached 30 years of age, the minimum Constitutionally eligible age to run for the seat. He had served for just a year as Assistant District Attorney. McCormack ran on the slogan: **"I back Jack, but Teddy ain't ready."** McCormack charged that if Kennedy's name were simply Edward Moore, **"It would be a joke."** U.S. Defense Secretary Robert McNamara at the request of President John F. Kennedy ordered staffers to try to find problems with McCormack's military record, but found none. Ted Kennedy won the race, then defeated George Cabot Lodge II, the brother of former U.S. Senator Henry Cabot Lodge (R-MA), who John F. Kennedy had unhorsed in 1952 when he was first elected to the U.S. Senate.

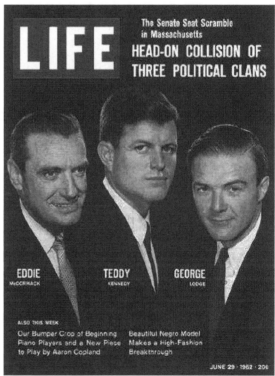

Eddie McCormack (L), Ted Kennedy (C), George Lodge (R)
Cover of Life Magazine

Chapter VII

Former Political Allies Turned Opponents

Former Political Allies Turned Opponents

Double-Edged Sword? Former Florida Governor Jeb Bush was once a benefactor of U.S. Senator Marco Rubio (R-FL). Bush donated to Rubio's first political campaign. In 2005, when Rubio was sworn in as Florida's House Speaker, Bush gave Rubio a sword, informing Rubio: **"I'm going to bestow to you the sword of a great conservative warrior"** (referring to the mythical warrior Chang). When he ran in the Republican U.S. Senate primary in 2010, Rubio garnered the support of many of Bush's prominent fundraisers. Though Bush remained officially neutral, his son, Jeb Bush Jr., supported Rubio. The day Rubio won the General Election, Jeb Bush stood at the podium introducing him.

In 2016, the two Floridians battled for support in the Republican Presidential primary. Some in the Florida political circuit thought Rubio would not run if Bush did, but in American politics, timing is everything, and Rubio, with his political star on the rise, saw this election as his time. Now the gloves came off, and Bush compared Rubio to Barack Obama, telling CNN: **"Look, we had a president who came in and said the same kind of thing — new and improved, hope and change — and he didn't have the leadership skills to fix things."**

Roosevelt v. Taft: In 1908, President Theodore Roosevelt used his political influence to secure the Republican Presidential nomination for U.S. Secretary of War William Howard Taft over other Republicans, including Vice President Charles Fairbanks. However, after Taft was elected and assumed the Presidency, Roosevelt became disillusioned with Taft, believing he was too tethered to the conservative bloodline of the party and the moneyed interests. The progressive Roosevelt launched a bid against Taft for the 1912 Republican Presidential nomination. He told news reporters: **"My hat's in the ring. The fight is on, and I'm stripped to the buff."** Roosevelt was not above *ad hominem* attacks on Taft, quipping that his former ally is: **"dumber than a guinea pig, a fathead."** Taft in turn branded Roosevelt's supporters **"destructive radicals and neurotics."**

After losing the nomination to Taft, Roosevelt did not make amends by supporting his party's nominee. Instead, he bolted from the GOP, running as the nominee of the newly created Progressive Party, a.ka. The Bull Moose Party. This move split the Republican vote and contributed to the victory of Woodrow Wilson.

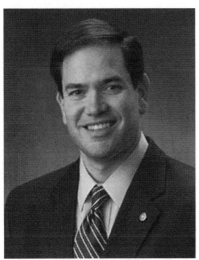

Marco Rubio
Official Photograph

Theodore Roosevelt (L), William Howard Taft (R)
Library of Congress

Former Political Allies Turned Opponents

FDR v. Farley and Garner: Franklin D. Roosevelt sought an unprecedented third term as president. Vice President John Nance Garner, a former ally, and James Farley (the Democratic National Committee Chairman and Post Master General) ran against him for the Democratic nomination.

Farley was a longtime Roosevelt loyalist, managing two successful campaigns for Roosevelt for Governor of New York and for President. He was dismayed that Roosevelt sought a third term. The ambitious Farley, who wanted to succeed Roosevelt, had been led to believe that Roosevelt would not seek a third term. Farley held that no President should seek more than two terms.

Gardner, a business-oriented conservative Democrat from Texas, thought that Roosevelt had veered too far to the left ideologically and called some elements of Roosevelt's New Deal (Domestic Program) **"Plain damn foolishness."** Roosevelt easily fended off both challenges.

Franklin D. Roosevelt (L), James Farley (R)
Franklin D. Roosevelt Presidential Library and Museum

Massachusetts Rough and Tumble Politics: In 1962, the Massachusetts Democratic Party nominated Endicott Peabody for Governor and Francis X. Bellotti for Lieutenant Governor. Though the tandem was not nominated as a team, they campaigned as a unified ticket. They won the election. However, as Lieutenant Governor, Bellotti broke with the Governor on a litany of issues, most notably capital punishment. Bellotti supported it, while Peabody opposed it. In 1964, Bellotti challenged Peabody for the nomination and won. Bellotti subsequently lost in the General Election to Republican John Volpe.

Francis X. Bellotti
Official Photograph

Humphrey v. Muskie: In 1968, the Democratic Presidential nominee Hubert Humphrey selected U.S. Senator Edmund Muskie (D-ME) as his vice presidential running mate. The ticket lost narrowly to Republicans Richard M. Nixon and Spiro Agnew.

Humphrey's presidential ambitions did not end after that election. In 1972, Humphrey again sought the Democratic Presidential nomination. He did this just six days after Muskie announced his intention to seek the nomination. Muskie was the early frontrunner and the choice of many members of the Democratic establishment, but he soon faded after a series of underperformances in the early primaries. Humphrey then became the defacto establishment favorite, but lost to the insurrectionist anti-Vietnam War candidate U.S. Senator George McGovern (D-SD). McGovern went on to lose badly to Nixon in the General Election.

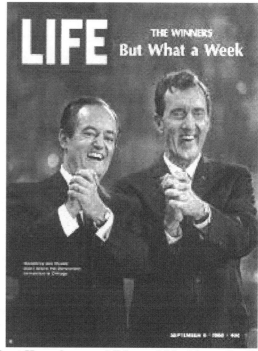

Hubert Humphrey and Edmund Muskie on the Cover of *Life Magazine* in 1968

Former Political Allies Turned Opponents

McGovern v. Hart: George McGovern won the 1972 Democratic primary with the help of the young campaign manager, Gary Hart. After McGovern lost in the General Election, Hart embarked on his own political career. In 1984, he sought the Democratic Presidential nomination as a moderate Democrat. That year, McGovern returned from the political wilderness and sought the nomination as well. He told Hart he did not believe any of the declared candidates were **"saying what needs to be said."** McGovern thought his message of full employment, curtailing defense spending, and freezing nuclear production was not being addressed adequately in the campaign.

McGovern, unlike Hart, stood little chance of winning the nomination, having lost badly in 1972, and having lost a re-election bid to the U.S. Senate in 1980. Hart ran as a moderate Democrat who was not a tribune of the labor unions and the **"special interest government in Washington."** McGovern ran as an unreconstructed liberal. The clash was ideological, not personal. McGovern belittled Hart's slogan **"new ideas"** by averring: **"Those are rather attractive slogans, but they really have no intellectual content."**

George McGovern
Library of Congress

Lincoln v. Alexander: Blanche Lincoln began her career as a receptionist in the office of U.S. Representative Bill Alexander (D-AR). In 1992, eight years after she left Alexander's office, Lincoln challenged her old boss. Alexander was embarrassed when it was revealed that he had run up overdrafts in the House bank of $208,546. Taking advantage of the opportunity, Lincoln maintained: **"I'll promise you one thing. I can sure enough balance my checkbook."** Alexander could not distance himself from the charges, and Lincoln easily defeated him.

Blanche Lincoln
Official Photograph

Condit v. Cardoza: In 2002, with U.S. Representative Gary Condit (D-CA) electorally vulnerable, State Assemblyman Dennis Cardoza, who had worked as Condit's Chief of Staff when Condit served as a State Assemblyman, challenged Condit in the Democratic primary. Believing Condit could not win in the General Election, many in the party's high command, (led by the state's Democratic Chairman Art Torres), took the unusual step of supporting the challenger against the incumbent.

Cardoza won the nomination. The Condit team was deeply hurt by Cordoza's candidacy, and there was no rapprochement after the election. Condit's son, Chad Condit, protested after his father's loss: **"Gary helped Dennis. Dennis backstabbed Gary. He took advantage of a tragedy . . . . He saw an opportunity to win an election and he did it."**

Gary Condit
Official Photograph

Chapter X

Political Insults

Political Insults

No Love for James Buchanan: Andrew Jackson, in explaining why he appointed James Buchanan to the post of Minister to Russia, said: **"It was as far as I could send him to get him out of my sight, and where he could do the least harm. I would have sent him to the North Pole if we kept a Minister there."**

Andrew Jackson
Library of Congress

John Adams Uncensored: John Adams had many quarrels with the U.S. Congress. Adams complained: **"In my many years I have come to a conclusion that one useless man is a shame, two is a law firm, and three or more is a Congress."**

John Adams
Library of Congress

Grammar Ain't Everything: After the 1923 death of Warren G. Harding, the esteemed poet Edward Estlin Cummings commented: **"The only man, woman, or child who ever wrote a simple declarative sentence with seven grammatical errors is dead."**

Edward Estlin Cummings
Library of Congress

The Barbarian President: In 1833, Harvard University awarded an honorary degree to President Andrew Jackson. John Quincy Adams, a Harvard University alumnus, boycotted the ceremony. Adams lost the Presidential election to Jackson in 1832. In his diary, Adams called Jackson, who had no college education: **"A barbarian who could not write a sentence of grammar and hardly could spell his own name."**

John Quincy Adams
Library of Congress

All is Fair in Love and War: U.S. House Majority Leader Tip O'Neill (D-MA) had no problem publicly belittling Republican President and friend Gerald R. Ford. He said Ford was **"worse than [Warren G.] Harding and [Herbert] Hoover put together."** Yet O'Neill and Ford had a friendly personal relationship. They often golfed together. Ford took O'Neill's criticisms in stride, knowing that they were not personal, just politics.

Gerald R. Ford (L), Tip O'Neill (R)
Library of Congress

Teddy Roosevelt Unplugged: President Benjamin Harrison did not support the particular version of Civil Service Reform favored by Theodore Roosevelt, then a Civil Service Commissioner. In response, Roosevelt blasted the President, branding him: **"a cold-blooded, narrow-minded, prejudiced, obstinate, timid old psalm-singing Indianapolis politician."** Harrison retorted that the young Roosevelt: **"wanted to put an end to all the evil in the world between sunrise and sunset."**

Theodore Roosevelt
Library of Congress

Davy Crockett, King of the Political Insults: U.S. Representative David "Davy" Crockett (Whig-TN) was a vociferous critic of Democratic President Martin Van Buren. He said of Van Buren: **"It is said that at a year old he could laugh on one side of his face and cry on the other, at one and the same time."**

David "Davy" Crockett
Library of Congress

Johnson Derides Ford: Future President Gerald R. Ford was U.S. House Minority Leader when President Lyndon B. Johnson was in the White House. Ford was a constant partisan critic of Johnson, and delivered the Republican response to Johnson's State of the Union Address in 1967. Johnson often mocked Ford in private, telling his associates that Ford had been the Center on the University of Michigan Football team, and jokingly said of Ford: **"He's a nice guy, but he played too much football with his helmet off."**

Gerald R. Ford on the Gridiron
Gerald R. Ford Library & Museum

Political Insults

Truman Gives Candid Assessment of Johnson: Harry S. Truman believed that Lyndon B. Johnson should have run for re-election in 1968. Truman said Johnson had: **"no guts . . . Instead, he let a mob of anti-war protestors run him out of the White House."**

Harry S. Truman (L), Lyndon B. Johnson (R)
Lyndon Baines Library and Museum

If you Don't Have anything nice to say, Don't say Anything at all: George Washington wanted no part of getting the U.S. into the French Revolution, whereas U.S. Secretary of State Thomas Jefferson supported U.S. intervention. James Callender, a journalist, sympathetic to Jefferson, and a critic of Washington, was invited to give a toast at a formal dinner. Not a man to mince words, Callender stood up and gave a toast **"To the speedy death of George Washington."**

George Washington
Painting by Gilbert Stuart

President Mocks Intellectuals: In an address to California Republicans in 1954, President Dwight D. Eisenhower mocked **"wise cracking intellectuals."** He mustered uproarious applause when he defined an intellectual as **"a man who takes more words than necessary to tell more than he knows."**

Dwight D. Eisenhower
Harry S. Truman Library and Museum

Robbers in the Senate, Not in the House: Prior to the ratification of the Seventeenth Amendment to the U.S. Constitution, U.S. Senators were elected by their respective state legislatures. Consequently, many Senators garnered their offices by bribing members of the Legislature to vote for them. This was "an open secret" in the nation's capital. One night, First Lady Francis Folsom Cleveland was startled and thought she heard burglars in the White House. She exclaimed to her husband, President Grover Cleveland: **"Wake up Grover, wake up, there are robbers in the house!"** Woken from his deep sleep, the President retorted: **"I think you are mistaken my dear. There are no robbers in the House, but there are lots in the Senate!"**

Grover and Frances Cleveland with "Baby Ruth"

The 'Chocolate Eclair' Analogy: As Assistant Secretary of the U.S. Navy, Theodore Roosevelt viewed President William McKinley as an indecisive leader. He said: **"McKinley had no more backbone than a chocolate eclair."** In 1900 Roosevelt became McKinley's Vice Presidential Running Mate.

Theodore Roosevelt
Library of Congress

How Dare you Vote Against This Treaty: Woodrow Wilson did not have much respect for those members of the U.S. Senate who opposed the ratification of the Treaty of Versailles, which would have allowed the U.S. to join the League of Nations. Wilson called these dissenting Senators: **"pygmy minds."** The treaty failed to secure ratification in the U.S. Senate.

Woodrow Wilson Returns From the Versailles Peace Conference
Library of Congress

Elegant Arthur: Democrat Woodrow Wilson made the following statement regarding "Elegant" Chester A. Arthur (one of his Republican Predecessors): **"Chester A. Arthur was the only President to sport muttonchop whiskers. He is a non-entity with side-whiskers."** Arthur earned the moniker "Elegant Arthur" for his fancy clothes and sense of fashion.

Chester A. Arthur
Library of Congress

I look Better Than That: In 1967, Lyndon B. Johnson was presented with his official portrait painted by artist Peter Hurd. Johnson was displeased with the portrait. He said it was **"the ugliest thing I ever saw."** Hurd was not offended and mentioned that he only had a half-hour to draw the painting and that the President kept falling asleep. The rejected portrait garnered a record amount of visitors at the Diamond Museum in Snyder, Texas.

Portrait of Lyndon B. Johnson Drawn by Peter Hurd

Political Insults

Telling What He Really Thinks: Andrew Jackson prevented the Bank of the United States from getting a new charter. He was against the fact that they wanted to regulate the money supply. Not a man to mince words, he wrote to the Bank Directors: **"You are a den of vipers and thieves . . . I intend to route you out and by the Eternal God, I will route you out."**

Andrew Jackson
Library of Congress

A Vacuous Mind is a Terrible Thing to Waste: U.S. Representative John Sherman (R-OH) had little use for Democratic President James Buchanan: He quipped: **"The Constitution provides for every contingency in the executive, except a vacancy in the mind of the President."**

John Sherman
Photograph by Mathew Brady

A Politician who does Not Mince Words: In 2010, after the organization "Americans for Tax Reform" alleged that U.S. Representative Gene Taylor (D-MS 1989-2011) had changed his position on Health Insurance Reform, Taylor issued a press release chastising the organization. It read: **"Americans for Tax Reform are lying sacks of scum, and anyone who knowingly repeats this false information is also a liar."** Taylor was a member of the conservative Blue Dog Caucus.

Gene Taylor
Official Photograph

Today's Letter 'B': In 1942, former Republican Presidential nominee Wendell Willkie compared the Neutrality Act to giving aid to German Chancellor Adolph Hitler. In response, U.S. Representative Dewey Short (R-MO) went to the House Floor to call Willkie: **"a Bellowing--Blatant---Bellicose---Belligerent---Blowhard."**

Dewey Short
Official Portrait

Political Insults

Passive Speaker: U.S. House Speaker Fredrick Gillett (R-MA 1919-1925) had a passive personality. A reporter once said: **"He did not drink coffee in the morning for fear it would keep him awake all day."**

Frederick Gillett
Official Photograph

Congress Drugged Most of the Time: In her 1970 book, *Unbought and Unbossed*, U.S. Representative Shirley Chisholm (D-NY) observed: **"Congress seems drugged and inert most of the time. The idea of meeting a problem is to hold hearings or, in the extreme case, to appointing a commission."**

Shirley Chisholm
Liberty of Congress

Don't Run in Baltimore: In 1989, Democrat Thomas V. Miller, the President of the Maryland State Senate, took a call from a reporter about why he was holding a fundraiser in Baltimore, outside of his suburban Washington, D.C., District. Miller responded: **"It helps educate my constituents as to why Baltimore needs the economic help. Baltimore is a goddamn ghetto. It's worse than Washington. It's Shit."** Miller was considered a possible contender for Governor of Maryland in 1990, prior to making that inappropriate comment.

Thomas V. Miller
Official Photograph

Presidential Backbone: President James Garfield took the side of James G. Blaine rather than U.S. Senator Roscoe Conkling (R-NY) on the appointment of William H. Robertson as the Collector of Customs of the Port of New York. Former President Ulysses S. Grant, an ardent ally of Conkling, said of Garfield: **"He is not possessed of the backbone of an angleworm [earthworm]."**

William H. Robertson
Engraving by George Edward Perine

Political Insults

Truman Doesn't Like Ike: Harry S. Truman thought little of his successor, Dwight D. Eisenhower, though the two made a rapprochement and became friends as former Presidents. Truman once said of Eisenhower: **"The General doesn't know any more about politics than a pig knows about Sunday."**

Harry S Truman (L), Dwight D. Eisenhower (R)
Harry S. Truman Library and Museum

As Cold as Ice: Benjamin Harrison had the reputation of being a distant and cold man. U.S. Senator Thomas Platt (R-NY) said of the President: **"Outside the White House and at dinner, he could be a courtly gentleman. Inside the Executive Mansion in his reception of those who solicited official appointments, he was as glacial as a Siberian stripped of furs. During and after an interview, if one could secure it, one felt even in the torrid weather like pulling on his winter flannels, galoshes, overcoat, mitts and earlaps."**

Benjamin Harrison
Library of Congress

President has a Sleeping Problem: U.S. Senator James E. Watson (R-IN) once said of his fellow Republican, President William Howard Taft: **"Most of the time, Taft simply did not and could not function in alert fashion. . . Often while I was talking to him after a meal, he would fall over on his breasts, and he would go sound asleep for ten or fifteen minutes. He would waken and resume the conversation, only to repeat the performance in the course of half an hour or so."**

James E. Watson
Official Photograph

Roosevelt Faces Cannibalism Charge: After reading a column by esteemed essayist H.L Mencken about the opportunism of President Franklin D. Roosevelt, conservative clergyman Gerald L.K. Smith commented: **"If he [Roosevelt] became convinced tomorrow that coming out for cannibalism would get him votes he sorely needs, he would begin fattening a missionary in the White House back yard come Wednesday."**

Gerald L.K. Smith
Library of Congress

Political Insults

Polk Takes on Congress: Though Democrat James K. Polk served in office with a democratically-controlled U.S. Congress, he sometimes got impatient with the Congress. In an 1846 diary entry, Polk wrote: **"The passion for office among members of Congress is very great, if not absolutely disreputable, and greatly embarrasses the operations of the Government. They create offices by their own votes and then seek to fill them themselves."**

James K. Polk
Photograph by Mathew Brady

Child's Play: U.S. House Minority Leader Gerald R. Ford (R-MI) was out front in opposing President Lyndon B. Johnson's Model Cities Program. For his part, Johnson did not think much of Ford's intellectual dexterity. Johnson said to an aide: **"You've got a little baby boy. Well, you take his little building blocks and go up and explain to Jerry Ford what we're trying to do."**

Gerald R. Ford Speaks. Lyndon B. Johnson and First Lady, Lady Bird Johnson Clap.
Gerald R. Ford Presidential Library and Museum

Misstatement or Clarification? During the 1996 Whitewater Trial, James McDougal, a former business partner of President Bill Clinton, was asked if he had said that Arkansas Governor Jim Guy Tucker, a lawyer, **"was a thief who would steal anything not nailed down?"** McDougal clarified his statement, insisting that he had positive feelings about Tucker, but not about lawyers. McDougal insisted: **"I think I said: like most lawyers, he would steal anything that's not nailed down."**

Jim Guy Tucker
Official Photograph

Reverse Evolution? In 1987, Arizona Governor Evan Mecham was under investigation for misuse of campaign funds, and was taking heat for voiding the Martin Luther King Holiday. His predecessor as Governor, Bruce Babbitt, told *Newsweek Magazine:* **"Evan Mecham proves that [Charles] Darwin was wrong."**

Evan Mecham
Official Photograph

118

Political Insults

A Frank Assessment of The Duke: State Representative Barney Frank (D-MA) was a vociferous critic of Massachusetts Governor Michael Dukakis during his first term in office. Frank excoriated Dukakis for budget cuts he believed hurt the poor. A reporter asked Frank if he had a problem with Dukakis riding the subway from his Brookline home to his office in the State House. Frank replied: **"No, I don't object that he rides the subway. I merely object that he gets off at the State House."** When Dukakis ran for re-election in 1978, Frank supported primary challenger Barbara Ackerman, who garnered just 6.72% of the vote in the primary. Dukakis lost to the other Democratic challenger in the race, Ed King.

Michael Dukakis
During First Term as Massachusetts Governor
Library of Congress

The wit of John Dingell: In 2018, Donald Trump met at the White House with Reality television star Kim Kardashian West. West successfully lobbied for a Presidential clemency for Alice Johnson serving a life sentence for a drug offence. Upon seeing a photograph of Trump and West in the Oval Office, former U.S. Representative John Dingell (D-MI) tweeted: **"I still can't believe they let this no-talent reality TV star into the oval office. Great to see my friend Kim is doing well though."**

John Dingell
Official Photograph

No Fan of Independence: U.S. House Speaker Sam Rayburn (R-TX) served as a mentor to a fellow member of the Texas Congressional Delegation, U.S. Representative Lyndon B. Johnson (D-TX). Rayburn witnessed Johnson's independent streak when Johnson was the only member of the Texas Congressional Delegation who refused to sign a letter supporting fellow Texan and Vice President John Nance Garner against charges of being anti-labor and a whisky drinker. After Rayburn failed to secure Johnson's vote, Rayburn called him: **"A damn independent boy; independent as a hog on ice."**

Sam Rayburn (L) Gets Kissed by his Protégé Lyndon B. Johnson (R)
From the Sam Rayburn Papers at the Dolph Briscoe Center for American History

Speaker References 'The Three Stooges': U.S. Representatives Newt Gingrich (R-GA), Robert Walker (R-PA), and Vin Webber (R-MN) often used Special Orders (Speaking in an empty House Chamber after the House has adjourned) to bash the Democratic Congressional Leadership. They often rankled U.S. House Speaker Tip O'Neill (D-MA). When a reporter asked O'Neill if he listened to this criticism, he replied: **"What are the names of The Three Stooges? I think I'll let Larry, Moe, and Curley talk to themselves."**

Tip O'Neill
Official Photograph

119

Political Insults

Not Mr. Popular: After William Henry Harrison passed away in 1841, John Tyler assumed the Presidency. He was the first President to face the prospect of impeachment. He was described by one newspaper as a: **"poor, miserable, despised imbecile."** *The New York Times* obituary read that Tyler was; **"the most unpopular public man that had ever held any office in the United States."**

John Tyler
Library of Congress

Wilson Holds Senate in Very Low Regard: In 1919 Woodrow Wilson was inflamed that the U.S. Senate did not ratify the Treaty of Versailles, which he had helped to negotiate to end WWI. Wilson said that the Senators: **"Have no use for their heads except to serve as a knot to keep their bodies from unraveling**

Woodrow Wilson
Library of Congress

U.S. Representative Tells Constituent to 'Go to Hell:' U.S. Representative John Steven McGroarty (D-CA 1935-1939) once wrote back to a constituent who sent him a critical letter saying he had not kept a campaign promise. McGroarty wrote: **"One of the countless drawbacks of being in Congress is that I am compelled to receive impertinent letters from a jackass like you in which you say I promised to have the Sierra Madre mountains reforested and I have been in Congress two months and haven't done it. Will you please take two running jumps and go to Hell."**

John Steven McGroarty
Official Photograph

Rhetorical Hyperbole: When Theodore Roosevelt was serving as President of the Board of the New York City Police Commissioners in 1894, he took great offense at opponents of his plan to vigorously enforce a law mandating that saloons be closed on Sundays. He called these opponents: **"Lynchers and Whitecrappers"** (White Hooded Klansman.)

Theodore Roosevelt
Norman Photographic Company
Albany, New York

Political Insults

Take That, Tsongas: In 1995, when former U.S. Senator Paul Tsongas (D-MA) chided President Bill Clinton for not focusing on balancing the federal budget, former Clinton campaign advisor Paul Begala stated: **"The notion that he** [Paul Tsongas] **is questioning the President's moral authority is like getting lectures from** [Conservative Talk Show Host] **Rush Limbaugh."**

Paul Begala
Photograph by Gage Skidmore

Bloodsucking Parasites: During Special Prosecutor Kenneth Starr's investigation of President Bill Clinton's involvement in the Whitewater Affair, James Carville, a former campaign advisor to Clinton, lashed out at Starr, stating: **"As with mosquitoes, horseflies, and most bloodsucking parasites, Kenneth Starr was spawned in stagnant water."**

Kenneth Starr
Official Photograph

Congressional Idiocy: American Author Mark Twain averred in a 1891 draft manuscript: **"Suppose you were an idiot and suppose you were a member of Congress. But I repeat myself."**

Mark Twain
Photograph by Mathew Brady

Losing Case With Brother on Jury: In 1999, U.S. Representative Asa Hutchinson (R-AR) was an Impeachment Manager during the U.S. Senate trial of Bill Clinton. Clinton was acquitted of perjury and obstruction of Justice. One of the jurors was U.S. Senator Tim Hutchinson (R-AR). In 2014, Democratic Gubernatorial candidate Mike Ross used the issue against Tim's brother, Asa Hutchinson, who was now his Republican opponent for Arkansas Governor. Ross told *The Associated Press*: **"He may be the only lawyer in America who has conducted a trial with his brother on the jury and lost."**

Mike Ross
Official Photograph

121

Political Insults

Taking on the Hippies: In 1968, when George Wallace, the nominee of the American Party, was heckled by young hippies, he responded: **"You come up when I get through and I'll autograph your sandals for you. That is, if you got any on . . . You need a good haircut. That's all that's wrong with you . . . There are two four-letter words I bet you folks don't know: 'work' and 'soap.'"** He got an uproarious ovation from his mostly blue-color supporters in the crowd.

George Wallace
Library of Congress

Dubya Frightens Gephardt: In 2003, while campaigning for the Democratic Presidential nomination, former U.S. House Majority Leader Richard Gephardt (D-MO) opined of President George W. Bush: **"He's incompetent. He frightens me. He's hard to help. I told him America founded the United Nations because I wasn't sure he knew the history, and if you'd been meeting with him every week since 9/11, you'd be running for president too. Because Bush refused to negotiate with Kim-Jong il,** (The Supreme Leader of North Korea) **North Korea is now weeks away from producing nuclear bombs. Bush abandoned the peace negotiations between Israel and Palestine, saying, it's not our problem. He's arrogant. He doesn't play well with others."** Gephardt lost the nomination to John Kerry, who in turn lost the General Election to Bush.

Richard Gephardt
Official Photograph

Kemp Bashes Dole's Intellectual Prowess: U.S. Representative Jack Kemp (R-NY) was an arch adversary of U.S. Senator Bob Dole (R-KS). This was exhibited in 1988 when the two men were candidates for the Republican Presidential nomination. Kemp said of Dole: **"When his library burned down, it destroyed both books. He hadn't finished coloring in the second."** Ironically, in 1996, Dole selected Kemp as his Vice Presidential Runningmate.

**Campaign button for the
Dole-Kemp Campaign**

Born With a Silver Foot: Texas State Treasurer Ann Richards made a name for herself in 1988 when she delivered the keynote address at the Democratic National Convention in Atlanta. Poking fun at the Republican Presidential nominee George H.W. Bush, who came from patrician stalk, Richards joked: **"Poor George, he can't help it. He was born with a silver foot in his mouth."**

Ann Richards
Official Photograph as Governor of Texas
By James Tennison

122

Political Insults

Are You Ready for some Football? During the heated Republican Presidential Primary between President Gerald R. Ford and former California Governor Ronald Reagan, Ford's media advisor, Don Penny, told the President that he was not as charismatic as Reagan and needed more one-liners in his speeches. The quick-witted Ford delivered the following one-liner: **"Governor Reagan and I do have one thing in common: We both played football. I played for Michigan; he played for Warner Brothers."** (Reagan was a former actor and played George Gipp, a famous Notre Dame football player, in the Warner Brothers Movie: *Knute Rockne—All American*).

Ronald Reagan (L) and Gerald R. Ford (R)
Time Magazine

Speaking Frankly about George W. Bush: In 2005, George W. Bush suggested that "intelligent design" should be taught in schools alongside creationism. This precipitated U.S. Representative Barney Frank (D-MA) to quip: **"People might cite George (W.) Bush as proof that you can be totally impervious to the effects of Harvard and Yale education."**

Barney Frank
Official Photograph

Take That: In 1929, some Southerners expressed disenchantment that First Lady Lou Hoover had invited an African-American woman to be a guest at the White House. Some segregationist members of the Texas Legislature called for her husband, Herbert Hoover, to be impeached for this act. The President commented to his wife: **"One of the chief advantages of orthodox religion is that it provides hot hell for the Texas Legislature."**

Herbert and Lou Hoover
Library of Congress

Borrowed Brains: In 1955, Dwight D. Eisenhower, in referring to his Special Assistant on Foreign Affairs, Nelson Rockefeller, told his Personal Secretary Ann Whitman: **"He is too used to borrowing brains instead of using his own."** Rockefeller's personal staff was considered highly intelligent.

Nelson Rockefeller
Department of Health Education and
Welfare Photograph

A Protective Father: In 1950, First Daughter Margaret Truman sang at Constitution Hall in Washington, D.C. *Washington Post* music critic Paul Hume wrote that she "**cannot sing very well, is flat a good deal of the time.**" In response, Harry S. Truman fired off a letter to Hume reading in part: "**It seems to me that you are a frustrated old man who wishes he could have been successful. When you write such poppycock, as were in the back section of the paper you work for, it shows conclusively that you're off the beam and at least four of your ulcers are at work. Some day I hope to meet you. When that happens you'll need a new nose, a lot of beefsteak for black eyes, and perhaps a supporter below!**"

Margaret Truman (R), with her Conductor (L) Before The Show
Harry S, Truman Library and Museum

Beyond Two Wrongs Don't Make a Right: Norman Cousins, the Editor of *Saturday Review,* told *The Daily Telegraph* in 1969, "**President** [Richard M.] **Nixon's motto was, 'if two wrongs don't make a right, try three.'**"

Norman Cousins
NASA Photograph

It's Only A Game -- Take it Easy: While on a trip to Paris in 1996, San Francisco Mayor Willie Brown was asked jokingly by a reporter if the French would ever invest in a new stadium for the San Francisco 49ers. This was on the heels of a game where the team's backup quarterback Elvis Grbac had made too many turnovers, giving the game to the Dallas Cowboys. Brown responded: "**Well, I'm trying to get the French to invest in a new quarterback. This guy Grbac is an embarrassment to humankind.**" A reporter then asked if he thought his comments were harsh. Brown doubled-down, averring: "**After that interception and that bonehead intellectual breakdown in the last game against Dallas, and we lost it 20-17, he can't play in any stadium that I'm going to assist to be built.**"

Willie Brown
Official Photograph

Representative Calls MIT Economist "A Nut": In referring to MIT Economist John Reilly's claim that instituting a cap-and-trade program for carbon emissions would cost only a fourth of what Congressional Republicans claim (based on a 2007 MIT study), U.S. Representative Louis Gohmert (R-TX) countered: "**Anyone who thinks you can pay $3,100 to the federal government and thinks you can get that money back completely in services -- like I said --he may go to M-I-T but he is an N-U-T.**"

Louis Gohmert
Official Photograph

Political Insults

The Pure Wit of George W. Bush: At a 2004 fundraiser for the Republican Governors Association, George W. Bush mocked the Democrats vying for their party's Presidential nomination. Bush mused: **"The candidates are an interesting group, with diverse opinions -- for tax cuts and against them, for NAFTA and against NAFTA, for the Patriot Act and against the Patriot Act, in favor of liberating Iraq and opposed to it. And that's just one senator from Massachusetts."** [John Kerry]

George W. Bush
White House Photograph by Eric Draper

"Cox and Cocktails:" In 1920, Republican Presidential nominee Warren G. Harding adopted the slogan: **"Cox and Cocktails."** Harding supported prohibition and in an effort to cultivate support in the prohibition community, Harding implied that if Democratic nominee James Cox were elected President, the Eighteenth Amendment to the U.S. Constitution, instituting Prohibition, would be repealed. Hypocritically, Harding consumed alcohol in private. Harding won the election in a landslide victory.

James Cox
Official Photograph

Piling On Willkie: On the last day of the 1940 Presidential campaign, New York City Mayor Fiorello La Guardia, who was campaigning for Franklin D Roosevelt in his attempt at winning a third term in Office, turned to a photographer as his picture was being taken and said: **"Go away, I did not come here to have my picture taken. He then told the crowd: "He thinks I'm Wendell Willkie."** Willkie was the Republican Presidential nominee known to like to have his picture taken. Responding to the uproarious laughter, La Guardia continued: **"Some men have their hair mussed because their brains are working, others because the photographers are working."**

Fiorello La Guardia (L)
Franklin D. Roosevelt (R)
National Archives
and Records Administration

Truman Bluntness: Campaigning for a full Presidential term on a whistle-stop tour in Spokane, Washington in 1948, a supporter told Harry S. Truman that he should throw eggs at his chief U.S. Senate critic Robert Taft (R-OH). Truman retorted: **"I wouldn't throw fresh eggs at Taft. You've got the worst Congress you've ever had. If you** [referring to the audience] **send another Republican Congress to Washington, you're a bigger bunch of suckers than I think you are."** Truman won the election, and the Democrats took control of both chambers of the U.S. Congress.

Harry S. Truman During His 1948 Whistle-Stop
Campaign Tour
Harry S. Truman Library and Museum

Political Insults

Helms Takes on Hippies: In 1972, Vice President Spiro Agnew campaigned for re-election as part of the Nixon/Agnew-ticket in Charlotte, NC. At one campaign event there were longhaired protestors outside the arena, visible from the stage where Agnew introduced Republicans running for office in North Carolina. Jesse Helms, the party's Senate nominee in the Tar Heel state, was jeered by the protestors when introduced. He got up to the podium and pointed to a group of young singers on the stage. Helms said: **"Isn't it nice that the majority of young people are represented by them instead of that"** [pointing to the protestors]. Helms then exclaimed: **"And that one with the real long hair, that's George McGovern."** McGovern was the Democratic Presidential nominee. The mostly Republican crowd erupted in pandemonium.

Jesse Helms
Official Photograph

Comparing Truman to a Jackass: Speaking against the election of Harry S. Truman to a full term as President in 1948, U.S. Representative Cliff Clevenger (R-OH) called Truman **"A nasty little gamin"** and **"A Missouri Jackass."**

Cliff Clevenger
Official Photograph

Of Karl and Groucho Marx: 1936 Republican Vice Presidential nominee Frank Knox ridiculed Democratic President Franklin D. Roosevelt calling him **"a blundering visionary and fanatic,"** and said that the New Deal contained **"something of Karl Marx equally as much as Groucho Marx."** (Karl Marx was the author of *The Communist Manifesto.* Groucho Marx was a comedian). Knox later became U.S. Secretary of the Navy under Roosevelt.

Frank Knox
Official Photograph

"Granting" his Vote to Buchanan: Prior to running for the Presidency, Republican Ulysses S. Grant was apolitical. His fist vote was in 1856, just 12 years before running for the Presidency. Grant voted for Democrat James Buchanan over Republican John C. Freemont. Grant had served with Freemont in the military and viewed him as an egotist. Grant said: **"I voted for Buchanan because I didn't know him and voted against Freemont because I did know him."**

Ulysses S. Grant
Library of Congress

126

Nixon and Sows: Bill Clinton was the Co-Chairman of 1972 Democratic Presidential nominee George McGovern's Texas campaign. Many Texas Democrats endorsed Republican President Richard M. Nixon. Former President Lyndon B. Johnson offered a tepid endorsement of McGovern but did not campaign with him. He told former aide Bobby Baker: **"George McGovern? Why, he couldn't carry Texas even if they caught Dick Nixon fu*** ng a Fort Worth sow."** McGovern lost Texas, garnering just 33.24% of the vote in the state.

George McGovern
Official Photograph

Fine, I Endorse McCain: U.S. Senator Thad Cochran (R-MS), a member of the Senate Appropriations Committee, had a strained relationships with his Senate colleague John McCain (R-AZ). McCain was an opponent of earmarks, which Cochran supported. The relationship turned personal. Cochran told *The Boston Globe:* **"The thought of his being President sends a cold chill down my spine. He is erratic. He is hotheaded. He loses his temper and he worries me."** Once McCain secured the Republican Presidential nomination in 2008, Cochran endorsed McCain.

Thad Cochran
Official Photograph

Reagan Compares Kennedy to Marx: In 1960, actor Ronald Reagan wrote a letter to the Republican Presidential nominee, Richard M. Nixon, wherein he suggested that Nixon not 'out liberal' Democratic nominee John F. Kennedy. Reagan suggested Nixon should run as a fiscal conservative, and wrote: **"Shouldn't someone tag Mr. Kennedy's bold new imaginative program with its proper age? Under the tousled boyish haircut is still old Karl Marx - first launched a century ago."**

Karl Marx
Library of Congress

Mocking George Romney: In 1967, George Romney, the early front runner for the Republican Presidential nomination, discussed his new found opposition to the U.S. role in Vietnam. He said that his past support for the war was because during a trip to Vietnam, **"I just had the greatest brainwashing that anybody can get, not only by the generals but also by the diplomatic corps over there. They do a very thorough job.** When Democratic Presidential aspirant Eugene McCarthy was told of Romney's comments, he averred: **"a light rinse would have sufficed."**

George Romney
Official Photograph

127

Political Insults

The Louisiana Nitwit: In 1991, Governor Kirk Fordice told Mississippi legislators that he favored a jungle primary system where all candidates run in a single primary. If no candidate pockets a majority of the vote, there would then be a runoff. However, Fordice said: **"Now everything's got downsides . . . and two or three people are sitting back there saying, 'Yeah, that's what got Louisiana so close to David Duke . . . and got 'em the nitwit that they got again . . . an old crook."** Duke was a former Grand Wizard of the Ku Klux Klan. He was defeated in the runoff by former Governor Edwin Edwards (Who Fordice called a crook) whose previous term as Governor was engulfed in scandals.

Kirk Fordice
Official Photograph

It's Howdy Doody Time: In 1995, U.S. Representative Marion Berry (D-AR) referred to his 30-year-old Republican colleague, U.S. Representative Adam Putnam (R-FL), as a **"Howdy Doody looking nimrod."** Berry was incensed that Putnam and some Republican colleagues attacked the conservative Blue Dog Democrats, saying they were not true fiscal conservatives. He blasted Putnam for saying the Blue Dogs were increasing spending. Putnam responded, saying: **"that was quite a performance, and I respect the gentleman's passion; but I do not respect the fact that he chose to personalize the debate, an important debate about the future of our Nation."**

Adam Putnam
Official Photograph

Comparing Republicans to the Taliban: At a 2009 rally for Democrats running for Executive offices in Virginia, U.S. Representative Jim Moran (D-VA) said: **"If the Republicans were running in Afghanistan, they'd be running on the Taliban ticket as far as I can see."**

Jim Moran
Official Photograph

The Olympic Tax & Spend Competition: During the 1988 Presidential race, Republican George H.W. Bush used an Olympic analogy against his Democratic opponent, Michael Dukakis. He said: **"My opponent ranks first in spending increases -- Second in tax hikes. If this were the Olympics, his composite score would make him the gold medal winner in the tax-and-spend competition."**

Olympic Rings

128

Political Insults

Spitball Warfare: Democrat Slams Democrat at Republican National Convention: In 2004, U.S. Senator Zell Miller (D-GA) endorsed Republican President George W. Bush over his own party's Presidential nominee, John Kerry. He delivered the keynote address at the Republican National Convention and belittled his Senate colleague, proclaiming: **"Listing all the weapon systems that Senator Kerry tried his best to shut down sounds like an auctioneer selling off our national security, but Americans need to know the facts . . . . This is the man who wants to be the Commander in Chief of our U.S. Armed Forces? U.S. forces armed with what? Spitballs?"**

Zell Miller
Official Photograph

The Little Man on the Wedding Cake: In 1944, Alice Roosevelt Longworth, the daughter of President Theodore Roosevelt, observed that the Republican Presidential nominee, Thomas E. Dewey: **"looks like the little man on the wedding cake."**

Thomas E. Dewey
Harry S. Truman Library and Museum

Texas Governor: A Good Looking Rascal: In a 2011 address to the International Association of Firefighters in New York City, Bill Clinton made fun of the campaign announcement of Texas Governor Rick Perry for the Republican Presidential nomination: **"I got tickled by watching Governor Perry announce for president. He's a good-looking rascal. And he's saying 'Oh, I'm going to Washington to make sure that the federal government stays as far away from you as possible ... while I ride on Air Force One and that Marine One helicopter and go to Camp David and travel around the world and have a good time.'"**

Rick Perry
Official Photograph

Duke Takes On Mitt: In a 2012 forum with students at the University of California at Davis, former Massachusetts Governor Michael Dukakis did not have any kind words to say about Mitt Romney, one of his Gubernatorial successors who was the Republican Presidential nominee. Dukakis said of Romney: **"He's Smart, he's slick, he's a fraud, simple as that . . . I think he'd be a disaster in the White House. I'm trying to be as subtle as I possibly can here."**

Michael Dukakis
Official Photograph

Corn Cobs and Ukuleles: While campaigning for the Democratic Presidential nomination in 1960, Hubert Humphrey told a crowd in La Croix, Wisconsin, *"Time, Look* and *Life* [Popular magazines at that time] **don't give a damn about dairy prices. They don't know the difference between a corn cob and a ukulele."**

Hubert Humphrey
West Virginia State Archives
Harry Brawley Collection

Brainless President: Democrat Woodrow Wilson had little respect for the intellectual acumen of his Republican successor Warren G. Harding. He said: **"Harding is incapable of thought, because he has nothing to think with."** Wilson also said of Harding: **"He has a bungalow mind."**

Woodrow Wilson (L) with Warren G. Harding (R)
National Archives

Pomposity Defined: William Gibbs McAdoo, who served as U.S. Treasury Secretary under the administration of Woodrow Wilson, said of President Warren G. Harding (who was known for his verbose prose): **"His speeches left the impression of an army of pompous phrases moving over the landscape in search of an idea; sometimes these meandering words would actually capture a straggling thought and bear it triumphantly as a prisoner in their midst, until it died of servitude and overwork."**

William Gibbs McAdoo
Library of Congress

Cabinet Burnout: In 1972 Richard M. Nixon was re-elected in a 49-state landslide. The day after the election, Chief of Staff H.R. Haldeman ordered a meeting of the President's Cabinet and called for the resignation of all Cabinet members. He told them: **"You are all a bunch of burned-out volcanoes."**

H.R. Haldeman
Official Photograph

Political Insults

"Cameron the Corrupt:" In 1861, newly elected President Abraham Lincoln nominated Simon Cameron to the post of U.S. Secretary of War. He made this appointment based on a political bargain with the Republican Party leaders. Once confirmed by the U.S. Senate, Lincoln asked U.S. Representative Thaddeus Stevens (R-PA) about the honesty of his new Secretary of War. Stevens had served with Cameron as a member of the Pennsylvania Congressional Delegation. Stevens was well aware of Cameron's corruption, and responded to Lincoln by saying: **"You don't mean to say you think Cameron would steal? No, I do not believe he would steal a red-hot stove."** When Lincoln told him that Cameron was offended by the comments and wanted an apology, Stevens replied: **"I believe I told you he would not steal a red-hot stove. I will now take that back."** Cameron was forced to leave office because of his notorious corruption.

Simon Cameron
Library of Congress

"Halitosis of the Intellect:" In 1933, U.S. Interior Secretary Harold Ickies said of U.S. Senator Huey Long (D-LA), who at that time was pushing legislation to place all federal spending under federal control: **"He is suffering from halitosis of the intellect; that's presuming he has an intellect."**

Harold Ickes
Official Photograph

How Coolidge Really Felt About Hoover: Although Calvin Coolidge campaigned for his Commerce Secretary, Herbert Hoover, in Hoover's successful bid to succeed Coolidge as President, Coolidge had a low opinion of Hoover's advice to him. As Coolidge left office, Coolidge said of Hoover: **"That man has offered me unsolicited advice for six years, all of it bad."**

Calvin Coolidge (L), Herbert Hoover (R)
Library of Congress

Poking Fun of John Adams: Thomas Paine, who wrote the 1776 pamphlet *Common Sense*, was a vociferous critic of John Adams. He enjoyed belittling the President. He once deadpanned: **"Some people talk of impeaching John Adams, but I am for softer measures. I would keep him to make fun of him."**

Thomas Paine
Oil Painting by Augusta Milliere

Former President Jackson Calls President Harrison an Imbecile: Former President Andrew Jackson, a Democratic-Republican, was distraught that the nation elected Whig William Henry Harrison as President in 1840. After Harrison's inauguration, Jackson said: **"The Republic may suffer under the present imbecile chief, but the sober second thought of the people will restore it at our next Presidential election."**

William Henry Harrison
Library of Congress

Comparing President Grant to a Horse: Former Georgia Governor Joseph Brown belittled President Ulysses S. Grant, stating: **"The people are tired of a man who has not an idea above a horse or a cigar."**

Joseph Brown
Library of Congress

Two John Kerry's: Speaking at the 2004 Republican National Convention in New York City, Vice President Dick Cheney, in trying to characterize Democratic Presidential nominee John Kerry as a flip-flopper, said: **"Senator Kerry says he sees two Americas. It makes the whole thing mutual -- America sees two John Kerry's."**

Dick Cheney
Official Photograph

Leaches and Insurance Companies: During a 2004 Presidential campaign speech in De Moines, Iowa, Dennis Kucinich said: **"Many years ago doctors would bleed patients with leeches. Today, the insurance companies do that."**

Dennis Kucinich
Official Photograph

Political Insults

Could It Be "Ditch?" In 1984, Barbara Bush, the wife of Vice President George H. W. Bush, was asked by *The New York Times* to give her opinion of Bush's opponent for re-election, Democratic Vice Presidential nominee Geraldine Ferraro (D-NY). Mrs. Bush responded: **"I can't say it, but it rhymes with 'rich.'"**

Barbara Pierce Bush
George Bush Presidential Library and Museum

Well, Ok: During a speech in Dodge, Iowa in 1952, Democratic Presidential nominee Adlai Stevenson, in referring to the campaign of his Republican opponent, Dwight D. Eisenhower, told the audience: **"The Republicans have a 'me too' candidate running on a 'yes but' platform, advised by a 'has been' staff."**

Adlai Stevenson
Library of Congress

Going Too Far: In 1994, Texas Governor Ann Richards, on a campaign stop in Texarkana, Texas, heaped approbation on Debbie Colman who was the recipient of the city's Teacher of the Year Award. Richards was inflamed that her Republican opponent, George W. Bush, had argued that the achievement scores for students were manipulated because it is an election year. Richards then asserted: **"You just work like a dog, do well, the test scores are up, the kids are looking better, the dropout rate is down. And all of a sudden, you've got some jerk who's running for public office [George W. Bush] telling everybody it's all a sham and it isn't real and he doesn't give you credit for doing your job. So far as he is concerned, everything in Texas is terrible."**

Ann Richards
Photograph by Kenneth C. Zirkel

Playing the Weight Card: During the last days of the 1932 Presidential campaign, Democratic Presidential nominee Franklin D. Roosevelt referred to his Republican opponent, Herbert Hoover, as a **"fat, timid capon."**

**Herbert Hoover (L),
Franklin D. Roosevelt (R)**
Franklin D. Roosevelt
Presidential Library and Museum

Political Insults

A Change of Rhetoric: In 2016, Republican Presidential candidate Donald Trump tweeted of his rival, U.S. Senator Ted Cruz (R-TX): **"Why would the people of Texas support Ted Cruz when he has accomplished absolutely nothing for them. He is another all talk, no action pol!"** In 2018, with Cruz enveloped in a tough fight for reelection to the U.S. Senate, Trump tweeted: **"I will be doing a major rally for Senator Ted Cruz in October. I'm picking the biggest stadium in Texas we can find. As you know, Ted has my complete and total Endorsement. His opponent is a disaster for Texas - weak on Second Amendment, Crime, Borders, Military, and Vets!"**

Ted Cruz
Photograph by Michael Vandon

Not an Insult One Would Normally Hear at the School Yard: Theodore Roosevelt was a harsh critic of Woodrow Wilson. The two had run against each other in 1912, and there was no love lost between the two Presidents. Roosevelt once branded Wilson: **"A Byzantine logothete backed by flubdubs and mollycoddles."** (Translation: A logothete is an administrator; a flubdud means non-sense; mollycoddle means pampered.)

Theodore Roosevelt
Library of Congress

Playing the Elitist Card: Political opponents of Massachusetts Governor Endicott "Chub" Peabody (1963-1965) joked that there were three municipalities in the Bay State named after him. They were: **"Peabody, Marblehead and Athol."** They also tried to exploit classism within the electorate by pointing to Peabody's patrician background, characterizing him as an elitist. During the Democratic Primary for re-election, supporters of Peabody's opponent, Lieutenant Governor Francis X. Bellotti, distributed bumper stickers which read: **"Vote for Peabody. He's better than you."** Bellotti won the primary, but lost the General Election to former Massachusetts Republican Governor Frank Volpe in the General Election.

Endicott "Chub" Peabody
Official Portrait

Two Mouths, Half a Brain: In 1983, Democrat Edwin Edwards was asked by his opponent David Treen: **"How Come you talk out of both sides of your mouth?"** Edwards replied: **"so people like you with only half a brain can understand me."**

Edwin Edwards
Official Photograph

Political Insults

A Real City Boy: During his failed 1982 run for the Democratic nomination for Governor of New York State, New York City Mayor Ed Koch asked Peter Manso of *Playboy Magazine:* **"Have you ever lived in the suburbs? I haven't but I've talked to people who have, and it's sterile. It's nothing. It's wasting your life, and people do not wish to waste their lives once they've seen New York** [City.]**"** When Manso asked Koch why people would live in New York City, given **"lousy city services and a late subway,"** Koch again exploded on the suburbs, asserting, **"As opposed to wasting time in a car? - Or out in the country, wasting time in a pickup truck? - When you have to drive 20 miles to buy a gingham dress or a Sears Roebuck suit. The rural American thing – I'm telling you, it's a joke."**

Ed Koch
Photograph by Rob C. Croes Anefo

Freeloading? During his successful 1966 campaign for the position of California Governor, Ronald Reagan told The *Sacramento Bee:* **"Unemployment insurance is a pre-paid vacation for freeloaders."**

Campaign Button for Ronald Reagan's 1966 Gubernatorial run

The Ignorance of the Constituents: In 1871, *Harper's Weekly* ran articles exposing the corruption of New York State Senator William "Boss" Tweed and his political machine. Tweed commented to a reporter: **"I don't care a straw for your newspaper articles, my constituents don't know how to read, but they can't help seeing them damned pictures."**

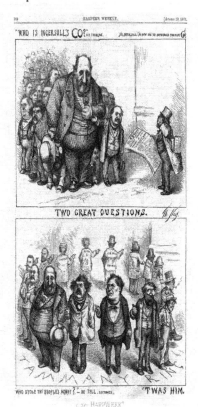

Political Cartoon by Thomas Nast of *Harpers Weekly*, Depicting a Corrupt Tweed Machine

Baby Talk: In 1966, Georgia Democratic Gubernatorial nominee Lester Maddox called his Democratic opponent, Howard Hollis "Bo" Calloway, **"a baby in his crib reaching for his rattler."** Maddox won the election.

Howard Hollis "Bo" Callaway
Official Portrait

Political Insults

Bi-Ignorant: When Democratic Texas Agricultural Commissioner Jim Hightower was informed that Republican Governor Bill Clements was studying Spanish, Hightower deadpanned: **"Oh Good. Now he'll be bi-ignorant."**

Jim Hightower
Photograph by Larry D. Moore

Vaseline? In 2013, Maine Governor Paul LePage became inflamed after State Senator Troy Jackson suggested that the Governor's veto threat of the State Budget was a "stunt." LePage responded: **"Jackson claims to be for the people, but he's the first one to give it to the people without providing Vaseline."**

Paul LePage
Photograph by Matt Gagnon

Time To Return to the Pigs: In 1998, when Democrat John Edwards defeated Republican U.S. Senator Lauch Faircloth (R-NC) in his re-election bid, Washington D.C. Mayor Marian Berry rejoiced. Faircloth by profession was a hog farmer. Berry had had a rocky relationship with Faricloth, who chaired the U.S. Senate Appropriations subcommittee for the District of Columbia. Speaking at a victory rally for Anthony Williams, who won the election to succeed Berry as Mayor, Berry told the crowd: **"Senator Faircloth has lost, lost, lost. Gone. Dead and buried . . . . He's so busy picking on me and the residents of the District of Columbia that he neglected his constituents in North Carolina. Now he can go back and deal with the pigs. Goodbye, Faircloth."**

Lauch Faircloth
Official Photograph

Senator Pays Political Price for Not Toeing the Party Line: In 1918, President Woodrow Wilson endorsed Pat Harrison in the Democratic U.S. Senate Primary against the incumbent Democrat James K. Vardaman (D-MS). Wilson was inflamed that Vardaman had voted against the Congressional Declaration of War with Germany. Vardaman did not take Wilson's endorsement of Harrison in stride. He called Wilson: **"the coldest blooded, most selfish ruler beneath the stars today."**

James K. Vardaman
Library of Congress

No Letting Bygones be Bygones: After losing to Democrat Barack Obama in a race for an open U.S. Senate Seat in Illinois in 2004, Republican nominee Allan Keyes refused to call Obama and concede the election, claiming it would be a **"false gesture."** Keyes said that Obama stands for **"a culture evil enough to destroy the very soul and heart of my country."**

**Bumper-sticker: Allan Keyes
for U.S. Senate**

Hillary Clinton Called The anti-Christ: In 2014, Republican Congressional candidate Ryan Zinke, to future Democratic Presidential candidate Hillary Clinton as the anti-Christ. In 2017, after the inauguration of President Donald Trump, Zinke, now a U.S. House member, came up to Clinton and introduced himself. Clinton writes in her book *What Happened* of the exchange. **"'You know, Congressman, I said. 'I'm not actually the anti-Christ. He was taken aback and mumbled something about not having meant it."**

Ryan Zinke
Official Photograph

An Odd Comparison: In his 2004 re-election bid, U.S. Senator Jim Bunning (R-KY) faced a firestorm of criticism for saying that his Democratic opponent, Daniel Monglaro, **"looks like one of Saddam Hussein's sons. . . . I mean before they were dead, of course . . . . I really mean that he looks like one of Saddam's sons, and he even dresses like them, too."**

Jim Bunning
Official Photograph

Lyndon B. Johnson was an Animal: During a recorded break on the CNN program *Crossfire* in 1982, former President Richard M. Nixon was discussing with host Pat Buchanan the book: *The Years of Lyndon Johnson: The Path to Power.* Nixon said to Buchanan about the portrayal of Johnson: **"It makes him look like a god damn animal. Of course he was."**

Richard M. Nixon (L), Lyndon B. Johnson (R)
Lyndon Baines Johnson Library and Museum

Political Insults

The Cuttlefish Analogy: During one of the Lincoln-Douglas U.S. Senate debates in 1858, Republican Abraham Lincoln said of his opponent, Democrat Stephen Douglas, who he believed was evading the issues: **"Judge Douglas is playing cuttlefish — a small species of fish that has no mode of defending himself when pursued except by throwing out a black fluid which makes the water so dark the enemy cannot see it, and thus it escapes."**

Cuttlefish
Photograph by Borazont

Who Woulda Thunk It? In 1964, Robert F. Kennedy easily won the Democratic New York U.S. Senate Primary. U.S. Representative Samuel S. Stratton (D-NY) had been the favorite before Kennedy moved to the state solely to run for the seat. After the election, Stratton joked: **"When Bobby Kennedy decided he was a New Yorker, that was the end of my campaign."**

Samuel S. Stratton
Official Photograph

Republican Calls Birthers "Dumbasses:" At a 2010 campaign event in Pueblo Colorado, Republican U.S. Senate candidate Ken Buck (Who enjoyed the support of many exponents of the Tea Party Movement) ignored a question about the birth certificate of President Barack Obama. At another event later that day, Buck saw a Democratic campaign tracker, who unbeknownst to Buck had a tape recorder in his pocket. Buck stated: **"Will you tell those dumbasses at the Tea Party to stop asking questions about birth certificates while I'm on the camera?"** After the remark became public, Buck's campaign apologized. Despite this incident, Buck won the Republican Primary. However, he lost in the General Election to incumbent Democratic U.S. Senator Michael Bennett.

Ken Buck
Official Photograph

Why Doesn't He Tell Him How He Really Feels: In the 1994 Virginia U.S. Senate race, Democratic incumbent Chuck Robb was challenged by Republican Oliver North who had been implicated in the Iran-Contra scandal during the Presidential Administration of Ronald Reagan. Senator Robb brought out the heavy rhetorical artillery, telling an audience in Alexander, VA that his Senate opponent: **"is a document-shredding, Constitution-trashing, Commander in Chief-bashing, Congress-thrashing, uniform-shaming, Ayatollah-loving, arms-dealing, criminal-protecting, résumé-enhancing, Noriega-coddling, Social Security-threatening, public school-denigrating, Swiss-banking-law-breaking, letter-faking, self-serving, election-losing, snake-oil salesman who can't tell the difference between the truth and a lie."** The next day, Robb won the Senate election.

Chuck Robb
Official Photograph

138

Political Insults

No Fan of Boxer: Speaking at a campaign rally for California's 2010 Republican Senate nominee Carly Fiorina, U.S. Senator John McCain chastised her opponent, U.S Senator Barbara Boxer (D-CA). He said: **"Barbara Boxer is the most bitterly partisan, most anti-defense senator in the United States Senate today. I know that because I've had the unpleasant experience of having to serve with her."**

Barbara Boxer
Official Photograph

Naked Politics: During the 2012 U.S. Senate campaign, challenger Elizabeth Warren was asked how she made money to get through college. She joked: **"I kept my clothes on."** She was joking about her opponent, U.S. Senator Scott Brown (R-MA), who had modeled nude to pay for college. During an appearance on *WZLX Radio* in Boston, Brown responded to Warren's dig about keeping her clothes on by stating: **"Thank God!"**

Scott Brown in *Cosmos Magazine*

In a State of Ambivalence: During a U.S Senate debate on NBC's *Meet the Press* in 2006, Democratic Nominee Claire McCaskill was asked by moderator Tim Russert: **"Bill Clinton raised money for you. Do you think Bill Clinton was a Great President?"** McCaskill responded: **"I think he's been a great leader but I don't want my daughter near him."** McCaskill later apologized to Clinton for the comments.

Claire McCaskill
Official Photograph

Kooks, Commies, and Egghead Professors: In 1966, future U.S. House Speaker Tip O'Neill (D-MA) addressed a rally at the Massachusetts State House in support of U.S. involvement in the Vietnam War. In his speech, O'Neil took aim at those who opposed the war, including many in academia who were his Cambridge constituents. O'Neill said: **"I believe in Academic Freedom, but not as it is expounded by kooks, commies, and egghead professors."** A year later, O'Neill became an opponent of the war.

Tip O'Neill
Official Photograph

Taking the Term 'Son of a Bitch' Literally: When told the Imperial Wizard of the Ku Klux Klan was going to come to Louisiana, U.S. Senator Huey Long (D-LA) said: **"You tell that imperial bastard in Mississippi to keep out of Louisiana. Tell that son of a bitch that I am not just using an expression; I am referring to the circumstances of his birth."**

Huey Long
Library of Congress

U.S. Senator gets into Eisenhower's Skull: U.S. Senator Thomas W. Bricker (R-OH) proposed a Federal Constitutional Amendment to limit the treaty-making power of the President. President Dwight D. Eisenhower put out a full court press to defeat it. He became annoyed at the time it was taking out of his Presidency to fight it. The amendment failed to be ratified by the U.S. Senate by just one vote. Eisenhower commented: **"If it's true that when you die the things that bothered you most are engraved on your skull, I am sure that I'll have there in the mud and dirt of France during the invasion and the name of Senator Bricker."**

Thomas W. Bricker
Official Photograph

Disparaging a Unitarian Candidate: In 1942, Former Massachusetts Governor James Michael Curley defeated incumbent U.S. Representative Thomas H. Elliot (D-MA) in the Democratic Primary. Curley exploited Elliot's religious background, which was Unitarian (Elliot was the son of a Unitarian Minister). In campaign speeches in the State's urban ethnic Eleventh Congressional District, Curley exclaimed to the crowd: **"My young opponent is a Unitarian. Do you know what a Unitarian is? A Unitarian is a person who believes that our Lord and Savior is a funny little man with a beard who runs around in his underclothes."**

James Michael Curley
Library of Congress

Helms Warns Clinton: U.S. Senator Jesse Helms (R-NC), a vociferous critic of President Bill Clinton, told *The Raleigh News and Observer* in 1995: **"Mr. Clinton better watch out if he comes down here. He'd better have a bodyguard."** He was referring to Clinton's unpopularity throughout military bases in North Carolina. He later said it was **"an offhand remark."**

Jesse Helms
Official Photograph

He's Got Ice Water for Blood: Though he shared an Irish heritage with Ronald Reagan and they shared a cordial personal relationship, U.S. House Speaker Tip O'Neill (D-MA) publicly held President Ronald Reagan in very low regard. He said of Reagan: **"The evil is in the White House at the present time. And that evil is a man who has no care and no concern for the working class of America and the future generations of America, and who likes to ride a horse. He's cold. He's mean. He's got ice water for blood."**

Ronald Reagan (L), Tip O'Neill (R)
Ronald Reagan Presidential
Foundation and Library

Is that Supposed to be a Compliment? Observing the actions of Freshman U.S. Senator Huey Long in 1933, U.S. Senate veteran Alben Barkley (D-KY) said to Huey Long (D-LA), **"You are the smartest lunatic I have ever seen in my whole life."**

Huey Long
Official Photograph

The Byrd and the Peckerwoods: U.S. Senator Robert C. Byrd (D-WV) was often chastised by fiscal conservative groups like Citizens against Government Waste for his propensity to allocate money to his home state of West Virginia. Byrd had little patience for these critics, believing that he was bringing needed resources to his home state. In 1995, Byrd told *ABC News,* **"What these peckerwoods call pork is infrastructure."**

Robert C. Byrd
U.S. Department of Transportation Photograph

Hey! At Least Truman Was Being Honest: When U.S. Senator Huey Long (D-LA) asked his colleague Harry S. Truman (D-MO), who was presiding over the Senate, what he thought of his fiery populist speech, Truman answered: **"I had to listen to you because I was in the chair and couldn't walk out."** Long was furious, and the two senators never spoke to one another again.

Harry S. Truman
Harry S. Truman Library and Museum

Congenitally Biased: President Lyndon B. Johnson said of U.S. Senator James Eastland (D-MS), an ardent segregationist and anti-communist: **"Jim Eastland could be standing right in the middle of the worst Mississippi flood ever known and blame it on the negroes helped by the communists."**

James Eastland (L),
Lyndon B. Johnson (R)
Lyndon Baines Johnson Library and Museum

The Most Dangerous Place in Washington: In 1995, U.S. Senate Minority Leader Bob Dole (R-KS) commented on U.S. Representative Charles Schumer (D-NY) and his many on-air appearances. Dole said: **"The most dangerous place in Washington is between Charles Schumer and a television camera."**

Charles Schumer
Official U.S. House Photograph

Goldwater Recommends all Good Christians Kick Ass: Reverend Jerry Falwell was a vociferous opponent of Ronald Reagan's nomination of Sandra Day O'Connor to the U.S. Supreme Court. Falwell thought her views on social issues were too liberal. He urged **"All Good Christians to oppose the nomination of Sandra Day O'Connor to the U.S. Supreme Court."** In response to Falwell's statement, U.S. Senator Barry Goldwater (R-AZ), a Libertarian-oriented conservative who virulently opposed social conservative inroads in the Republican Party, quipped: **"All Good Christians should kick Jerry Falwell's ass."**

Barry Goldwater
Official Photograph

Trash Talking Senators: U.S. Senators Daniel Webster (Whig-MA) and Henry Clay (Whig-KY) witnessed a pack of mules walking by. Webster commented: **"There goes a number of your Kentucky constituents."** Clay retorted: **"Yes, they must be on their way to Massachusetts to teach school."**

Henry Clay
Official Photograph

Political Insults

Political Trash-Talking: In 1919, U.S. Senate Majority Leader Henry Cabot Lodge Sr. (R-MA) called Democratic President Woodrow Wilson, who he had feuded with over the ratification of the Treaty of Versailles, **"the most sinister figure that ever crossed the country's path."**

Henry Cabot Lodge Sr.
Library of Congress

No Political Pandering Here: U.S. Senator Stephen M. Young (D-OH 1959-1971) was known for his blunt and sometimes sarcastic responses to constituents who challenged his views. One letter-writer ended his letter by saying: **"I would welcome the opportunity to have intercourse with you."** Senator Young responded: **"You sir, can have intercourse with yourself."**

Stephen M. Young
Official Photograph

Words Taken Back: In 2005, at an event at Del Sol High School in Las Vegas, U.S. Senate Minority Leader Harry Reid (D-NV) said of George W. Bush: **"This man's father was a wonderful human being. I think this guy is a loser."** Reed later apologized to Deputy Chief of Staff Karl Rove for making this remark.

Harry Reid
Official Photograph

He is No Gentleman: In 1995, during a fiery debate on the elimination of an exemption for nuclear carriers and submarines under the Clean Water Act, U.S. Representative Patricia Schroeder (D-CO) said: **"Mr. Chairman, do we have to call the gentleman 'The gentleman' as he is not one?"** Schroeder's remarks were sparked after Democratic Socialist Representative Bernie Sanders (I-VT) asked his colleague Randy Duke Cunningham (R-CA) to yield. Rather than yield, Cunningham responded: **"Sit down, you Socialist."**

Patricia Schroeder
Official Photograph

143

Political Insults

Not in a New York State of Mind: In 1834, U.S. Representative David "Davy" Crocket (Whig-TN) visited New York City for the first time. He commented: **"I would rather risk myself in an Indian fight than venture among these creatures after night. God deliver me from such constituents or from a party supported by such."**

David "Davy" Crockett
Library of Congress

No Friend of Bill Clinton: U.S. Representative Robert K. Dornan (R-CA) refused to watch the Inauguration of President Bill Clinton in 1993. He told *The Los Angeles Times*: **"As much as I love history, I could not physically watch a decorated Navy combat carrier attack pilot** [George H. W. Bush] **passing on the torch to a draft dodger."**

Inauguration of Bill Clinton
Library of Congress

Gangsta Rap: In 1988, U.S. Representative Mario Biaggi (D-NY) was convicted for taking illegal gratuities while in office. During his trial, the Assistant U.S. Attorney called Biaggi: **"A thug in a Congressman's Suit."**

Mario Biaggi
Official Photograph

Keeping It Classy! In 2002, U.S. House Minority Leader Richard Gephardt (D-MO) said that U.S. Representative James Traficant (D-OH) should resign from office after he was convicted of filing false tax returns, taking bribes, racketeering, and forcing his Congressional aides to do chores on his Ohio farm and on his houseboat. When a reporter asked Traficant to respond to Gephardt's request, Traficant responded: **"Gephardt has no balls and he can go f--k himself."** Later when he defended himself before the House prior to being expelled, Traficant said: **"Mr. Gephardt, if you're here, I apologize for my comments; it was in the heat of battle. If you had been there, I probably would have hit you too. But I apologize for these words."**

James Traficant
Official Photograph

Political Insults

Weird Analogy: In 2013, U.S. Representative Steve Stockman (R-TX) tweeted: **"About 110,000 people contract Chlamydia each month, more than signed up for Obamacare. Stated another way, Obamacare is less popular than Chlamydia."** Chlamydia is a Sexually Transmitted Disease.

Steve Stockman
Official Photograph

Great Comeback: In 1972, during a hearing on Home Rule for the District of Columbia, U.S. Representative John Rarick (D-LA) testified against Home Rule for the District, calling it: **"a sinkhole, rat infested . . . the laughing stock of the free and Communist world."** U.S. Representative Charles Diggs (D-MI) disagreed and retorted: **"We are stretching the First Amendment even to permit 'you' to speak before this committee."**

John Rarick
Official Photograph

The Barefoot Boy From Wall Street: 1940 Presidential candidate Wendell Willkie spoke often about his humble roots growing up in Longwood, Indiana, but managing to become a corporate lawyer and top Utilities executive. He managed to develop many ties to Wall Street. Joking about Willkie's humble beginnings story, U.S. Interior Secretary Harold Ickies dubbed him: **"The barefoot boy from Wall Street."** Furthering this joke, Alice Roosevelt Longworth, the daughter of Theodore Roosevelt, said Willkie has: **"grassroots in every country club in America."**

Wendell Willkie
Library of Congress

Governor Judas: In 2008, New Mexico Governor Bill Richardson, who dropped out of the Presidential sweepstakes, endorsed Barack Obama over Hillary Clinton for President. Hillary's husband Bill had nominated Richardson to the posts of U.S. Ambassador to the U.N. and to the position of U.S. Secretary of Energy. Political Consultant James Carville, a supporter of Hillary, observed: **"Mr. Richardson's endorsement came right around the anniversary of the day when Judas sold out for 30 pieces of silver, so I think the timing is appropriate, if ironic."**

Bill Richardson
Official Photograph

Political Insults

The Dunce Stands Alone: For much of Franklin D. Roosevelt's second term, there was speculation that he would run for an unprecedented third term. Roosevelt was circumspect in not revealing his decision. He would craftily brush off the question. However, he would sometimes get annoyed. At a 1937 press conference, White House Correspondent Robert Post of *The New York Times* asked Roosevelt if he would seek a third term. An irritated Roosevelt responded: **"Bob, go put on the dunce cap and stand in the corner."** In 1940, when Roosevelt accepted the Democratic Party nomination for a third term, Mr. Post wrote him a letter reading: **"Who's The Dunce Now?"**

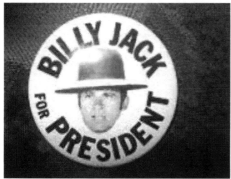

Franklin D. Roosevelt (C) Takes Questions at a Press Conference
Franklin D. Roosevelt Presidential
Library and Museum

Harsh Words Indeed for Presidential Candidate: In 1992, actor and Democratic Presidential candidate Tom Laughlin (of *Billy Jack* film fame) told High School students at Iowa City West High School that one of his opponents, U.S. Senator Tom Harkin (D-IA), **"doesn't care for anybody but Harkin. I think he's a sleazebag. I despise him."**

Tom Laughlin for President Pin
Using His Movie Character Billy Jack

Dukakis Agrees With Bush and Dole: In a speech prior to the Iowa caucuses in 1988, Democratic Presidential candidate Michael Dukakis poked fun of Republican candidates George H.W. Bush and Bob Dole. Dukakis told a crowd in Cedar Rapids, Iowa, **"Vice President Bush and Senator Dole have been saying some rather nasty things about each other. Senator Dole says the Vice President is not much of a leader and the Vice President says Senator Dole is not much of a leader. I don't ordinarily agree with those guys but in this case I agree with both of them. Neither of them is much of a leader."**

Michael Dukakis on the Cover of
Time Magazine

Taking on Trump: In 2018, Donald Trump branded Tallahassee Mayor and Florida Gubernatorial nominee Andrew Gillum **"a stone cold thief."** To this, Gillum took to twitter to retort: **"I heard @realDonaldTrump ran home to lie about me. But my grandmother told me – never wrestle with a pig. You both get dirty, but the pig likes it. So ignore him and vote, Florida."**

Andres Gillum
Official Photograph

Political Insults

Master of Alliteration: Dean Acheson, U.S. Secretary of State under the administration of Democrat Harry S. Truman, advocated a policy of **"containment"** with respect to communism. In 1952, Republican Vice Presidential candidate Richard M. Nixon argued that the U.S. should work to roll back, rather than contain communism. Nixon railed against what he characterized as **"Acheson's College of Cowardly Communist Containment."**

Dean Acheson
Lyndon Baines Johnson Library and Museum

Doggy Humor: During a 2011 debate amongst Republican Presidential aspirants, Gary Johnson brought down the house by stating: **"My next-door neighbor's two dogs have created more shovel-ready jobs than this current administration."** After garnering little attention in the Republican Primary, Johnson became a Libertarian and mustered that party's Presidential nomination. However, he garnered less than 1% of the vote in the General Election.

Gary Johnson
Official Photograph

Strong and Vague: Former U.S. Senator Eugene McCarthy (D-MN) was a critic of President Jimmy Carter and Carter's opponent for renomination in 1980, U.S. Senator Ted Kennedy (D-MA). He said of the two: **"The difference between Carter and Kennedy: Carter has this vague religion which he believes in strongly, while Kennedy has this strong religion which he believes in vaguely."**

Ted Kennedy (L), Jimmy Carter (R)
The National Archives and Records Administration

Catchy Political Tune: In 1884, Republican Presidential nominee James G. Blaine was enveloped in accusations that when he served as Speaker of the U.S. House of Representatives, he had influenced legislation benefitting the railroad companies, and had allegedly profited from the bonds he owned in the railroad companies. Democrats chanted: **"Blaine Blaine, James G. Blaine, The continental liar from the state of Maine."** Blaine lost the election to Democrat Grover Cleveland.

James G. Blaine
Library of Congress

147

Political Insults

Just Blame The Workers: During the 1988 Democratic Presidential Primary, candidate Richard Gephardt said of one of his rivals: **"Governor [Michael] Dukakis has an ad on the air in which he basically blames American workers for our trade problems. I [Gephardt] have a motto in my campaign: 'It's your fight too.' I wonder if his (campaign) has a motto, 'It's your fault too.'"**

Richard Gephardt for President Pin

So is he Undecided? During a 2017 conversation on election hacking, Democratic Political strategist James Carville was asked how he felt on Donald Trump. His response: **"I feel like he's a lying felonious sack of s##t."**

James Carville
Office of James Carville

Clinton Suggests Representative Needs Rabies Shot: One of the harshest Critics of Bill Clinton during the 1992 Presidential campaign was U.S. Representative Robert K. Dornan (R-CA). Clinton told reporters: **"Every time I see Bob Dornan - he looks like he needs a rabies shot."**

Bob Dornan
Official Photograph

Don't Let the Door hit You on the Way Out of the Country: In 1976, former President Richard M. Nixon traveled to China as a private citizen. The trip occurred during the New Hampshire Primary season. Nixon's successor, Gerald R. Ford, was facing a redoubtable challenge from former California Governor Ronald Reagan. Nixon's trip reminded primary voters that Ford had pardoned the unpopular Nixon. When U.S. Senator Barry Goldwater (R-AZ), a Ford supporter, was asked about Nixon's trip, he averred: **"As far as I'm concerned, Nixon can go to China and stay there."** Despite the Nixon episode, Ford still won the New Hampshire Primary and the GOP Presidential nomination.

Barry Goldwater
Library of Congress

Political Insults

Orange Hair? In 1976, Gerald R. Ford joked of his Republican Primary opponent: **"Ronald Reagan doesn't dye his hair, he's just prematurely orange."**

Ronald Reagan (L), Gerald R. Ford (R)
Gerald R. Ford Presidential Library and Museum

You Must Know Dewey to Dislike Him: The Republican Presidential nominee in 1944 and 1948 was Thomas E. Dewey. He was viewed as prickly, aloof, and distant. U.S. Senator Robert A. Taft (R-OH) who competed with Dewey three times for the Republican Presidential nomination commented: **"You really have to get to know Dewey to dislike him."**

Thomas E. Dewey
Library of Congress

The Heart Versus the Gut: In 1964, the campaign slogan of Republican Presidential nominee Barry Goldwater was: **"In your heart you know he's right."** The campaign of Goldwater's opponent, Democratic President Lyndon B. Johnson, retorted: **"In your gut, you know he's nuts."**

Pin Mocking Barry Goldwater

Truman Lets Nixon Have It: Former President Harry S. Truman had little respect for Richard M. Nixon. When Nixon was the Republican Presidential nominee in 1960, the former President said: **"Richard Nixon is a no-good lying bastard. He can lie out of both sides of his mouth at the same time, and if he ever caught himself telling the truth, he'd lie just to keep his hand in."**

**Richard M. Nixon (L),
Harry S. Truman (R)**
Harry S. Truman Library and Museum

Political Insults

Panda Bear or Pander Bear? During the 1992 Presidential election, former U.S. Senator Paul Tsongas accused Bill Clinton of pandering to Connecticut voters by saying he would support a scaled back version of the Sea Wolf Nuclear Submarine Program. Then Tsongas told Florida voters: **"It was a cynical attempt to get votes from Connecticut. The American people are just hearing how cynical and unprincipled Bill Clinton is. He knows full well it will never be built."** At a campaign rally in Fort Lauderdale, Florida, Tsongas held up a teddy bear and said, **"This is my opponent, Pander bear."** Unfortunately for Tsongas, many voters watching the event thought he was saying **"panda bear"** and did not understand why he was calling Bill Clinton a **"panda bear."**

Bill Clinton and Paul Tsongas on cover of *Time Magazine*

Presidential Ham: In 1840, Whig Presidential nominee William Henry Harrison was viewed by his opponents as a ham that loves the limelight. After Harrison won the election, U.S. Senator John C. Calhoun (D-SC) commented: **"He seems to enjoy this election as a mere affair of personal vanity."**

William Henry Harrison
Photograph by Albert Sand Southorth and Josiah Johnson Hawes

The New Nixon, Again: During the 1968 Presidential campaign, Democratic nominee Vice President Hubert Humphrey made fun of the reinvention of his Republican opponent, former Vice President Richard M. Nixon: **"They had a renewal job in 1952** (When Nixon won the GOP Vice Presidential Nomination). **There was some reason for it too. Then they had another renewal job in 1956** (When Nixon ran for reelection as Vice President). **Then they had another renovation operation in 1960** (when Nixon was the Republican Presidential nomine). **Then when he ran for Governor in California in 1962, they renewed him again. Then in 1964 another touchup, and now I read about the new Nixon of 1968. Ladies and gentleman, anybody who had his political face lifted so many times can't be very new."**

**Richard M. Nixon (L),
Hubert Humphrey (R)
Cover of *Veja Magazine***

Making light of Candidate's Costly Hair Care: Making light of recent revelations that Democratic Presidential candidate John Edwards had taken $800 out of his campaign war chest for two haircuts, Republican Presidential candidate Mike Huckabee said in a Republican debate: **"We've had a Congress that spent money like John Edwards at a beauty shop."**

Mike Huckabee
Photograph by Greg Skidmore

No Fan of Romney: During his address to the Democratic National Convention in 2012, former Ohio Governor Ted Strickland drew plaudits from the partisan crowd for saying of the Republican Presidential nominee Mitt Romney: **"Mitt Romney has so little economic patriotism that even his money needs a passport."**

Ted Strickland
Official Photograph

Getting Off On The Wrong Foot: During the 1932 Democratic National Convention, the Indiana Delegation, led by future Indiana Governor Paul V. McNutt, refused to support Franklin D. Roosevelt's Presidential nomination until the very last ballot. Roosevelt claimed McNutt was rude to him when he asked for support from the Indiana Delegation. Ironically, McNuttt was elected Governor that year and Roosevelt was elected President. The two Democrats had a rocky relationship. Roosevelt referred to McNutt as: **"That platinum blond S.O.B. from Indiana."**

Paul V. McNutt
Library of Congress

As Partisan as it Gets: During the 1948 Presidential election, U.S. Representative John F. Kennedy (D-MA) waded into extreme partisan territory when he made the following statement about the Republican Party: **"They follow the Hitler Line – no matter how big the lie; repeat it often enough and the masses will regard it as true."**

John F. Kennedy (L), and Harry S. Truman (R) in his Later Years
National Archives and Records Administration

A Man of Monumental Littleness: Theodore Roosevelt was no fan of one of his predecessors, John Tyler. The sarcastic Roosevelt quipped: **"He has been called a mediocre man; but this is unwarranted flattery. He was a politician of monumental littleness."**

John Tyler
Official Portrait

151

Political Insults

Truman Chides Dewey: In a speech in Phoenix, Republican Presidential nominee Thomas E. Dewey asserted: **"America's future, like yours in Arizona, is still ahead of us."** His Democratic opponent, Harry S. Truman, chided Dewey for making this remark. During a campaign address in New York City, Truman said: **"Well I hope the future will last a long time for all of you, and I hope it will be a very happy future – and I hope it won't be a future under Republicans, either."**

Harry S. Truman (L) Thomas E. Dewey (R) Shaking Hands
Harry S. Truman Library and Museum

Candidate Asks Heckler to Kiss His Ass: When Democratic Presidential nominee George McGovern was harassed by a heckler in Battle Creek, Michigan, he whispered in his ear: **"Listen, you son of a bitch, why don't you kiss my ass."** His supporters then manufactured campaign buttons with the acronym "KMA" emblazoned on them. U.S. Senator James Eastland (D-MS) later told McGovern: **"That was the best line in the campaign."**

George McGovern
Library of Congress

President Calls Opponents "Bozos:" At a 1992 campaign rally in Warren, Michigan, President George H.W. Bush lashed out at his Democratic opponents Bill Clinton and Al Gore saying: **"My dog Millie knows more about foreign affairs than these two bozos."** Bush lost the election.

Millie
George Bush Presidential
Library and Museum

Fly Swatter Politics: In a campaign speech in Ames Iowa in 1976, President Gerald R. Ford mocked statements by his Democratic opponent Jimmy Carter. Carter had said he would cut the nation's defense budget. Ford told the crowd: **"Teddy Roosevelt once said, 'Speak softly and carry a big stick.' Jimmy Carter wants to speak loudly and carry a fly swatter."**

Jimmy Carter (L), Gerald R. Ford (R)
Gerald R. Ford Presidential Library and Museum

Political Insults

Congress is Just as Stupid as the People: In a 1971 interview with Theodore A. Wilson and Richard D. McKenzie, Dean Acheson, (former U.S. Secretary of State during the Truman administration,) blasted the American people: **"People say, If the Congress were more representative of the people it would be better. I say the Congress is too damn representative. It's just as stupid as the people are; just as uneducated, just as dumb, just as selfish."**

Dean Acheson
Harry S. Truman Library and Museum

No Love Lost Here: When future U.S. Secretary of State John Foster Dulles was a lawyer at Sullivan & Cromwell, he chose not to hire future U.S. Supreme Court Justice William O. Douglas, saying he **"didn't seem sharp enough."** Douglas later recalled the job interview saying: **"I was so struck with Dulles' pomposity that when he helped me on with my coat as I was leaving the office, I turned and gave him a quarter tip."** Douglas later said, **"I'm not sure I want to go to Heaven. I'm afraid I might meet John Foster Dulles there."**

John Foster Dulles
Official Photograph

Spiro Agnew Alliterates: In an address to the California Republican State Convention delivered on September 11, 1970, Vice President Spiro Agnew excoriated the American news media, saying: **"In the United States today, we have more than our share of the nattering nabobs of negativism. They have formed their own 4-H Club – The hopeless, hysterical hypochondriacs of history."** Speechwriter William Safire wrote these words for Agnew.

Spiro Agnew
Official Photograph as Governor of Maryland

The Bureaucratic Senate: Vice President Henry Wilson, who served under President Ulysses S. Grant, made the following comment about the U.S. Senate that he in fact presided over: **"I believe if we introduced the Lord's Prayer here, senators would propose a large number of amendments to it."**

Henry Wilson
Library of Congress

153

Political Insults

Is This the U.S. Senate or the Jerry Springer Show? In 2004, Vice President Dick Cheney, while serving in his constitutional role as President of the U.S. Senate, was on the Senate floor for the official Senate photograph. After the photograph, U.S. Senator Patrick Leahy (D-VT) greeted Cheney. In response, Cheney said to Leahy: **"Go f*** yourself."** Cheney was indignant at Leahy for excoriating him in his role as ranking member of the U.S. Senate Judiciary Committee for the alleged profiteering of Halliburton (formerly led by Cheney) in Iraq.

Patrick Leahy
Official Photograph

Waging a War Against Intellectuals: Following the 1969 Moratorium to end the War in Vietnam, Vice President Spiro Agnew ginned up conservative populist indignation against intellectuals. He told a Republican Party fundraiser in New Orleans: **"A spirit of national masochism prevails, encouraged by an effete corps of impudent snobs who characterize themselves as intellectuals."**

Spiro Agnew
Official Photograph

Great Analogy: U.S. Senator Barry Goldwater (R-AZ) once commented about Vice President Hubert Humphrey: **"He talks so fast that listening to him is like trying to read *Playboy Magazine* with your wife turning the pages."**

Playboy Magazine

President Calls Texas Oil Tycoons "Stupid:" In a 1954 letter written to his brother Newton Eisenhower, Dwight D. Eisenhower upbraids conservatives who want to abolish the social safety net. He writes: **"There is a tiny splinter group, of course, that believes you can do these things. Among them are H.L. Hunt, a Texas oil tycoon, a few other Texas oil millionaires, and an occasional politician or businessman from other areas. Their number is negligible and they are stupid."**

Dwight D. Eisenhower
The Eisenhower Presidential
Library and Museum

154

Political Insults

Quick-Witted Andrew Jackson Smacks Down His Vice President: Vice President John C. Calhoun broke with President Andrew Jackson over the issue of nullification (The right of a State to nullify a federal law which that state deems unconstitutional). Calhoun, a native South Carolinian, supported it, while Jackson opposed it. Calhoun publicly said that he would even support his state's succession from the Union if necessary, to which Jackson responded: **"John Calhoun, if you secede from my nation, I will secede your head from the rest of your body."**

Andrew Jackson
Library of Congress

Insecure: John F. Kennedy told a White House aide to follow this advise when dealing with Vice President Lyndon B. Johnson: **"You are dealing with a very insecure, sensitive man with a huge ego. I want you literally to kiss his fanny from one end of Washington to the other."**

John F. Kennedy (L) and Lyndon B. Johnson (R)
Lyndon Baines Johnson Library and Museum

Creative Name Calling: In 1912 former President Theodore Roosevelt, running as the nominee of the Progressive Party labeled his Republican opponent President William Howard Taft, **"a puzzlewit."** Taft returned fire, calling Roosevelt: **"an egotist and a demagogue."** The two had been close friends prior to Taft's Presidency. In fact, Roosevelt supported Taft for the Republican Presidential nomination in 1908.

Theodore Roosevelt (L) and William Howard Taft, (R)
Saturday *Evening Post*

Abe Lincoln Behind the Bar: Abraham Lincoln was a licensed bartender. He once co-owned a bar in his hometown of Springfield, Illinois. During a 1858 debate for the U.S. Senate, his opponent, Stephen A. Douglas (D-IL), mentioned that he first met Lincoln as a customer at his bar. Lincoln deadpanned: **"I have left my side of the counter. But, Mr. Douglas still sticks as tenaciously as ever, to his."**

Abraham Lincoln
Library of Congress

Political Insults

Pancake Diplomacy: At the 1992 Republican National Convention, Pat Buchanan, who failed to garner the nomination, spoke in favor of the victor, President George H. W. Bush. Buchanan mocked the Democratic nominee, Bill Clinton, for his dearth of foreign policy experience. Buchanan declared: **"Bill Clinton's foreign policy experience stems mainly from having breakfast at the International House of Pancakes."**

International House of Pancakes Official Logo

Nixon – Johnson Feud: In September of 1966, President Lyndon B. Johnson announced that he would be traveling to Manila, Philippines to meet with South Vietnamese President Nguyen Van Thieu. At the time, Johnson's job approval ratings were slipping, as there appeared no end in sight for the U.S. in the Vietnam War. Former Republican Vice President Richard M. Nixon, a potential challenger to Johnson in 1968 lampooned the timing of the meeting, right before the mid-term elections. Nixon mused: **"There have been many firsts in the Johnson administration, but this is the first time a president may have figured the best way to help his party is to leave the country."**

Johnson returned fire, blasting Nixon at a press conference. Johnson averred: **"I do not want to get into a debate on a foreign policy meeting in Manila with a chronic campaigner like Mr. Nixon. It is his problem to find fault with his country and with his government during a period of October every two years. If you will look back over his record you will find that to be true. He never did really recognize and realize what was going on when he had an official position in the government. You remember what President** (Dwight D.) **Eisenhower said, that if you would give him a week or so he would figure out what he was doing."**

Richard M. Nixon (L), Lyndon B. Johnson, (R)
Lyndon B. Johnson Library and Museum

Today's Word of the Day is "Dotard: "In 2017, Donald Trump called North Korean President Kim Jong Un **"Little Rocket Man."** Un retorted by saying: **"I will surely and definitely tame the mentally deranged dotard with fire."** This caused many Americans to go to Merriam-Webster dictionary in search of the meaning of the word: **"dotard."** The dictionary defines it as a person with dotage." Dotage is defined as being "a state or period of senile decay marked by decline of mental poise and alertness.

Kim Jung Un
P388388 on Winkimedia Commons

Mincing no Words: In 2016, former Major League Baseball pitcher Curt Schilling said of Democratic Presidential nominee Hillary Clinton: **"There is No other option. Killary is the most despicable, corrupt, felonious, lying evil human to ever run for President."**

Curt Schilling
Photograph by Google Man

Chapter XI

Hot Microphones

Hot Microphones

Locker-room Jokes: In 1991, U.S. Senator Bob Kerrey (D-NE) told a dirty joke to his fellow Democratic Presidential aspirant Bill Clinton while both men waited to address a roast for U.S. Representative Dick Swett (D-NH). A C-SPAN microphone picked up the joke about fellow Presidential candidate Jerry Brown and two lesbians. Kerry joked that Brown (who was single at the time) went into a bar and expressed interest in one of two women sitting at the bar. The bartender told Brown both women are lesbians. Brown asked the bartender how he knew. The bartender proceeded to illustrate a graphic sex act he witnessed between the two women. The punch line had Brown saying he would like to perform the same act on the woman and asking: **"Does that make me a lesbian?"**

Bob Kerrey
Official Photograph

In A Firing Mood: In the wake of the September 11, 2001 hijackings, Acting Massachusetts Governor Jane Swift delivered an address to the Commonwealth, announcing that State Police Superintendent John DiFava would replace Joe Lawless as Airport Security Chief. With the microphone still on, Swift said: **"They Work for me and they know I'm in a firing mood. Just kidding. I hope my mic wasn't on."**

Jane Swift
Official Photograph

Whoops: Immediately before a 1984 weekly radio address, Ronald Reagan joked: **"My fellow Americans. I've signed legislation that will outlaw Russia forever. We begin bombing in five minutes."** He later found out his microphone was on and that his statement was broadcast worldwide.

Ronald Reagan
Official Photograph

Ouch: In 2008, during a commercial break, while being interviewed on *Fox News*, the Reverend Jesse Jackson made the following off-hand comment about Democratic Presidential nominee Barack Obama: **"See, Barrack's been talking down to black people on this faith-based. . . I want to cut his nuts off."** Unbeknownst to Jackson, the microphone was still on.

Jesse Jackson
Library of Congress

Hot Microphones

Big Time Open Microphone: At a campaign rally in Naperville, Illinois in 2000, where the Republican nominees for President and Vice President, George W. Bush and Dick Cheney, were on the podium waving to the assembled crowd and getting ready to speak, Cheney noticed Adam Clymer of *The New York Times* with other members of the press in the crowd. Cheney said to Bush: **"There's Adam Clymer, Major League Asshole from *The New York Times*."** Bush responded: **"Oh yeah, he is, big time."** Unbeknownst to them, the microphone picked up the conversation and it became front-page news. The reason Bush and Cheney had such a negative view of Clymer is that he wrote an article concluding that Cheney donated just 1% of the money he had earned in the energy industry to charity.

Dick Cheney (L), George W. Bush (R)
White House Photograph by David Bohrer

Boxer Believes in Yesterday: In 2010, California U.S. Senate candidate Carly Fiorina was caught on an open microphone lampooning, U.S. Senator Barbara Boxer's hair. Boxer was her opponent. Talking with aides, Fiorina discussed the observation by a friend. **"It seems, had seen Boxer on TV earlier in the morning. And she "said what everyone says, God, what is that hair? So yesterday!"**

Barbara Boxer
Official Photograph

New England Senators Get Candid: Following a hearing of the U.S. Senate Appropriations Subcommittee on Transportation, Housing and Urban Development, and Related Agencies, Chairwoman Susan Collins forgot to turn her microphone off. Accordingly, America got to hear what she really thinks during a conversation with U.S. Senator Jack Reed (D-RI), the committee's ranking member. During the conversation, Collins said to Reed: **"I swear, [the Office of Management and Budget] just went through and whenever there was 'grant,' they just X it out. With no measurement, no thinking about it, no metrics, no nothing. It's just incredibly irresponsible."** Reed responded, referring to President Donald Trump: **"I think he's crazy, I mean, I don't say that lightly, and as kind of a goofy guy. "**

Later in the conversation, referring to a statement by U.S. Representative Blake Farenthold (R-TX) where he said if Collins were not a female he would challenge her to a duel, Collins said to Reed: **"Well, he's huge and he — I don't mean to be unkind, but he's so unattractive it's unbelievable."**

Blake Farenthold
Official Photograph

Hot Microphones

Barack Obama Unplugged: A hot mic at the 2011 G20 summit caught President Barack Obama saying to French President Nicholas Sarkozy (referring to Israeli Prime Minister Benjamin Netanyahu): **"You're tired of him. What about me? I have to deal with him every day."**

Benjamin Netanyahu
U.S. State Department Photograph

Getting Fresh: U.S. Representative Martin R. Hoke (R-OH) was about to be interviewed jointly with U.S. Representative Eric Fingerhut (D-OH) after President Bill Clinton's 1994 State of the Union Address. A female television producer asked Hoke to unbutton his jacket. Hoke responded: **"You can ask me to do anything you want."** Hoke then said to Fingerhut: **"She's got ze beega breasts."** The incident was taped, though not broadcast live. The tape was soon played on Cleveland television stations, prompting Hoke to publically apologize and declare: **"I need a 2-by-4 to the head."**

Martin Hoke
Official Photograph

Republican Calls Trump and Idiot: A private conversation between U.S. Senator Jeff Flake (R-AZ) and Mesa, Arizona Mayor John Giles was picked up by Mesa *ABC15 KNXV-TV*, a Mesa Television station. In the discussion, Flake told Giles; **"If we've become the party of Roy Moore** (Alabama U.S. Senate GOP nominee) **and Donald Trump, we are toast."** Giles then suggested to Flake that he should run **"And I'm not blowing smoke at you, but you're the guy that could a just for fun, how much fun it would be just to be the foil, and you know and to point out what an idiot this guy (Donald Trump) is."**

Trump then tweeted: **"Sen. Jeff Flake(y), who is unelectable in the Great State of Arizona (quit race, anemic polls) was caught (purposely) on "mike" saying bad things about your favorite President. He'll be a NO on tax cuts because his political career anyway is "toast."**

Jeff Flake
Official Photograph

It is just that Simple: In 2011, in between network interviews, U.S. Secretary of State Hillary Clinton was informed that Libyan President Muammar al-Gaddafi was killed by an aide. She said: **"We came, we saw, he died."**

Muammar al-Gaddafi
Photograph by Ricardo Stuckert/PR

Hot Microphones

From the U.S. House to the Big House: In 1980, U.S. Representative Michael Myers (D-PA) was seen on videotape accepting a $50,000 bribe from an undercover FBI agent. In the recording, Myers averred: **"money talks and bullshit walks."** Myers was expelled for his actions by the House, becoming the first member since 1861 to suffer that fate. Myers served a three-year prison sentence for bribery and conspiracy.

Michael Myers
Official Photograph

Of God and Guns: During the 2008 Presidential campaign, Democratic Presidential aspirant Barack Obama said at a private fundraiser in San Francisco regarding Americans who lose their jobs after factories in their municipalities shut down: **"It's not surprising then they get bitter, they cling to guns or religion or antipathy to people who aren't like them, or anti-immigrant sentiment, or anti-trade sentiment, as a way to explain their frustrations."** At an NRA convention in 2011, Texas Governor Rick Perry, seeking the Republican Presidential nomination, asserted: **"I happily cling to my guns and my God, even if President Obama thinks that that is a simpleminded thing in his elitist heart."**

Rick Perry
Official Photograph

Just Get Me Out of Here: Before speaking at a dinner ahead of a straw pole in Maine, Republican Presidential candidate John Anderson whispered to reporter Walter Shapiro: **"This is a hellhole. I would sneak out, but I'm afraid they are going to introduce me and someone would notice I was gone."** Anderson garnered just six votes at the event.

John Anderson
Library of Congress

It Was Only a Joke: In 1999, Texas Governor George W. Bush, on the precipice of declaring his Presidential campaign, announced he would visit Israel. After meeting with the Republican Governors Association in New Orleans, Bush joked to *Austin American-Statesman* journalist Ken Herman: **"You know what I'm going to tell those Jews when I get to Israel Don't you Herman? I'm telling' 'em they're all going to Hell."** Bush had fostered a friendly relationship with Harman. Still, as a journalist, Herman knew that the comment by Bush was not off the record. Herman mentioned the comment in an article. Bush showed his displeasure at Harman by telling him: **"You know, I could have kept you from writing that, Herman, I could have just not said it."** Bush was telling Herman that the jocular relationship the two men shared was over.

George W. Bush Official Portrait as Governor of Texas

Chapter XII

Politicians and Elitism

Politicians Battle Elitism

Romney Tape Released: At a 2012 $50,000-a-plate private fundraiser in Baca Raton, FL, prospective Republican presidential nominee Mitt Romney told the crowd: **"There are 47 percent of the people who will vote for the president no matter what. All right, there are 47 percent who are with him, who are dependent upon government, who believe that they are victims, who believe the government has a responsibility to care for them, who believe that they are entitled to health care, to food, to housing, to you-name-it. That's an entitlement. The government should give it to them. And they will vote for this president no matter what. And I mean the president starts off with 48, 49 . . . he starts off with a huge number. These are people who pay no income tax. Forty-seven percent of Americans pay no income tax. So our message of low taxes doesn't connect. So he'll be out there talking about tax cuts for the rich. . . . My job is not to worry about those people. I'll never convince them they should take personal responsibility and care for their lives. What I have to do is convince the 5–10% in the center that are Independents, that are thoughtful, that look at voting one way or the other depending upon in some cases emotion, whether they like the guy or not."** The video of this speech was leaked to *Mother Jones Magazine* and solidified the Democratic narrative that Romney was an out-of-touch elitist.

Mitt Romney
U.S. House of Representatives Photograph

Mrs. Bill Clinton: In 1980, Bill Clinton lost his bid for re-election, making the 34-year-old the youngest ex-Governor in American history. Bill Clinton's Republican opponent, Frank White, exploited the maiden name issue by continuously introducing his own wife as **"Mrs. Frank White."**

In 1982, Bill Clinton regained the Governorship, defeating White. Hillary became more engaged in the campaign and changed her name to Hillary Clinton, telling a reporter: **"I'll be Mrs. Bill Clinton."** During the next nine years of her husband's Governorship, Hillary gradually shed the elitist label, as she chaired the Arkansas Education Standards Committee and was successful in bringing a neonatal clinic to Arkansas's Children's Hospital in Little Rock. By 1990, there was even talk of Hillary running to succeed her husband as Governor of Arkansas. Bill instead ran and won re-election.

Hillary Clinton (L), Bill Clinton (R)
Butler Center for Arkansas Library System

Domestic Affairs: In 1991, Democratic Presidential candidate Tom Harkin joked about the patrician President George H.W. Bush: **"Bush's idea of solving a domestic problem is to fire the maid and yell at the butler."**

Tom Harkin
Official Photograph

Politicians Battle Elitism

Just Say Thanks: in his first campaign for New York Governor in 1958, wealthy businessman Nelson Rockefeller would tell voters who praised him: **"Thanks a thousand"** rather than his customary **"Thanks a million"** so that voters would not associate Rockefeller with his vast inherited wealth.

Nelson Rockefeller
Official Photograph

Taking the Bull by the Horns: In a rare case of taking the issue of Elitism head-on, Massachusetts Republican Governor Bill Weld, after losing a hard-fought U.S. Senate race in 1996 to incumbent Democrat John Kerry, made light of his patrician pedigree and cultural elitism. He told *New York Times* reporter Sara Rimer: **"It was not my first defeat. There was the Rhodes scholarship, the Marshall scholarship, the Harvard Law Review. My life is a tangled wreck of failures."**

Bill Weld
Official Photograph

Pot Calling the Kettle: George H.W. Bush, the son of a U.S. Senator, learned to take the offensive when it came to his wealth. Before being branded as an "elitist," Bush would suggest the same of his opponents. Bush was reared in Greenwich Connecticut, was educated at the prestigious Philips Academy in Andover, Massachusetts and then graduated from Yale University.

Despite Bush's own privileged background, when he ran for the Republican Presidential nomination in 1988, he derisively referred to one of his opponents, Pierre (Pete) S. du pont (a fellow ivy leaguer from a patrician background) as **"Pierre."** Mr. DuPont always referred to himself as **"Pete,"** knowing that "Pierre" triggers elitist connotations. His other opponents referred to DuPont as "Pete." Despite Bush's background, his first name did not denote elitism in voter's minds like the name "Pierre."

Pierre (Pete) S. DuPont
Photograph by MPdoughboy153

Tribune of the People: Thomas Jefferson went out of his way to act like he was one of the people. So as not to appear too dignified or elite, he would often greet foreign dignitaries at the door wearing his pajamas.

Thomas Jefferson
Painting by Mather Brown

Politicians Battle Elitism

Clinton Excoriates Brown: During his successful 1992 Presidential campaign, Hillary's husband Bill emphasized his humble background and pledged to be a voice for the plight of "the forgotten middle-class." During a primary debate, former California Governor Jerry Brown accused Bill Clinton of using his power as Governor to funnel money to the Rose Law Firm, where Hillary worked. In response, Clinton portrayed Brown as an elitist, retorting: **"Jerry comes here with his family wealth and his $1,500 suit, making lying accusations about my wife."**

Jerry Brown (L), Bill Clinton (R)
Public Domain

Bring Massachusetts Into It: 1988 Republican Presidential Nominee George H.W. Bush successfully countered his patrician heritage, including his accent and elite pedigree. Bush often referred to his Democrat opponent Michael Dukakis as **"that liberal Governor from Massachusetts."** Interestingly, though Bush was an Ivy leaguer himself, he bashed Dukakis, who graduated from Harvard Law School, asserting: "His foreign policy views born in Harvard Yard's boutique, would cut the muscle of Defense. These charges helped Bush turn a seventeen-point deficit into a ten-point victory over Dukakis. Although Dukakis tried to suggest Bush was a "financial elitist," his charges gained him little political traction. Dukakis averred: **"George Bush plays Santa Claus to the wealthy and Ebeneaser Scrooge to the rest of us."** In the end, the American people chose the "financial elitist over the cultural elitist."

Michael Dukakis
Photograph by Hal O'Brien

Calling "Dubya" Elite: In 1978, when Bush ran for an open Congressional seat, his Democratic opponent, Kent Hance, was successful in branding Bush as an **"Ivy Leaguer."** Hance used his own humble background to lambast Bush's elite upbringing. Hance lamented: **"Yale and Harvard don't prepare you as well for running for the 19th Congressional District as Texas Tech [Hance's alma mater] does."** Hance also said: **"My daddy and granddad were farmers. They didn't have anything to do with the mess we're in right now, and Bush's father has been in politics his whole life."** Hance won the race.

However, George W. Bush learned his lesson, and when he ran for Governor of Texas in 1994, he turned the tables by presenting himself as the antithesis of his background. He even succeeded in talking in colloquialisms, calling parents **"moms and dads"** and calling voters **"folks."** In his race for Governor in 1994, Bush beat popular incumbent Governor Ann Richards despite her personal approval ratings, which exceeded 60%. He did this with a disciplined message, focusing on issues which struck a resonant chord with socially conservative Texans, including welfare reform, tort reform, and juvenile justice reform. Moreover, Bush excoriated Richards for vetoing a concealed carry handgun bill. Lone Star state voters came to see Bush as one of their own, not as some "phony Texan" from Yale.

Kent Hance
Official Photograph

Politicians Battle Elitism

Bush Masters the Anti-Elitist Card: In 1999, as Texas Governor George W. Bush was beginning his Presidential campaign, he purchased the Prairie Chapel Ranch near Crawford, Texas. This was a strategic and political *tour de force*. The Bush team successfully effectuated a master narrative of Bush as a rugged individualist and a rhinestone cowboy clearing brush from his ranch while the Eastern elite sit in their ivory tower with air-conditioned offices mocking working class Americans. Bush exploited the undercurrent of virulence in Middle America toward the people he had gone to school with, and he did it brilliantly.

Bush knew that Harvard and Hollywood don't play well in America's heartland. By emphasizing his slight Western accent, his love for the outdoors, and his devout Christianity, Bush became public enemy number one in the eyes of the coastal establishment. They mocked him as obtuse, ignorant, and anti-intellectual. In both 2000 and 2004, Bush ran against two fellow patricians, Ivy Leaguers Al Gore and John Kerry, respectively. In both cases, Bush won the election, in part by creating a master narrative where he was a plain-talking Texan challenging "intellectual out-of-touch elites."

George W. Bush at the Prairie Chapel Ranch
Executive Office of the President

Ivy Leaguer Makes a "Splash" at a Truck Stop: George H.W. Bush had trouble trying to relate to the average voter. In 1991, when seeking re-election, he requested **"a splash more of coffee"** at a New Hampshire Truck stop.

Pin for George H.W. Bush Re-Election Campaign

Know the Fans, Not the Owners: In 2008, Republican Presidential candidate Mitt Romney was interviewed by Alabama Sports Talk Radio Host Paul Finebaum. Romney was asked his thoughts on the possibility that quarterback Peyton Manning could be traded to the Denver Broncos. Romney's response was: **"Well, you know I'm surprised to hear that Denver's thinking about him. They're — I don't want him in our neck of the woods [New England]. Let's put it that way. I don't want him to go to Miami or to the Jets. But I've got a lot of good friends, the owner of the Miami Dolphins, and the New York Jets — both owners are friends of mine."**

Mitt Romney
Official Photograph

Chapter XIII

Political Debate Moments

Political Debate Moments

What's a Junk Bond? During a 1990 debate for the Office of Treasurer and Receiver General of the Commonwealth of Massachusetts, Democrat William Galvin, trying to show that his Republican opponent, Joe Malone, was ignorant of economic issues, asked Malone the question: **"What's a junk bond?"** Without hesitation, Malone responded: **"That's what we'll have if you're elected."** Malone won the election.

Joe Malone
Official Photograph

Linguistic Legerdemain: During a debate for the 1988 race for the Democratic Presidential nomination, U.S. Representative Richard Gephardt turned to U.S. Senator Al Gore and tried to blast him for moving to the right to secure Southern votes. Gephardt said: **"When you started this race, you decided you needed a southern political strategy. So you decided that you'd better move to the right on defense and a lot of other issues. And lately you've been sounding more like Al Haig than Al Gore"** (Al Haig was U.S. Secretary of State in the Reagan administration and was also a GOP Republican Presidential Candidate). Without missing a beat, Gore said: **"That line sounds more like Richard Nixon than Richard Gephardt."**

Al Gore
Official Photograph

Don't Shoot for the Moon: In a 2012 Presidential debate in Jacksonville, Florida, U.S. Representative Ron Paul (R-TX) was asked by host Wolf Blitzer about a proposal offered by one of his opponents, former U.S. House Speaker Newt Gingrich (R-GA), to colonize the moon. Paul mustered uproarious laughter for his response: **"Well, I don't think we should go to the moon. I think we maybe should send some politicians up there."**

Ron Paul
Photograph by David Carlyon

FanGate: In 2014, Republican Florida Governor Rick Scott did not enter the debate stage for the first seven minutes of a Gubernatorial debate because his Democratic opponent Charlie Crist had a fan underneath his podium. The debate rules had forbid the use of props. Scott finally came on stage.

Rick Scott
Official Photograph

171

Political Debate Moments

Shaming Ted Kennedy: In 1982, Republican Ray Shamie used a creative tactic that embarrassed Democrat Ted Kennedy into agreeing to debate him. Shamie hired a plane to fly around the country with a trailing banner that read: **"$10,000 reward -- Get Ted Kennedy to debate Ray Shamie."** The stunt mustered national media attention.

Ray Shamie for U.S. Senate Pin

A Biting Zinger: During the 1988 Vice Presidential debate, Republican Dan Quayle suggested that he had more experience than John F. Kennedy had in 1960 when he was elected President. In what became one of the most remembered lines in Presidential debate history, the Democratic nominee Lloyd Bentsen deadpanned: **"Senator, I served with Jack Kennedy. Jack Kennedy was a friend of mine. Senator, you're no Jack Kennedy."** Quayle called the remark **"uncalled for."**

Lloyd Bentsen
Official Photograph

Reagan Turns the Tables on the Age Question: During a Presidential debate between President Ronald Reagan and Walter Mondale, Reagan was asked this question by Henry "Hank" Trewitt of *The Baltimore Sun,* **"You already are the oldest President in history, and some of your staff say you were tired after your most recent encounter with Mr. Mondale. I recall, yes, that President Kennedy, who had to go for days on end with very little sleep during the Cuba missile crisis. Is there any doubt in your mind that you would be able to function in such circumstances?"** Reagan answered: **"Not at all Mr. Trewhitt, and I want you to know that also I will not make age an issue of this campaign. I am not going to exploit for political purposes my opponent's youth and inexperience."** Trewhitt then exclaimed: **"Mr. President, I'd like to head for the fence and try to catch that one before it goes over."**

Walter Mondale (L), Ronald Reagan (R)
Ronald Reagan Presidential
Library and Museum

Political Debate Moments

One-Liner Time: During the 1988 Presidential race, Republican nominee George H.W. Bush tried to use the fact that Boston Harbor was the dirtiest harbor in the U.S. against his Democratic opponent, Massachusetts Governor Michael Dukakis. During one of the Presidential debates, after Democratic nominee Michael Dukakis delivered a long answer to a question about the bulging Federal Budget Deficit, Bush quipped: **"Is this the time for one-liners? That answer is about as clear as Boston Harbor."**

George H. W. Bush (L), Michael Dukakis (R)
George Bush Presidential Library and Museum

Leave it to Beavers: During a 1990 Massachusetts Gubernatorial debate, Republican nominee Bill Weld exploited a claim by the Democratic nominee, John Silber Ph.D., that beavers created so much wetland that preserving wetlands should not be of concern. Weld quipped: **"Would you tell us doctor, what plans, if any, you have for the preservation of open spaces in Massachusetts, other than leave it to beavers?"**

William F. Weld
Photograph by Mathew W. Hutchins, *Harvard Law Review*

Clinton Forced to Make a Pledge: Sometimes a candidate is forced to make a pledge in a debate for political survival, which could hurt him/her in future races. In his 1990 bid for a fifth term as Arkansas Governor, Bill Clinton was neck-and-neck with his Republican opponent Sheffield Nelson. While Clinton enjoyed respectable job approval ratings, voters wondered if it was time for a change in the Governorship, and if Clinton would be a full-time Governor if re-elected. There was speculation that Clinton would seek the Democratic Presidential nomination in 1992, taking him away from the state. When Clinton was asked in a Gubernatorial debate if he promised to serve out his full term, he replied: **"You bet."** After easily beating Nelson, Clinton met with Arkansas voters the next year, and asked to be released from that pledge. He eventually defied the pledge and declared his Presidential candidacy.

Brochure for the Re-Election Campaign of Bill Clinton in 1990

Other-Worldly: During a 1984 debate of aspirants for the Democratic Presidential nomination, U.S. Senator John Glenn (D-OH) boasted of his role as an astronaut, to which U.S. Senator Ernest "Fritz" Hollings (D-SC) retorted: **"But what have you done in 'this' world?"**

Ernest "Fritz" Hollings
Official Photograph

Political Debate Moments

Don't Want to Debate Me, Watch This: In 1990, U.S. Senator Rudy Boschwitz (R-MN) appeared to be a shoe-in for re-election. Political consultant Bill Hillsman engineered a brilliant advertising campaign wherein his Democratic challenger Paul Wellstone could not locate Boschwitz. He even visited Boschwitz's campaign headquarters and state offices, asking staffers where Boschwitz was. When they told him he was not there, Wellstone asked the staffers to tell Boschwitz he would like to debate him. Wellstone also interviewed Minnesota residents, who told him how debates were healthy for the political process. Using the interviews, Wellstone developed an advertising campaign which garnered national attention, precipitously increasing Wellstone's name recognition and forcing Boschwitz to agree to multiple debates. That year, Wellstone scored one of the biggest upsets in the country, defeating the once near immutable Boschwitz.

Paul Wellstone
Official Photograph

The Chicken Strategy: In 2014, Oklahoma City Mayor Mick Cornett was well ahead in the polls in his re-election bid. He refused to show up for the debates with this three opponents. While he was safely re-elected, supporters of his opponents had fun with Cornett's absence. At one debate at the Fairview Missionary Baptist Church, a man seated in the front row sporting a chicken suit made local headlines by clucking: **"Why won't Mick debate?"**

Mick Cornett
Photograph by Ed Schipul

Who Let the Dogs In? In 1994, U.S. House Minority Whip Newt Gingrich (R-GA), in his quest to become the first Republican House Speaker in forty years, spent little time in his Congressional District. Instead, Gingrich barnstormed the nation, campaigning for Republican Congressional candidates in 125 other districts. Gingrich refused to debate his Democratic opponent, Ben Jones, a former U.S. Representative. Jones traveled to Gingrich's campaign stops around the country, trying to get to meet Gingrich and demand that he come back home to Georgia to debate. At one stop, Jones brought bloodhounds. However, Jones could not get close enough to Gingrich to confront him about participating in a debate. Jones lost the race by over 25 percentage points.

Ben Jones
Official Photograph

Bad Luck: In 1986, popular Massachusetts Governor Michael Dukakis afforded his Republican challenger, George Kariotis, one debate. The debate was scheduled to be held on the day after the last game of the World Series between the Boston Red Sox and the New York Mets. However, the Seventh game was rained out and re-scheduled for the next day. Consequently, while about 1.5 million households in the Boston media market turned their television sets to the game, only about 46,000 viewers watched the debate. In good humor, Kariotis said in his concession speech, after pocketing just 31.2% of the vote: **"In fairness to Mike, I should clear up something. He was criticized, I think, for giving me only one televised debate during the seventh game of the World Series** [Between the Boston Red Sox and the New York Mets]. **I should point out that that was really his second choice; his first choice was tomorrow."** (The day after the election)

George Kariotis for Governor Pin

Political Debate Moments

Interesting Justification: During a 2016 Democratic Presidential debate, candidate Lincoln Chafee was asked why he voted for the repeal of parts of the Glass-Steagall Act in 1999. Chafee responded this way: **"The Glass-Steagall was my very first vote. I'd just arrived. My dad had died in office. I just arrived to Senate. I think we get some takeovers and that was one. It was my very first vote, and it was 95, 90 to 5. The record."**

Lincoln Chafee
Official Photograph

Chlorofluorocarbon Carbon Abatement Enters a Presidential Debate: In his opening statement in the 1996 Vice Presidential debate, Democrat Al Gore looked at his Republican debate counterpart Jack Kemp, a former NFL Quarterback, and stated: **"I'd like to start by offering you a deal, Jack. If you won't use any football stories, I won't tell any of my warm and humorous stories about chlorofluorocarbon abatement."**

Al Gore
Photograph by Greg Michaud

Flip Flop Charge: The day after a 1992 Presidential debate that was held in East Lansing, MI, President George H.W. Bush campaigned in Holland, Michigan. Bush noted that a Michigan furniture company, the Herman Miller Corporation, made the furniture for the debate: three podiums, one for each of the three candidates. Bush joked: **"Governor [Bill] Clinton has a tendency to take two positions on every issue. So maybe Herman Miller should make a fourth podium, one for Clinton when he's for something and one for Clinton when he's against it."**

George H.W. Bush (L), Bill Clinton (M), H. Ross Perot (R) and Jim Lehrer
George Bush Presidential
Library and Museum

Playing Her Cards Too Close to the Vest: Barack Obama was unpopular in Kentucky. Secretary of State Alison Lundergan Grimes was the Democratic Senate nominee. She did not want to be tethered to Obama, but knew that abandoning him would alienate her fellow Democrats. During a debate with U.S. Senate Minority Leader Mitch McConnell, Grimes would not say if she had voted for Obama, averring: **"This is a matter of principle. Our constitution grants, here in Kentucky, the constitutional right for privacy of the ballot box, for a secret ballot."** She pleased very few voters with that answer, and lost the election to McConnell.

Alison Lundergan Grimes
Photograph by Cage Skidmore

Chapter XIV

Whisker-Close Elections

Whisker-Close Elections

The Winding Road to Success: In 1918, Peter Francis Tague Jr. (D-MA) became the first person to be elected to the U.S. House of Representatives by a write-in vote. After losing the Democratic primary to former Boston Mayor John F. Fitzgerald, Tague then ran as a write-in candidate in the General Election, losing by just 238 votes. Tague then contested the results. The U.S. House of Representatives Election Committee ruled that there was fraud in the election. Tague was ruled the winner by 525 votes. The Committee voted 5-2 to unseat Fitzgerald and to seat Tague.

Peter Francis Tague
Official Photograph

The Mount Rushmore State Close Ones: South Dakota has been the epicenter of close elections. In 1962, George McGovern was elected to the U.S. Senate by just 597 votes out of 254,139 cast. In 1978, Tom Daschle was elected to the U.S. House by just 139 votes out of 129,227 votes cast. In 2002, South Dakota Democrat Tim Johnson was re-elected by just 524 votes out of 334,458 votes tabulated.

Tim Johnson
Official Photograph

Protracted Election Process: Many Americans are still reeling from the protracted and still disputed Presidential election of 2000, where Republican George W. Bush was certified by Florida Secretary of State Katharine Harris as the winner of the Florida Presidential election, and thus the winner of the national election. Officially, Bush had just 597 more votes in the sunshine state out of more than six million votes cast in Florida.

George W. Bush (L), and Al Gore (R) on the Cover of
Time Magazine

One Vote Wonder: There was actually an election where one vote literally decided the winner of a statewide election. The closest Gubernatorial election ever recorded in U.S. history occurred in Massachusetts in 1839. At the time, a candidate was required to garner a majority of the votes to win the election. Otherwise, the State legislature would choose the winner. The legislature was controlled by the Whig Party, which would almost assuredly have voted to re-elect incumbent Governor Edward Everett, the Whig nominee.

However, his opponent, Democrat Marcus Morton, garnered 51,034 votes of 102,066 votes cast, giving Morton a majority by a single vote margin. Had just one vote switched, Morton would not have won the majority, and thus would have lost the election. Amazingly, the Secretary of the Commonwealth, H.A.S. Dearborn, a devoted Whig and Everett supporter, failed to cast a vote. Ironically, neither did some members of the Whig high command, prompting Everett to bemoan: **"A better mode of showing (their support) would have been to vote."**

Marcus Morton
United States Democratic Review

Whisker-Close Elections

Landslide Bunning: In 1998, Jim Bunning quipped: "It's great to have a landslide victory" after winning an open U.S. Senate in Kentucky by just 6,766 votes out of 1,145,414 cast. In 2004, Bunning was re-elected by just 22,652 votes out of 1,724,362 votes cast.

Jim Bunning
Official Photograph

Lucky Box 13: In 1941, Lyndon B. Johnson lost a special election to fill the seat of the late U.S. Senator Morris Sheppard by just 1,311 votes out of 988,295 cast. In 1948, Johnson was on the other side of a photo finish, defeating former Governor Coke Stevenson by just 87 votes out of 988,395 cast.

Decades later, Louis Salas, who served as an elections judge in Jim Wells County, told author Robert Caro that he had certified 202 fraudulent ballots for Johnson, enough to give him the race. Johnson earned the alliterative moniker: **"Landslide Lyndon."** Because of that 87-vote victory, Johnson went to the U.S. Senate, and subsequently became exceedingly influential, as evinced by his meteoric rise to the top of the Senate hierarchy. Just four years into his Senate term, Johnson became Minority Leader. Two years later, he became Majority leader. In 1960, he was elected Vice President, and in 1963 he assumed the Presidency upon the death of President John F. Kennedy.

Lyndon B. Johnson in 1948
Lyndon Baines Johnson Library and Museum

Close Popular Vote Total, Despite Landslide in the Electoral College: In 1880, Republican James Garfield defeated Democrat Winfield S. Hancock in the popular vote by just 7,368 popular votes out of 9,217,410. However, in the Electoral College, the margin was much wider, with Garfield garnering 214 votes and Hancock mustering just 155 votes.

James Garfield
Library of Congress

Really, Really Close: In 1974, a U.S. Senate election in New Hampshire was decided by just two votes out of 223,363 votes cast. On Election Day, Republican Louis Wyman was declared the winner by just 355 votes. His Democratic opponent, John A. Durkin, subsequently asked for a recount. The recount showed Durkin had actually won the election by 10 votes. Wyman then asked for another recount.

This time it was Wyman who was the winner by a measly two votes. Undeterred, Durkin then appealed the election to the Democratically-controlled U.S. Senate. But the Senate could not resolve the dispute. Finally, after a seven-month deadlock, Wyman asked Durkin to run in a Special election. Durkin agreed.

The election garnered national attention because it was the only Congressional election during the off year. It became a referendum on the economic policies of President Gerald R. Ford. In fact, Ford participated in a 136-mile motorcade in the state five days prior to the election in a futile attempt to keep the seat in Republican hands. Durkin won the Special election by 27,000 votes.

John A. Durkin
Official Photograph

Chapter XV

What's in a Name?

What's in a Name?

Two Men, Same Name, One Ballot: In 1946, after entering a race for an open seat in the U.S. House of Representatives, future President John F. Kennedy used a creative tactic to muster an electoral advantage. A popular candidate in the race was Boston City Councilor Joe Russo. To siphon support from Russo, the Kennedy campaign persuaded and bankrolled a custodian domiciled in the district with no political experience or political aspirations to enter the race. His name was also Joe Russo. The City Councilor Joe Russo complained, **"that someone had seen fit to buy out a man who has the same name as mine."** But the City Councilor had no recourse. John F. Kennedy won the race.

John F. Kennedy for Congress Poster, 1948

Vote Tim for Treasurer: In 2002, there were four candidates running in the Democratic Primary for the office of Treasurer and Receiver-General in Massachusetts. The race flew under the radar, being overshadowed by the hotly contested Democratic Gubernatorial Primary. The Treasurer candidates had little name recognition. Two of the candidates shared the last name: 'Cahill.' One was State Representative Michael P. Cahill (D-Beverly); the other candidate was Norfolk County Treasurer Tim Cahill. To clear up any ballot confusion, Tim Cahill aired a very cute advertisement ending with his young daughter Kendra Cahill sitting on the porch next to her father telling voters to **"vote Tim for Treasurer."** That campaign ad helped to effectuate a Tim Cahill victory over Michael P. Cahill and the others in that race.

Tim Cahill
Photograph by Jim Gillooly

The Other Joe Kennedy: In 2009, during the Special Election to fill the term of the late U.S. Senator Edward M. Kennedy (D-MA), speculation emerged that Kennedy's nephew, the former U.S. Representative Joe Kennedy, would seek the Democratic nomination. However, Joe stayed out of the race and the nomination went to Attorney General Martha Coakley. However Libertarian-oriented Joe Kennedy (No relation to the famous Kennedy family) secured ballot status as an Independent in the General Election. During the campaign, an unidentified recorded message was sent to some Democratic households, urging voters to vote for Joe Kennedy. However, Kennedy's role in the General Election was *de minimis*, as he pocketed less than 1% of the vote.

Joe Kennedy
Photograph by Dan Kennedy

What's in a Name?

Everyone named John Kennedy Can Run in Massachusetts: In 1954, two years after the very popular John Fitzgerald Kennedy was elected to the U.S. Senate, a stockroom supervisor at Gillette Company named John Francis Kennedy entered the race for Massachusetts Treasurer and Receiver General. Despite his lack of political experience, or a significant campaign war chest, Kennedy stunned the political establishment by winning a six-candidate primary and going on to win the General Election. Kennedy's upset victory was likely due to low-information voters who thought that John Fitzgerald Kennedy was running for state Treasurer. John Francis Kennedy did little campaigning for the post, spending just $300. John Francis Kennedy became known as **"The maverick with the Magic name,"** a moniker bestowed upon him by Bay State politicians.

In 1960, John Francis Kennedy ran for Governor the same year John Fitzgerald Kennedy ran for President. John Francis Kennedy was not so lucky this time around. He lost the Democratic Primary. Interestingly, in the race to succeed John Francis Kennedy for the post of Treasurer and Receiver General, two candidates named John Kennedy entered the race. They were John M. Kennedy and John B. Kennedy. However, both of these Kennedys lost the primary. It could be that even low-information voters did not believe that John Fitzgerald Kennedy would want to carry out the duties of State Treasurer and Governor, while also serving as President.

Obama/The Other Edwards: In 2008, one of the four finalists to be Barack Obama's Vice Presidential runningmate was U.S. Representative Chet Edwards (D-TX). On paper, he was a redoubtable contender. Edwards exhibited widespread bipartisan appeal representing a conservative Congressional District in Texas, where George W. Bush garnered 70% of the vote in 2004. Edwards was charismatic and made a name for himself in Congress as a champion of veterans' issues. He could have brought the ticket gravitas with veterans, blue-collar voters, and Southerners. There was one problem however. His last name is Edwards. The Democratic Party had recently been embarrassed when it was revealed that former Presidential Candidate and U.S. Senator John Edwards (D-NC) had had an extramarital affair with film producer and campaign staffer Rielle Hunter, while Edwards' wife, Elizabeth Edwards, was suffering from breast cancer. The Obama campaign chose U.S. Senator Joe Biden (D-DE) instead. Chet Edwards later admitted to reporters that his last name was a major factor in his not being selected as Obama's runningmate, averring: **"I would have to think that a bumper sticker that said 'Obama/The Other Edwards' would be difficult."**

Chet Edwards
Official Photograph

John Fitzgerald Kennedy
Library of Congress.

184

Chapter XVI

Political Dirty Tricks

Political Dirty Tricks

Impish Dirty Trick: In 1970, 19-year old Republican operative Karl Rove, using a false identity, broke into the campaign office of Allan J. Dixon, the Democratic nominee for State Treasurer of Illinois, and purloined Dixon campaign stationary. Knowing when Dixon had scheduled a rally, Rove proceeded to use the stolen stationary to advertise: **"Free beer, free food, girls, and a good time for nothing."** He distributed the homemade flyers at rock concerts and homeless shelters, inviting these people to the rally. Rove later become Deputy Chief of Staff under the administration of George W. Bush. Dixon later became a U.S. Senator from Illinois. Rove later apologized for his actions.

Karl Rove
Official Photograph

Deceptive Dirty Tricks: After the first Presidential debate between Democrat John F. Kennedy and Republican Richard M. Nixon, Democratic Strategist and political prankster Dick Tuck hired an elderly woman to wear a Nixon button and embrace Kennedy in front of TV cameras. She said, **"Don't worry, son! He beat you last night, but you'll get him next time."**

John F. Kennedy (L), and Richard M. Nixon (R)
Richard M. Nixon Foundation

That's "Not" What I Said: It was reported first by *Time Magazine* that U.S. Representative George Smathers (D-FL) made the following charge about U.S. Senator Claude Pepper (D-FL) while campaigning to defeat him in the 1950 Democratic Primary: **"Are you aware that the candidate is known all over Washington as a shameless extrovert? Not only that, but this man is reliably reported to have practiced nepotism with his sister-in-law and he has a sister who was once a wicked thespian in New York. He matriculated with co-eds at the University, and it is an established fact that before his marriage he habitually practiced celibacy."** Smathers denied making the quote and offered $10,000 to anyone who could prove he made it. No one could prove it. Smathers won the election.

George Smathers
Library of Congress

Political Intervention- - - - Not Divine Intervention: After his razor-thin victory in 1888 (Winning the Electoral Vote but not the National Popular Vote), President-Elect Benjamin Harrison said to Republican National Committee Chairman Matthew Stanley Quay: **"Providence has given us victory."** Quay later said to a news reporter: **"He ought to know that Providence didn't have a damn thing to do with it. Harrison will never know how many men were compelled to approach the penitentiary to make him President."**

Mathew Stanley Quay
Official Portrait

Political Dirty Tricks

Getting Muskie to Cry? In 1972, much of the Democratic establishment was aligned with the candidacy of U.S. Senator Edmund Muskie (D-ME). Republican President Richard M. Nixon feared Muskie would muster the nomination. To prevent this possibility, his campaign tried to derail his candidacy before the New Hampshire Presidential Primary. They wanted to run against the insurrectionist candidate George McGovern who was well to Muskie's left. Shannanagators in the Nixon campaign penned a letter written to the Editor of the influential *Manchester Union Leader*. It was published just two weeks prior to the New Hampshire Primary. The letter-writer alleged in the missive to have asked Muskie how he could represent African-Americans as President when there were so few African-Americans in Muskie's home state of Maine. This letter went on to state that Muskie had responded: **"No Blacks, but we have Canucks."** (A derogatory term for French Canadians who have a large representation in Maine).

The letter proved effective in that Muskie challenged the letter-writer and the newspaper by standing outside its headquarters and branding the paper's editor, William Loeb, **"A gutless coward."** It was reported in the media the next day that Muskie cried, though some observers maintain that the water on Muskie's face was from snowflakes. However, after the incident some New Hampshire voters began questioning if Muskie had the temperament to be President.

Consequently, many Muskie supporters defected to McGovern. While Muskie won the primary, he garnered an underwhelming 46.4% of the vote. Muskie never reclaimed his early electoral momentum. He dropped out of the race in late April, telling news reporters: **"I do not have the money to continue."** McGovern eventually pocketed the nomination.

Edmund Muskie
Library of Congress

Faking a Russian Accent: In 1934, Supporters of Republican Frank Merriam mocked Upton Sinclair, the Socialist Party Gubernatorial nominee in California. Sinclair was lampooned in newsreels playing in movie theaters. The theater owners were solicitous that if Sinclair were elected Governor, disgruntled studio heads would move their industry to another state. In one such newsreel, an actor portrayed an uncouth man with a thick Russian accent asserted his support for **"Sean-clair."** The man said (using a broken English accent): **"I am foting for Seenclair. His system vorked vell in Russia, vy can't it vork here?"** Merriam won the election.

Upton Sinclair
Library of Congress

Bringing "Advice Columnists" Into The Election Process: In 1964, Democratic President Lyndon B. Johnson ordered aides to write letters to "advice columnists" Ann Landers and Dear Abby posing as ordinary voters trepidatious of a victory by Republican nominee Barry Goldwater.

Lyndon B. Johnson on Election Night in 1964
Lyndon Baines Johnson Presidential Library and Museum

Political Dirty Tricks

Fortune For Hart: In 1984, supporters of insurrectionist Democratic Presidential candidate Gary Hart emplaced fortune cookies at a fundraiser for Democratic front-runner Walter Mondale in Pennsylvania. When the donors opened them up, they read: **"Hart Wins Pennsylvania."**

Gary Hart
Photograph by Nancy Wong

Forgery: Twelve days before the 1880 Presidential election, a forged letter surfaced purportedly written by Republican nominee James Garfield addressed to H.L. Morey of the Employers Union in Lynn, Massachusetts, asserting his support for unfettered Chinese immigration into the U.S. Garfield did not remember if he had actually written the letter, so he did not deny it at first. Across the U.S., there was fear of Chinese-Americans. Meanwhile, the campaign of Garfield's opponent Winfield Scott made political hay out of the issue by suggesting that the new immigrants would purloin jobs from Americans. Once the Garfield team stated that he had not written the letter, they sent the media copies of a letter that he did write on another topic so they could see the difference in handwriting.

James Garfield
Library of Congress

Treason? In 1968, Democratic Presidential nominee Hubert Humphrey was gaining momentum and nearly caught his Republican counterpart Richard M. Nixon. President Lyndon B. Johnson, Humphrey's boss, made a last-ditch effort to effectuate peace in Vietnam. If a peace treaty was signed, Humphrey likely would have won the election. The Johnson administration agreed to halt the bombing of North Vietnam. However, the South Vietnamese delegation left the talks. According to the FBI, Nixon sabotaged the peace talks to avoid a Humphrey victory. The FBI bugged the phone of Anna Chennault, a Nixon aide. They found that she told South Vietnamese government officials that they could get a better deal under Nixon. Johnson, having received the information from the FBI, did not release it. According to Nixon biographer John Farrell, the President did not disclose his findings because he lacked **"absolute proof"** that Nixon had personal involvement, and did not want to disclose to the public that the FBI intercepted calls between the South Vietnamese Ambassador to the U.S. and Chennault.

Anna Chennault
Harbart Schelinger Library

FDR Playing Fidelity Card: During the 1940 Presidential campaign, Democratic President Franklin D. Roosevelt ordered his advisor Lowell Mellett to disseminate rumors about Republican Presidential nominee Wendell Willkie having an extra-martial affair. **"Spread it as a word-of-mouth thing, or by some people way, way down the line. We can't have any of our principal speakers refer to it."** Ironically, Roosevelt was himself engaged in an extra-marital relationship with secretary Lucy Mercer. This conversation was reveled in 1982, when American Heritage released tapes the President secretly recorded.

Wendell Willkie
Library of Congress

189

Political Dirty Tricks

Nixon Tries to Scar Wallace: After winning the Presidency in 1968, Richard M. Nixon and his coefficients were obsessed with enfeebling their potentially formidable opponents for re-election. Former Alabama Governor George Wallace had run for President in 1968 as the nominee of the American Independence Party. Nixon wanted to monopolize the populist blue-collar conservative message that Wallace had preached in 1968. He feared Wallace would become either the Democratic nominee or would again be the American Independence Party nominee, and would once again become the tribune of the message.

To stop Wallace, the Nixon forces subversively tried to have him defeated in his 1970 bid to recapture the Alabama Governorship. Accordingly, Nixon ordered his lawyer, Herbert Kalmbach, to clandestinely funnel $100,000 to Wallace's opponent, incumbent Democrat Albert Brewer. Brewer defeated Wallace in the primary, but did not garner the requisite majority of the vote to avoid a runoff with Wallace. In the Runoff election, Kalmbach secretly sent a $330,000 donation to Brewer. However, the scheme proved feckless as Wallace won the General Election comfortably. Wallace then ran for President two years later, but his campaign came to a halt when he was shot and paralyzed at a campaign rally in Laurel, Maryland.

George Wallace
Lyndon Baines Johnson Library and Museum

How Low Can You Go? In the 1844 Presidential election, Thurlow Weed, a prominent member of the Whig Party, circulated a mendacious story that Democratic Presidential nominee James K. Polk had sold slaves to pay for his campaign. Weed also falsely spread a rumor that Polk had branded his slaves with his initials.

Thurlow Weed
From *An Iron Will* by Orisen Sweet Mardin (1901)

Getting on Nixon's Nerves: In 1962, former Vice President Richard M. Nixon was running for Governor of California. Dick Tuck, an inveterate political dirty trickster, gave children in the Chinatown section of Los Angeles a sign reading: **"Welcome Nixon. What about the Hughes Loan in Chinese?"** (This was a reference to a controversial 1956 $205,000 loan Nixon's' brother Donald had secured from Hughes Tool Co., to avert bankruptcy of his grocery and restaurants businesses.) Nixon, who could not speak Chinese, posed with the children. Tuck then gave Nixon the translation. When he found out what the sign said, an inflamed Nixon tore up the sign in public view.

Richard M. Nixon
Library of Congress

Chapter XVII

Political Bloopers

Political Bloopers

Someone Needs To Do Her American History Homework: In 2011, Republican Presidential aspirant Michele Bachmann spoke to a crowd in Concord, New Hampshire. In the address, she said: **"You're the state where the shot was heard around the world at Lexington and Concord, and you put a marker in the ground and paid with the blood of your ancestors."** She was referring to the first shot fired during the Revolutionary War, which did not happen in Concord New Hampshire, but in Concord, Massachusetts.

Michele Bachmann
Official Photograph

San Francisco? At an October rally, 1996 Republican Presidential nominee Bob Dole told a San Diego audience: "We're honored to be back in San Francisco" Members of the audience yelled **"San Diego"** prompting Dole to shoot back: **"Oh San Diego, Sure."**

Bob Dole 1996 Campaign Button

The Man Who Did Not Invent the Internet: In March of 1999, as Vice President Al Gore was beginning his quest for the Democratic Presidential nomination against former New Jersey Senator Bill Bradley, he was asked by CNN's Wolf Blitzer: **"Why should Democrats looking at the Democratic nomination — the process, support you instead of Bill Bradley** [Gore's opponent for the nomination], **a friend of yours, a former colleague in the Senate? What do you have to bring to this that he doesn't necessarily bring to this process?"** Gore Responded in part: **"During my service in the United States Congress, I took the initiative in creating the Internet."** Gore was referring to his role as the lead sponsor of the 1991 High-performance Computing and Communications Act, which appropriated $600 million for high-performance computing and co-sponsored the Information Infrastructure and Technology Act of 1992. Critics chided Gore for his statement about **"creating the internet"** and falsely claimed that Gore had said he **"invented the Internet."** U.S. House Majority leader Dick Armey (R-TX) joked: **"If the Vice President created the Internet then I created the Interstate."**

Al Gore
Official Photograph

Catching Pancakes Not As Easy as it Looks: During the 2000 New Hampshire Bisquick Pancake Presidential Primary Flip-off, Republican Gary Bauer, trying to catch a pancake with his spatula, fell backwards through a curtain. Mocking a popular Visa commercial from the time, Bauer quipped: **"Cost of spatula and skillet, $32. Candidate falling off platform: Priceless."**

Gary Bauer
Photograph by Graig Mhaud

Political Bloopers

Big Difference Between Michael Jordan and Michael Jackson: While speaking at a fundraiser in Washington, D.C. in 1998, Vice President Al Gore took a moment to discuss Basketball legend Michael Jordan. Gore said: **"I tell you that Michael Jackson is unbelievable, isn't he. He's just unbelievable."**

Al Gore
Executive Office of the President

Rick Scott's Bizarre Statement: In 2012, Spanish King Juan Carlos was being excoriated by the public for taking a lucrative elephant-hunting trip in Botswana. Spain was embroiled in economic turmoil at the time. The King was walking with crutches from injuring his hip on the trip. He was forced to apologize for the insensitivity of the trip. Florida Governor Rick Scott bizarrely introduced himself to the King by asserting: **"I've ridden elephants. I've never tried to shoot one."**

King Juan Carlos
Espana

Right Airport, Wrong Person: During the 1948 Presidential campaign, President Harry S. Truman dedicated a new airport in Carey, Idaho. Truman was led to believe by Veterans in the audience that the airport was being named for William Smith, a WWII airman. Truman announced that the airport was being named for Williams. In actuality, the airport was to be named for Wilma Smith a young girl who had recently died. Her mother corrected the President.

Harry S. Truman
Harry S. Truman Presidential Library and Museum

Really? At a 1992 campaign rally for the re-election of George H.W. Bush, Michigan Governor John Engler introduced the president by saying: **"My friends, its with a great deal of pride that I present to you a President who wants to cut jobs, who wants to cut taxes and cut jobs, who wants to stop the regulations and cut the jobs."**

John Engler
Official Photograph

Political Bloopers

A Freudian Slip? In 2016, while campaigning for his wife Hillary Clinton in Washington State, Bill Clinton told the crowd to support Hillary: **"If you believe we've finally come to the point where we can put the awful legacy of the last eight years behind us and the seven before that."** Democratic President Barack Obama, extremely popular with Democratic primary voters was President for the last seven years. Clinton spokesman Angel Urena tried to minimize the damage by telling members of the media: **"After President Obama was elected, Republicans made it their number one goal to block him at every turn. That unprecedented obstruction these last eight years is their legacy, and the American people should reject it by electing Hillary Clinton to build on President Obama's success so we can all grow and succeed together."**

Bill Clinton
Photograph by Gage Skidmore

Presidential Candidate Cannot Recall Her College Major: In a 2003 interview, Democratic Presidential candidate Carol Mosley Braun was asked by a news reporter what her major was in College. Braun responded: **"I don't remember what I majored in in college. . . . I hate to guess. I'm gonna guess it was Political Science, but I'm not sure. It might have been history. I'll check. I hadn't thought of that one."** She did in fact major in Political Science at the University of Illinois.

Carol Mosley Braun
Official Photograph

Bad Way to Kick-Off a Campaign: In 2011, Michele Bachmann returned to Waterloo, Iowa where she was born to announce her bid for the Republican Presidential nomination. In an interview at the event with *Fox News*, Bachmann said: **"What I want them to know, just like John Wayne was from Waterloo, Iowa, that's the kind of spirit that I have too."** Actually, John Wayne the tough guy actor, was not from Waterloo, Iowa, but from Winterset Iowa. Ironically, however, serial killer John Wayne Gacy did live in Waterloo, Iowa during his twenties.

John Wayne Gacy (R) Pictured With Frist Lady Roslyn Carter (L)
White House Photograph

Need to Learn Spanish Civics: During a 2003 trip to Madrid, Spain, Florida Governor Jeb Bush referred to King Juan Carlos as **"The President of the Republic of Spain."** In actuality, the nation has not been a Republic since the Spanish Civil War, which ended in 1939 with General Francisco Franco defeating the Republicans.

Jeb Bush
Photograph by Gage Skidmore

Political Bloopers

Hunting Tale: In 2007, Republican Presidential aspirant Mitt Romney told a voter: **"I purchased a gun when I was a young man. I've been a hunter pretty much all my life."** It was later reveled that Romney had only hunted twice in his life. Romney later said: **"I'm not a big-game hunter. I've made that very clear. I've always been a rodent and rabbit hunter, small varmints, if you will."**

Mitt Romney
Official Photograph

It Ain't So Joe: In a 2008 interview with *NBC*'s Katie Couric, Democratic Vice Presidential nominee Joe Biden stated: **"When the stock market crashed, Franklin Roosevelt got on the television and didn't just talk about the princes of greed. He said, 'Look, here's what happened."** Actually, Herbert Hoover, not Franklin D. Roosevelt, was President when the Stock Market crashed in 1929. In addition, television was an experimental medium at the time and very few Americans had access to it.

Joe Biden
U.S. Congress Photograph

Wrong and Weird: During a 2009 interview with *Pajamas TV*, U.S. Representative Michele Bachmann (R-MN) observed: **"I find it interesting that it was back in the 1970s that the swine flu broke out under another, then under another Democrat president, Jimmy Carter. I'm not blaming this on President Obama, I just think it's an interesting coincidence."** Actually, the last swine flu outbreak occurred in 1976, when Gerald R. Ford was President.

Michele Bachmann
Official Photograph

Dole Dates Himself: 1996 Republican Presidential nominee Bob Dole addressed a crowd in Los Angeles, home to the "Los Angeles" Dodgers." This was the day after Dodgers pitcher Hideo Nomo pitched a no-hitter against the Colorado Rockies. Dole told the crowd: **"The 'Brooklyn' Dodgers had a no-hitter last night, and I'm going to follow what Nomo did. And we are going to wipe them out between now and November 5."** The Dodgers had moved from Los Angeles to Brooklyn 39 years before. Dole's Press Secretary suggested Dole had made the statement on purpose, telling assembled reporters: **"You've covered Bob Dole long enough to know he likes to mix up a serious address like this with a little mirth."**

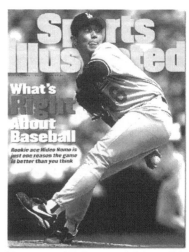

Hideo Nomo on the Cover of *Sports Illustrated*

Political Bloopers

Ouch: In 1996, Republican Presidential nominee Bob Dole fell off a railing on a stage while shaking hands at a campaign rally in Chico, California. His fall was broken by photographers.

Bob Dole
Robert J. Dole Archive and Special Collections

Biden: Obviously, I Don't Know What the Hell I'm Talking About: In 1977, U.S. Senator Joe Biden (D-DE) offered an amendment to the U.S. Criminal Code. He began reading the amendment and discovered that his staff had changed the wording of the amendment. Biden then admitted to his colleagues: **"Obviously I don't know what the hell I'm talking about. I thought I had a two-for-one provision there. The staff, in its wisdom, rewrote it, so I guess I did not want that after all."**

Joe Biden
Official Photograph

Did I Say That? During the 1976 Presidential debate between Republican Gerald R. Ford and Democrat Jimmy Carter, Max Frankel of *The New York Times* suggested that because of the Helsinki Accords: **"The Russians have dominance in Eastern Europe."** Ford mendaciously asserted: **"There is no Soviet domination over Eastern Europe and there never will be under a Ford administration."** Frankel gave Ford a chance to correct his misstatement, but instead Ford doubled-down, exclaiming: **"I don't believe Mr. Frankle that the Yugoslavians consider themselves dominated by the Soviet Union. I don't believe that the Romanians consider themselves dominated by the Soviet Union. I don't believe that the Poles consider themselves dominated by the Soviet Union. Each of those countries is independent, autonomous. It has its own territorial integrity and the United States does not concede that those countries are under the domination of the Soviet Union."** The President's team went into damage control mode and asserted that the President simply meant that the U.S. would never recognize Soviet control of Eastern Europe. But the damage was done, and this gaffe was one of the reasons Ford lost this razor-thin election.

Jimmy Carter (L), and Gerald R. Ford (R) at the 1976 Presidential Debate
Executive Office of the President

John McCain and the Beach Boys: During a 2007 campaign appearance in Murrells, South Carolina, Republican Presidential candidate John McCain was asked by an audience member: **"When do we send them an airmail message to Tehran?"** McCain began singing: **"That old Beach Boys song, Bomb Iran, Bomb Bomb Bomb."** The actual name of the song was **"Barbara Ann."**

John McCain
Official Photograph

Political Bloopers

Oops: During a debate, 2012 Republican Presidential aspirant Rick Perry stumbled when trying to name the three departments of the Federal Government he would abolish. **'It's three agencies of the government that when I get there that are gone, Commerce, Education, and the uh, um, what's the third one there, let's see. . . The third agency of government I would do away with, Education, the uh, Commerce, and let's see. I can't, the third one, sorry. Oops.'** The agency Perry could not come up with was the Department of Energy. Ironically, Perry later became Energy Secretary.

Rick Perry Campaigning for President in 2012
Iowa Politics.com

Someone Needs to Enroll in Civics 101: In 2015, the Oklahoma Supreme Court ruled that having the Ten Commandments posted on the grounds is unconstitutional. Oklahoma Governor Mary Fallin responded by averring: **"You know, there are three branches of our government. You have the Supreme Court, the legislative branch and the people, the people and their ability to vote. So I'm hoping that we can address this issue in the legislative session and let the people of Oklahoma decide."** The three branches are actually the Executive, legislative, and Judiciary.

Mary Fallin
Official Photograph

Caught up in Words: In a 2010 debate, Arizona Governor Jan Brewer screwed up her opening statement. She said: **"Thank you all for watching us tonight. I have a** (then she blanks out for a few seconds) **done so much and I just cannot believe that we've changed everything since I've become your Governor in the last 600 days. Arizona has come back from the abyss. We have cut the budget. We have balanced the budget, and we are moving forward. We have done everything that we could possibly do.** (Then comes a nine second blank out) **We have a did what was right for Arizona. I will really tell you that I have done the best that anyone can do."**

Jan Brewer
Official Photograph

Translation: That's Not What I Meant: On a 1977 trip to Poland, Jimmy Carter suffered the misfortune of having a shaky translator. Carter told the Polish people in a speech: **"I have come to learn your opinions and understand your desires for the future."** The translator said: **"I desire the Poles carnally."**

Jimmy Carter
Official Photograph

Political Bloopers

Aleppo: During an appearance on MSNBC's Morning Joe, 2016 Libertarian Presidential nominee Gary Johnson was asked by panelist Mike Barnacle: **"What would you do, if you were elected, about Aleppo?"** A befuddled Johnson asked; **"What is Aleppo?"** prompting Barnacle to aver: **"You're kidding me."** Aleppo is an important city in the war-torn country of Syria. Johnson later apologized, saying he just blanked.

Gary Johnson
Campaign Portrait

It has the Wrong 'Buz' to it: In 1989, Vice President Dan Quayle Told a Nashville crowd: **"As America celebrates the twentieth anniversary of Neal Armstrong, Buzz Lukens and walking on the moon."** Quayle meant to refer to Buzz Aldren. Lukens was a U.S. Representative from Ohio not Buzz Lukens who was convicted of paying an underage girl for sex.

David "Buz" Lukens
Official Photograph

Bush Plugs CBS Show on NBC: In 1987, the Republican Presidential debate was held after the Democrats debate. Both debates were broadcast on NBC. In the Republican debate, Vice President George H.W. Bush lambasted the Democrats: **"To hear the Democrats wringing their hands about all that's wrong—I'm sorry. I'm depressed. I want to switch over and see 'Jake and the Fatman' on CBS."** Jake and the Fatman was a production about a prosecutor and an investigator.

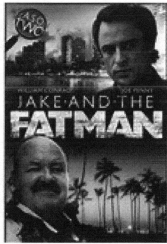

Jake and the Fatman Video

PotatoE: In 1992, Vice President Dan Quayle was administering a spelling bee at Rivera Elementary School in Trenton, NJ. Student William Figueroa spelled the word **"potato"** correctly on the board. Quayle then told him to put an E at the end of the word. Quayle saw the word with the E at the end on a flashcard.

Dan Quayle
U.S. Department of Defense Photograph

Political Bloopers

Words in the Margin Not Meant to Be Uttered: Campaigning for a full term in 1976, Gerald R. Ford mistakenly read words in the margin of his speech ("with emphasis"): **"I say to you this is nonsense with emphasis!"**

Gerald R. Ford
Gerald R. Ford Presidential Library and Museum

Unemployed Presidential Candidate: During a 2011 meeting with unemployed Americans in Tampa, Florida, Republican Presidential candidate Mitt Romney declaimed: **"I should tell my story. I too am unemployed."** Many unemployed were offended by Romney's joke.

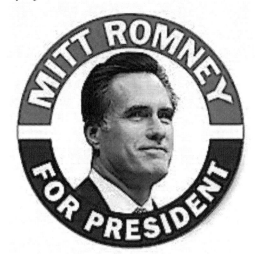

Pin Promoting Mitt Romney For President

McCain Will Veto Beer? When showing his seriousness about eliminating earmarks, 2008 Republican Presidential nominee John McCain declared: **"I will veto every single beer."** He meant to say he will veto every single **"bill."**

John McCain
Official Photograph

Slip of the Tongue: Campaigning for the Republican Presidential nomination in 2000, George W. Bush told the Greater Nashua, N.H. Chamber of Commerce: **"I know how hard it is for you to put food on your family."**

George W. Bush
White House Photograph by Pete Souza

Political Bloopers

Same Name, Wrong Guy: In 2013, Boston voters elected State Representative Marty Walsh Mayor. Vice President Biden called Walsh to congratulate him. Biden exclaimed: **"You son of a gun, Marty, You did it."** However, Biden called the wrong Marty Walsh. The Marty Walsh Biden congratulated was a Democratic operative and a former aide to U.S. Senator Ted Kennedy (D-MA.)

Marty Walsh
Official Photograph

What? Ronald Reagan mistakenly said: **"We are trying to get unemployment to go up, and I think we're going to succeed:"**

Ronald Reagan
Ronald Reagan Presidential Foundation and Institute

Why won't this thing Work?; In 1945, First Lady Bess Truman was christening two new ambulance planes to be used by the Army and Navy. Mrs. Truman had a bottle of Champaign, and began to hit it on the plane's nose. However, the bottle would not break. No one scored the glass before the event. Accordingly, Mrs. Truman continued to try to break the bottle to no avail.

Bess Truman with Bottle
Harry S. Truman Presidential Library and Museum

"FORE!" Gerald R. Ford was arguably the most athletic President in American history. His athletic prowess was exhibited on the football field. He was a star football player at the University of Michigan. Ford was offered contracts by both the Detroit Lions and the Green Bay Packers. He turned them down to attend Yale Law School instead. Ford was also a good golfer, having played the sport for most of his life. He sported a handicap of 12. However, while President, Ford took a shot that went off course and hit a spectator on the head. The press had a field day with this, characterizing Ford as a klutz. Comedian Bob Hope quipped: **"It's not hard to find Jerry Ford on the Golf course – You follow the wounded."** Ford, in his self-deprecating humor, deadpanned: **"I know I am getting better at golf because I am hitting fewer spectators."**

Gerald R. Ford
Gerald R. Ford Library and Museum

Political Bloopers

Bush says he and Reagan had some Sex: During a campaign rally in 1988, Republican Presidential nominee George H.W. Bush made the following malapropism: **"For seven and a half years I've worked alongside President Reagan. We've had triumphs. Made some mistakes. We've had some sex...uh...setbacks."**

George H.W. Bush
George Bush Presidential Library and Museum

57 States? At a campaign event in Beaverton, Oregon, Democratic Presidential candidate Barack Obama meant to say that he had visited 47 states. Instead, he said he visited 57 states. His political opponents had a field day with this, suggesting that Obama legitimately thought there were 57 states in the U.S. The actual quote is: **"It is wonderful to be back in Oregon. Over the last 15 months, we've traveled to every corner of the United States. I've now been in 57 states. I think [I have] one left to go. Alaska and Hawaii. I was not allowed to go to even though I really wanted to visit, but my staff would not justify it."**

Barack Obama
U.S. Air force Photograph

Shouldn't it be 'Puck' Players? After the Boston Bruins won the Stanley Cup Championship in 2011, Boston Mayor Tom Menino said at a press conference: **"Congratulations to the Boston Bruins for a great series bringing the Stanley Cup back to Boston . . . and great ballplayers on the ice and also great ballplayers off the ice."**

Tom Menino
Official Photograph

Crime Report: Doing Great Outside of the Murders: At a 1989 address to the National Press Club, Washington D.C. Mayor Marion Barry asserted: **"Outside of the killings, D.C. has one of the lowest crime rates in the nation."**

Marion Barry
Official Photograph

Political Bloopers

Voted for it -- Before Voting Against It: While at an appearance at Marshall University in Huntington, West Virginia, a heckler asked Democratic Presidential candidate John Kerry about his vote against an $87 billion appropriation to pay for the wars in Afghanistan and Iraq. Kerry responded: **"I actually did vote for the $87 billion before I voted against it."** Kerry later explained that he had meant to say that he voted for a Democratic version of the appropriation which would have paid for the wars by eliminating tax cuts signed by George W. Bush in 2001 on those making over $200,000. That measure did not pass, and Kerry voted against a subsequent proposal, which would have borrowed the money. Yet the damage was done, and the campaign of Republican President George W. Bush ran advertisements highlighting Kerry's inarticulate quote. This helped Bush's campaign to perfect the master narrative that Kerry is a flip-flopper.

John Kerry
Official Photograph

The Ongoing Asparagus Feud: During a 2013 U.S. Judiciary Committee meeting, a confrontation broke out between U.S. Attorney General Eric Holder and U.S. Representative Louie Gohmert (R-TX) about the FBI's investigation of the alleged Boston bomber Tamerlan Tsarnaeev. Gohmert said: **"The Attorney General will not cast aspersions on my asparagus."** During another hearing almost a year later, the two once again clashed, and Holder, remembering Gohmert's previous malapropism, said in a sarcastic tone to Gohmert: **"Good luck with your asparagus."**

Louie Gohmert
Official Photograph

To be Blunt about It: In 1992, George H. W. Bush, reading from a cue card at a town hall in Exeter, NH exclaimed: **"Message, I care."** This was during an economic downturn, and some Republicans were turning to his Republican Primary opponent, Pat Buchanan.

George H.W. Bush
Official Photograph

On and On and On: Arkansas Governor Bill Clinton was scheduled to deliver a 15-minute speech in support of Democratic Presidential nominee Michael Dukakis at the 1988 Democratic National Convention. Instead, Clinton droned on for 33 minutes. The audience booed him. When Clinton declared: **"In conclusion"** the audience cheered. Some political observers predicted Clinton had ended his political future, but Clinton regained his political star by appearing on the Late Show with Johnny Carson, making fun of the event.

Bill Clinton
William J. Clinton Presidential Library and Museum

Chapter XVIII

Political Firsts

Political Firsts

First African-American Governor: The first African-American Governor in U.S. history was Louisiana's Pinckney Benton Stewart Pinchback. Pinchback was the state's Lieutenant Governor and was promoted to Governor when Governor Henry Clay Warmoth was forced to resign for his role in election fraud. Governor Pinchback served the last thirty-five days of Warmoth's unexpired term.

Pinckney Benton Stewart Pinchback
Library of Congress

Arizonan Makes History: In 2012, Democrat Krysten Sinema won a U.S. House seat in Arizona, making her the first outward bisexual to be elected to Congress.

Krysten Sinema
Official Photograph

First Use of Presidential Veto Power: In 1792, George Washington issued the first Presidential Veto. He vetoed the *Apportions Bill of 1792*. The legislation would have fixed the size of the United States House of Representatives based on the United States Census of 1790. Washington believed the bill was unconstitutional.

George Washington
Library of Congress

The First Attempt to Assassinate a President: In January of 1835, Richard Lawrence, who was mentally ill and believed he was King Richard lll of England, attempted to assassinate President Andrew Jackson at a funeral. Lawrence believed that Jackson was keeping money from him and had killed his father. His shot misfired. This is the first known attempt to assassinate a U.S. President.

Andrew Jackson
Library of Congress

207

Political Firsts

First Hispanic House Member: The first Hispanic American to serve in the U.S. House of Representatives was Joseph Marion Hernandez (Whig-Florida.) He entered office in 1822.

Joseph Marion Hernandez
Library of Congress

An Indian-American First: In 1956, Democrat Dalip Singh Saund became the first Indian-American elected to the U.S. Congress. Saund won a seat in the U.S. House of Representatives by voters in the Twenty-Ninth Congressional District of California, which included Riverside and Imperial Counties. He served until 1963.

Dalip Singh Saund
Official Portrait

Asian-American First: The only Asian American ever to preside over a state legislative body in U.S. history was Colleen Hanabusa. Her colleagues elected the Hawaii State Senator as President of the State Senate in 2006. In that capacity, she wielded the gavel and presided over the State Senate. Hanabusa was elected to the U.S. House of Representatives in 2010.

Colleen Hanabusa
Official Photograph

Out of The Closet: The first openly Gay person to be elected as a freshman to the U.S. Congress was Jared Polis in 2008. He was elected to represent the Boulder-based Second Congressional District of Colorado.

Jared Polis
Official Photograph

Political Firsts

Electrophobia: Benjamin Harrison was the first President to have electricity installed in the White House. But fearing his own electrocution, he was unwilling to touch any of the White House light switches.

Benjamin Harrison
Library of Congress

Clinton attends a game of Hoops: In 1994 President Bill Clinton became the first sitting President to attend a college basketball game. He attended a game between the University of Arkansas Razorbacks and the Texas Southern Tigers in Fayetteville, Arkansas.

Bill Clinton wearing an Arkansas Razorbacks Jacket
William J. Clinton Presidential Library and Museum

One Giant Leap for Bloggers: Barack Obama was the first President to call on a blogger during a Presidential News Conference. He called on Sam Stein from the *Huffington Post* during his first Primetime Press Conference.

Barack Obama
White House Photograph by Pete Souza

First Jewish Governor: Washington Bartlett was the first person of Jewish descent elected Governor of a U.S. state. The San Francisco Mayor was elected as Governor of California in 1886. He died of a kidney disease less than a year into his term.

Washington Bartlett
Official Photograph

209

Political Firsts

First Female Governor: Nellie Ross was the first female Governor elected in the United States. She was elected Governor of Wyoming in 1924 and served from 1925-1927.

Nellie Ross
Library of Congress

First Jewish Congressman: In 1845, Lewis Charles Levin became the first Jewish American to serve in the U.S. Congress. The U.S. House member represented Pennsylvania's First Congressional District. Levin was a member of the Nativist American Party (a.k.a. Know Nothing Party.) He was defeated for re-election in 1850.

Lewis Charles Levin
Portrait by Rembrant Peale

Cajun Diversity: In 2008, Anh "Joseph" Cao (R-LA) became the first American of Vietnamese descent elected to the U.S. Congress. He was elected to the House of Representatives by voters in Louisiana's First Congressional District centered in New Orleans. The district is 64% African-American.

Anh "Joseph" Cao
Official Photograph

First Jewish Congresswoman: Florence Kahn was the first Jewish Woman to serve in the U.S. Congress. The Democrat represented San Francisco in the U.S. House of Representatives from 1925-1937.

Florence Kahn
Library of Congress

Political Firsts

The First Chinese-American Congresswoman: U.S. Representative Judy Chu (D-CA), elected in a Special election in 2009, became the first Chinese-American to serve in the U.S. Congress.

Judy Chu
Official Photograph

May I Say "Madam Chairwoman?" U.S. Representative Mae Ella Nolan (R-CA 1923-1925) was the first female to chair a Congressional Committee. She chaired the House Committee on Expenditures in the Post Office Department. She represented the same Congressional District later represented by Nancy Pelosi, the first female House Speaker.

Mae Ella Nolan
Official Photograph

Socialist and Proud of it: In 1910, voters from the Fifth Congressional District of Wisconsin elected Victor L. Berger of the Socialist Party of America to represent them in the U.S. House of Representatives, making him the first Socialist elected to the U.S. Congress.

Victor L. Berger
Library of Congress

Korean-American First: In 1992, Chang-jun "Jay" Kim became the first Korean-born American elected to the U.S. Congress. He represented the Forty-First Congressional District of California until losing a bid for re-election in 1998.

Chang-jun "Jay" Kim
Official Photograph

Political Firsts

Historic Lady in the Garden State: Mary Norton was the first Democratic woman elected to the U.S. House of Representatives. In 1924 she was elected to represent New Jersey's Twelfth Congressional District, which included her home in Jersey City. She served from 1925-1951.

Mary Norton
Official Portrait

Montana's Maverick Trailblazer: The first woman elected to the U.S. Congress was Republican Jeannette Rankin. She served as the at-large representative for Montana in the U.S. House of Representatives from 1917-1919. During that term Rankin, a devout pacifist, voted against U.S. involvement in WWI. Rankin did not run for re-election, choosing instead to run for the U.S. Senate. She lost. After a two-decade congressional hiatus, Rankin won back her House seat in 1940. In 1941, she was the only member of the U.S. Congress to vote against a declaration of War on Japan following the Pearl Harbor invasion. Rankin questioned if President Franklin D. Roosevelt had provoked the attack.

Jeannette Rankin
Library of Congress

Senator for a Day: The first woman to serve in the United States Senate was Georgia Democrat Rebecca Ann Felton (1922). Peach State Governor Thomas Hardwick appointed her to replace Senator Thomas E. Watson, who died in office. Senator Felton was 87 years of age and was a veteran of the Woman's Suffrage Movement. Unfortunately her tenure in the U.S. Senate was short, only lasting one day. A day later the newly elected U.S. Senator, Walter George, was sworn into office.

Rebecca Latimer Felton
Library of Congress

First African-American U.S. Senator: In 1870, Mississippi Republican Hiram Revels became the first African-American to serve in the U.S. Senate, filling the seat vacated by U.S. Senator Albert G. Brown. Brown resigned when the South succeeded at the beginning of the U.S. Civil War in 1861.

Hiram Revels
Library of Congress

Political Firsts

Nancy Does It "Her Way:" In 1978, Kansas voters made Republican Nancy Kassebaum the first female elected to the U.S. Senate whose husband had not been a U.S. Senator.

Nancy Kassebaum
Official Photograph

Transracial Appeal: In 1966, the voters in Massachusetts made state Attorney General Edward W. Brooke the first popularly elected African-American U.S. Senator in American History. At that time, the African-American population in the Commonwealth was just 2%.

Edward W. Brooke
Library of Congress

Nepotism Alabama Style: U.S. Senator Hugo Black (D-AL) resigned his seat in 1937 to assume a seat on the U.S. Supreme Court. Alabama Governor Bibb Graves appointed his wife, Democrat Dixie Bibb Graves, to the vacant Senate seat. Mrs. Graves became the first married woman U.S. Senator in U.S. history. She served for less than one month and then resigned from the Senate.

Dixie Bibb Graves
Library of Congress

A Five-Term Senator: U.S. Senator Thomas Hart Benton (Democratic-Republican and Democrat-MO, 1821-1851) was the first U.S. Senator to serve five full terms.

Thomas Hart Benton
Portrait by Bill Hathorn

Chapter XIX

Political Linguistic Legacy

Political Linguistic Legacy

That's OK with Me: Martin Van Buren was nicknamed "Old Kinderhook" simply because he hailed from Kinderhook, New York. Van Buren became known as **"OK"** for short. During his 1840 re-election campaign, his supporters created OK clubs. Although the expression OK had been around for some time, Van Buren's Campaign popularized the expression. Van Buren's political adversaries mendaciously claimed that OK originated from his predecessor and ally Andrew Jackson. They alleged that Jackson was a poor speller, and that Jackson believed that OK was the abbreviation for **"all correct."**

Martin Van Buren
Library of Congress

The Origin of Booze: Whisky distiller E.G. Booze supported William Henry Harrison's 1840 Presidential campaign. In promoting Harrison, he sold whisky in log-cabin-shaped bottles. This is where the word Booze came from.

William Henry Harrison
Library of Congress

First Lady: Zachary Taylor coined the term "First Lady" at the funeral of Dolly Madison in 1849. Taylor eulogized her by saying: **"She will never be forgotten, because she was truly our First Lady for a half-century."**

Zachary Taylor
Library of Congress

A Shermanesque Statement: In 1884, there was an active effort by some Republican Party activists to draft former Civil War General William Tecumseh Sherman to seek the Republican nomination for President. Sherman stated definitively: **"I will not accept if nominated and will not serve if elected."** This unequivocal language left no wiggle room for Sherman to explore a candidacy. This absolute language is today called a **"Shermanesque statement."** When an individual says he/she will not run for a certain office, reporters often ask if the candidate will make a **"Shermanesque statement"** that he/she will not run.

William Tecumseh Sherman
Library of Congress

Political Linguistic Legacy

Mending Fences: The phrase "Mend fences" was coined by U.S. Treasury Secretary John Sherman in 1879. He told an audience in his native Ohio: **"I have come home to look after my fences."** While Sherman likely meant that he was coming home to look after the fences on his farm, the line came to mean that he was trying to consolidate political support in his home state.

John Sherman
Library of Congress

The Cold War: The term **"Cold War,"** describing the rivalry between the United States and the Soviet Union, was coined by financier Bernard Baruch at the unveiling of his portrait in the South Carolina House of Representatives in 1947. Baruch was a native South Carolinian. In describing the rivalry between the United States and the Soviet Union, Baruch referred to the rivalry as **"The Cold War."**

Bernard Baruch
Library of Congress

The Founding Father of the term "Founding Father": The term **"Founding Fathers"** was coined by then U.S. Senator Warren G. Harding (R-OH) during his keynote address at the 1916 Republican Convention.

Warren G. Harding
Library of Congress

GOBBLEDYGOOK! The term **"gobbledygook"** was coined by former U.S. Representative Maury Maverick (D-TX 1935-1939). Maverick was serving as the head of the United States Smaller War Plants Corporation during WWII. Maverick had little tolerance for technocratic language that he could not understand. Accordingly, Maverick wrote a memorandum to his employees saying: **"Stay off the gobbledygook language. It only fouls people up. For Lord's sake, be short and say what you're talking about ... anyone using the words 'activation' or 'implementation' will be shot."** The word **"gobbledygook"** was the brainchild of Maverick, imitating the noise a turkey makes.

Maury Maverick
Library of Congress

218

"The GOP." Today, the acronym GOP (which stands for Grand Old Party) is synonymous with the Republican Party. The term has an interesting history. In fact, the Democratic Party originally used the acronym. A loyal Georgia Democrat coined it in 1878. The term became synonymous with the Republican Party after the 1888 presidential election in which Republican Benjamin Harrison defeated incumbent Democratic president Grover Cleveland. *The Chicago Tribune,* sympathetic to the Republican Party, declared: **"Let us be thankful that under the rule of the Grand Old Party. . . these United States will resume the onward and upward march which the election of Grover Cleveland in 1884 partially arrested."**

GOP Symbol
Public Domain

Goody-Goody: The term "goody-goody" was originally coined in the 1890s as a term of derision for **"good government guys"** or **"goo-goos."** These "goody-goodies" were politicians who supported government reform and an end to government graft and corruption. About a hundred years later, Chicago columnist Mike Royko revivified the term.

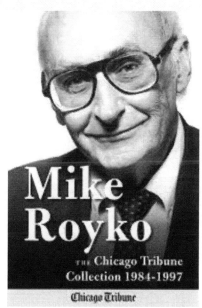

Mike Royko
Chicago Tribune Collection

What a Teddy Bear: The term "teddy bear" was named after President Theodore Roosevelt. In 1902, the president accepted an invitation from Mississippi Governor Andrew H. Longino to join a bear hunting expedition in the Mississippi Delta. The president had an unsuccessful hunting trip. The nationally acclaimed hunter Holt Collier was one of the guests on the trip. He was also serving as an animal-tracker for the President. Collier managed to capture a bear cub, and instead of shooting it, he hit the cub on the head with his rifle, and tied it to a tree. He wanted the president to shoot it so the president could boast of a successful hunting trip. When Roosevelt saw the little bear, he refused to shoot it, arguing that it would not be a fair fight. Political cartoonist Clifford Berryman got word of the episode and published a cartoon of Roosevelt declining to shoot the bear. Ever the opportunists, candy store proprietors Morris and Rose Michtom made a stuffed bear and coined it **"Teddy's bear."** It is now simply called **"Teddy bear."**

A *Washington Post* Cartoon showing Theodore Roosevelt ordering a Teddy Bear free

Chapter XX

Political Hyperbole

Political Hyperbole

At least he Never said it had a Basement: Lyndon B. Johnson had a fascination with the Alamo. His father, State Legislator Samuel Johnson, Jr., wrote legislation to give control of the Alamo to the Daughters of the Republic of Texas. In 1966, while visiting U.S. troops in South Korea, Lyndon B. Johnson accurately said that there is a picture of his father inside the Alamo. He then went too far by mendaciously claiming that his great-great-grandfather had died in the Alamo. In actuality, the great-great-grandfather that Lyndon B. Johnson was referring to was a real-estate trader who died at home. Johnson creatively told the press: **You all didn't let me finish. It was the Alamo Bar and Grill in Eagle Pass, Texas."**

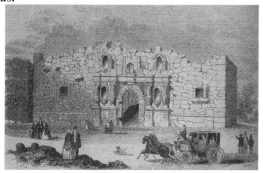

The Alamo
Printed in Gleason's Pectoral Drawing Room

Technically True: During his two Presidential campaigns, Mitt Romney continuously claimed that as Governor of Massachusetts he made the **"tough choices and balanced the budget without raising taxes."** Romney was referring to the projected $3 billion budget shortfall he inherited when he assumed office in 2003. Romney did not mention that he raised over $500 million in **"fees."** Romney also raised corporate taxes under the guise of closing corporate loopholes and truncating local aid to the state's municipalities. This forced municipalities to cut services and/or raise property taxes on their residents.

Mitt Romney
Official Portrait

Military Hyperbole: Candidates with military experience often brandish this experience on the campaign trail, and occasionally get themselves into trouble. During his 2008 bid for an open U.S. Senate seat in Connecticut, it was revealed that the Democratic nominee Richard Blumenthal had on two occasions claimed he served as a Marine **"in Vietnam."** Blumenthal had in fact served in the Marines during the Vietnam era, but never served in Vietnam. He apologized for the remarks and despite this exaggeration was elected to the Senate by twelve points.

Richard Blumenthal
Official Photograph

Fatherly Tails: In 2014, David Perdue, the Republican nominee for an open U.S. Senate seat representing Georgia, told Morehouse College students that his father, in his role as a Superintendent of Schools, desegregated the Houston County schools. Perdue said his father **"integrated I think the first — if not the first or second — county school system in Georgia, and he did it before they had to. He did it right after he got elected, and he did it because it was the right thing to do."** Perdue failed to mention the fact that the desegregation plan was instituted after the NAACP successfully challenged the **"Freedom of Choice"** plan instituted by the Houston County School Board, which allowed but did not mandate integration.

David Perdue
Official Photograph

Political Hyperbole

Reporting Exaggeration: During his failed 1988 bid for the Democratic Presidential nomination, Al Gore told the *Des Moines Register* that in his early days as a reporter for the *Nashville Tennessean*, he got **"a bunch of people indicted and sent to jail."** However, it was later revealed that Gore's reporting resulted in just two municipal officials being indicted, and neither was jailed.

Pin for Al Gore For President in 1988

I Can Be Sanctimonious: An amusing exaggeration came from Mark Roosevelt, the Democratic nominee for Massachusetts Governor in 1994. In an interview with the *Boston Globe*, he made the following comment about his tenure in the Massachusetts State Legislature: **"A record of accomplishment probably unsurpassed by any legislator in the 20th century in Massachusetts."** Roosevelt later retracted the comment, stating: **"I can be sanctimonious."** Roosevelt lost the Gubernatorial election to Republican incumbent William Weld, garnering less than 30 percent of the vote.

Mark Roosevelt
Official Photograph

Running Ahead of Himself: In 2012, Republican Vice Presidential nominee Paul Ryan claimed to have ran a sub-three-hour marathon. Actually, he ran the Grandma's Marathon in Duluth, MN as a twenty-year-old in just over four hours. Ryan issued a statement to *Runners World* reading: **"The race was more than 20 years ago, but my brother Tobin—who ran Boston last year— reminds me that he is the owner of the fastest marathon in the family and has never himself ran a sub-three. If I were to do any rounding, it would certainly be to four hours, not three. He gave me a good ribbing over this at dinner tonight."**

Paul Ryan
Official Photograph

They All Exaggerate: Robert Strauss, who served as chairman of the Democratic Party, captured this phenomenon of political exaggeration best when he said: **"Every politician wants every voter to believe he was born in a log cabin he built himself."**

Log Cabin
Photograph by DrunkDriver

Chapter XXI

Presidential Election Fate

Presidential Election Fate

Only Sitting House Member to be Elected President. One of the Republican candidates vying for the 1880 presidential nomination was U.S. Treasury Secretary John Sherman. The nomination at the time was decided at each party's National conventions. U.S. Representative James Garfield (R-OH) was a member of the Ohio delegation to the Republican National Convention. His role was to deliver an address on behalf of the Ohio delegation nominating Sherman, a native son of Ohio. Garfield was not a candidate for president. In fact, he had just been elected by the Ohio State Legislature to the U.S. Senate (At that time, the legislatures, not citizens, elected their U.S. Senators). Earlier that year, Garfield and Sherman had agreed to a deal whereby Garfield would support Sherman's presidential bid if Sherman endorsed Garfield for the U.S. Senate. The Republican Convention was deadlocked between Sherman, former President Ulysses S. Grant, and James G. Blaine. Garfield, unlike the person he was nominating (Sherman was nicknamed the Ohio Icicle), electrified the crowd, and a chorus of **"We Want Garfield"** ensued. Stunned by the chant, Garfield insisted that his name not be placed for nomination. However, by the second day, with no end in sight to the stalemate, Blaine and Sherman both agreed to support the rising star, James Garfield. The nation was astounded by this set of unlikely events as was Garfield himself. Garfield mustered the nomination on the 36th ballot.

James Garfield
Library of Congress

Don't Listen to Roscoe Conkling: In 1884, there was a schism in the GOP over Civil Service Reform. The leading supporter of the current system was the Omni powerful U.S. Senator Roscoe Conkling (R-NY). The Party's Presidential nominee, James Garfield, offered the Vice Presidency to U.S. Representative Levi Morton (R-NY), who strongly desired becoming president. However, Conkling persuaded Morton, his protégée, that Garfield was destined to lose the election, and that Morton would share the blame for the loss and would never win the Republican presidential nomination. Morton reluctantly heeded that advice and declined the offer. Garfield's second choice was Chester A. Arthur, also a supporter of Conkling. As with Morton, Conkling beseeched Arthur not to accept the nomination. Arthur refused Conkling's request and was nominated as Vice president. The ticket scraped out a victory and Garfield assumed the Presidency. Garfield was subsequently assassinated in just his first year in office. Arthur assumed the Presidency.

Roscoe Conkling
Library of Congress

It Wasn't in the Cards: The name Irvine Lenroot is not exactly a household word, but had the Republican Party high command and the GOP presidential nominee had their way, he may have become president. U.S. Senator Warren G. Harding garnered the Republican presidential nomination in 1920. Harding came from the conservative bloodline of the GOP. The Republican Party establishment wanted to balance the ticket with Lenroot, a U.S. Representative from Wisconsin and a tribune of the party's liberal bloodline. However, conservative delegates to the Republican National Convention rebelled against the high command and nominated Massachusetts Governor Calvin Coolidge. Coolidge was a rising star in conservative circles for his role in standing up to organized labor during the Boston Police Strike. Ironically, Harding died in 1923, allowing Coolidge to ascend to the Presidency, winning a term in his own right a year later. Irvine Lenroot faded back into political obscurity.

Irvine Lenroot
Library of Congress

Presidential Election Fate

The Minister who lost his Candidate an Election: In 1884, Republican Presidential nominee James G. Blaine made a strategic blunder by not dissociating himself from a supporter. This *faux pas* likely cost Blaine the election. A few days before the 1884 presidential election, Republican presidential nominee James G. Blaine made a campaign appearance in New York, where Presbyterian Minister Samuel D. Burchard, a Blaine supporter, excoriated the Democrats as the Party of **"Rum, Romanism, and Rebellion."** Blaine sat silent during this tirade, making no effort to disassociate himself from these volatile remarks. Unfortunately for the unsuspecting Blaine, many Irish voters took umbrage by the use of the word **"rum,"** believing that the Minister was perpetuating a stereotype that Irish-Americans, who were mostly Democrats, were alcoholics. This galvanized the Irish vote against Blaine in the swing state of New York, where Democrat Grover Cleveland eked out a razor-thin victory, defeating Blaine by just 1,047 votes. New York proved to be the state that made the electoral difference in this razor-close presidential election.

Be Careful What you Wish For: Vice President Garret Hobart had died in office of heart disease, resulting in the Republican Party needing a new vice presidential running mate for President William McKinley in 1900. New York Republican Party boss and U.S. Senator Thomas C. Platt, a rival of New York Governor Theodore Roosevelt, successfully urged the Republican Party to select Roosevelt as the running mate to President William McKinley in 1900. Platt did this to get Roosevelt out of the Governorship because Roosevelt was challenging the Platt political machine in New York. Platt thought with Roosevelt gone that Lieutenant Governor Benjamin Barker Odell Jr. would become the Governor and would be more compliant to Platt's political machine. The thinking was that Roosevelt would be rendered inconsequential in that the Vice Presidency has little power. As circumstances would have it, President McKinley was assassinated in 1901, during the first year of his second term in office, and Roosevelt became president. Upon hearing the news, a shocked Platt exclaimed: **"Oh God, now that dammed cowboy is President of the United States."** To add insult to injury, Governor Odell, similar to Theodore Roosevelt, became a crusader for reform, shunning the Thomas C. Platt political machine.

Samuel D. Burchard
Contemporary Photograph

Thomas C. Platt
Library of Congress

228

Chapter XXII

Miscellaneous

Miscellaneous

Fast Eddy: In 1975, Massachusetts State Representative Ed Markey, a member of the House Judiciary Committee, led the charge in passing legislation to end the practice of allowing state judges to be associated with law firms while serving as judges. Markey shepherded legislation through the House to end this practice. Governor Michael Dukakis signed the legislation. However, House Speaker Thomas McGee was vociferously opposed to the legislation and kicked Markey off the committee. Markey's desk was placed in the hall. Markey, a Congressional candidate stood in front of the desk in a political television advertisement and said: **"The bosses can tell me where to sit, but nobody tells me where to stand."** Markey won the Congressional seat.

Ed Markey
Official Photograph

Blame is the Art of Politics: In 1967, ABC News anchor David Brinkley observed: **"To err is human, to blame it on the other party is politics."**

David Brinkley
Library of Congress

No Twinkling: In 1998, U.S. Representative Michael Pappas (R-NY), a supporter of the impeachment of President Bill Clinton, sang an ode to Special Prosecutor Kenneth Starr on the House Floor. The verse: **"Twinkle Twinkle Kenneth Starr, now we know how brave you are"** was used against Pappas by his Democratic opponent Rush Holt, for re-election in 2000. Clinton was popular with Pappas' constituents, Starr was not. Consequently, Holt defeated Pappas for re-election.

Michael Pappas
Official Photograph

Sarah's Fish Story: In her 2009 speech in which she resigned the Governorship of Alaska, Sarah Palin told members of the Press: **"Only dead fish go with the flow."**

Sarah Palin
Official Photograph

231

Miscellaneous

"Lock Him Out:" When Republican Mike Huckabee assumed the Lieutenant Governorship in then Democratic Arkansas in 1993, he tried to enter his new office, only to find **"The doors to my office were spitefully nailed shut from the inside, office furniture and equipment were removed, and the budget spent down to almost nothing prior to our arriving. After fifty-nine days of public outcry, the doors were finally opened for me to occupy the actual office I had been elected to hold two months earlier."**

Mike Huckabee
Official Photograph

Michael Jordan Enters the Political Court: In 2004, Barack Obama, running for an open U.S. Senate seat in Illinois, received a check from Chicago Bulls legend Michael Jordan. Upon seeing the check, Obama mused: **"I wasn't sure whether I should cash it or frame it."**

Michael Jordan (L), Barack Obama (R)
Photograph by Pete Souza

Who is this Hillary? In 1982, former Arkansas Governor Bill Clinton was running to recapture the Governorship he had lost in 1980. He was scheduled to show up at a debate with one of his primary opponents, U.S. Representative Jim Guy Tucker (D-AR). Instead, Hillary Clinton showed up. Tucker had never met her. Tucker told *The Guardian* in 2016: **"I was expecting Bill, and he sent her ... and she stomped on me. She was well prepared, and she went after me hard, and I was not prepared to respond. I have no question in that little mountain community she whipped me that day."**

Jim Guy Tucker
Official Photograph

Too Many Wars: In 2017, U.S. Senator Rand Paul (R-KY) observed, (while referring to his bellicose colleague Republican Lindsey Graham of South Carolina): **"You know you are in too many wars in too many places when even warmonger Lindsey Graham can't keep track anymore."**

Lindsey Graham
Official Photograph

Miscellaneous

The Omnipotent *Boston Globe*: *The Boston Globe* was a constant thorn in the side of Massachusetts Governor Ed King. The paper delivered a torrent of criticism of the Governor for charges of cronyism, mainly hiring fellow Irish Catholics for state positions. King remarked: **"If God is with you, who can be against you, except *The Boston Globe*."**

Ed King
Official Portrait

Coming Back to bite Him: One of the advocates of enacting the 17th Amendment to the U.S. Constitution, which provided for the direct election of U.S. Senators, was U.S. Senator John W. Kern (D-IN). Kern actually became a victim of the amendment in 1916, when he lost the popular vote to Harry S. New.

John W. Kern
Official Photograph

Poland is Not that Great: In 1933, former Boston Mayor James Michael Curley was told by President Franklin D. Roosevelt that he would receive his wish, becoming U.S. Navy Secretary. However, the President's son, James Roosevelt later told Curley the position was not available. As a consolation prize, the President offered Curley the Ambassadorship to Poland, telling Curley how interesting Poland was. An inflamed Curley retorted: **"If it is such a god damn interesting place, why don't you resign the Presidency and take it yourself."** Curley did not accept the offer.

James Michael Curley
Official Photograph

The Man With the Green Hat: During Prohibition, Congress had a bootlegger, George L. Cassidy, who had the moniker **"The man in the green hat"** because he dawned a green hat when he was arrested for his actions. Cassidy later wrote of his experience: **"I would say that four out of five senators and congressmen consume liquor either at their offices or their homes."** He also maintained: **"The fact that the Capital Police and the door guards were appointed by members of Congress seemed to assure me of protection in getting into the building."**

George Cassidy
Library of Congress

Miscellaneous

What's so Bad About Stealing a Few Dollars? While serving as Military Governor of New Orleans, Louisiana, Benjamin Franklin Butler requisitioned $8,000 from a local bank without accounting for where the money went. At trial, the bank's attorney asked Butler what his neighbors in Lowell, Massachusetts would think of his actions to which Butler replied: **"The people would think I was a fool for not having taken twice as much."**

Benjamin Franklin Butler
Library of Congress

It's a Small World After All: When a coterie of German editors visited his office in Providence, Rhode Island, Governor John O. Pastore (1945-1950), who stood at just 5-foot-4 inches tall, stated: **"Rhode Island is the smallest state in the Union, and I am the smallest governor in the United States."**

John O. Pastore
Official Photograph

You Have a Point There: Vice President Dan Quayle once observed: **"If we don't succeed, we run the risk of failure."**

Dan Quayle
Official Photograph

Chock Full of Nuts: The Democratic nominee for the U.S. Senate in Wyoming in 2012 was Tim Chestnut. He had an inimical campaign slogan: **"Chestnut, the best nut for Senate."** Cowboy State Voters strongly disagreed, giving him just 22% of the vote. Chestnut is an Albany County Commissioner.

Tim Chestnut
Official photograph

Miscellaneous

Who Would Want to be a Patriot Under this Definition? Nationally Syndicated Columnist William E. Vaughan observed: **"A real patriot is the fellow who gets a parking ticket and rejoices that the system works."**

William E. Vaughan
Official Photograph

The Adventures of Alabama Bill: Before serving as a member the U.S. Congress from Florida, Bill Lehman appeared in television advertisements for his used car business in the Miami area, where he lived. He referenced himself as **"Alabama Bill."** The nickname continued, even though Lehman had moved out of his boyhood state. Toward the end of his career, Lehman suffered a stroke. He joked: **"I'm the only politician who can speak out of one side of his mouth."**

Bill Lehman
Official Photograph

That's Why He Failed: In 1974, Twenty-year-old Helicopter school flunkout Robert Preston stole a U.S. Army Bell UHB-D1 Helicopter from an U.S. army base, went on a wild ride and landed on the White House Lawn. Lucky for him he was not shot down.

An Army Bell UHB-D1 Helicopter
U.S. Army Photograph

Really Tough on Crime: In 1990, successful Massachusetts Gubernatorial candidate Bill Weld advertised himself as **"Attila (The Hun) on Crime."** Weld averred he would **"reintroduce prisoners to the joys of busting rocks."**

Bill Weld
Official Portrait

235

Miscellaneous

Neatness Isn't Everything: In 1974, State Representative Barney Frank, known for his disordered appearance, ran for re-election with the campaign slogan: **"Neatness Isn't Everything."**

Barney Frank Campaign Poster

The House and Sex Appeal: Serving from 1925-1937, U.S. Representative Florence Prag Kahn (R-CA) was the first Jewish woman ever to serve in the U.S. Congress. When she was asked about her achievements and popularity in the House, Kahn answered: **"Sex appeal."**

Florence Prag Kahn
Library of Congress

Filibuster Al: In 1992, U.S. Senator Alfonse D'Amato (R-NY) filibustered for 15 hours and 14 minutes against a tax proposal. At one point, he began singing the song: **"South of the border"** as a way to ridicule the outsourcing of American jobs to Mexico.

Alfonse D'Amato
Official Photograph

Nothing to Worry About: In 1978, Massachusetts Democratic Gubernatorial candidate Ed King promised the Massachusetts business community that he would repeal all environmental regulations implemented by his main primary opponent Governor Michael Dukakis. King was a vociferous supporter of nuclear power, despite the potential link to cancer. When he was asked about its potential dangers, King answered: **"I'm sure we'll find a cure for cancer."**

Ed King
United States Department of Transportation

Miscellaneous

Gay Marriage Should Be Between a Man and a Woman: In a 2003 interview with conservative radio talk show host Sean Hannity, California Gubernatorial candidate Arnold Schwarzenegger misspoke in trying to state his opposition to same-sex marriage. He said: **"I think that gay marriage is something that should be between a man and a woman."**

Arnold Schwarzenegger on the Cover of *Time Magazine*

Not the Best Way to Cultivate the Hispanic Vote: When 1990 Republican Texas Gubernatorial nominee Clayton Williams was asked why the state's Hispanic voter should support him, he responded: **"I met Modesta [Williams' wife] at a Mexican restaurant."**

Clayton Williams on the Cover of *Texas Monthly*

Deep Thoughts with Roman Hruska: During the 1970 confirmation hearings for Richard M. Nixon's failed U.S. Supreme Court nominee Harold Carswell, U.S. Senator Roman Hruska (R-NE) defended allegations that Carswell was of mediocre intelligence by stating: **"Even if he were mediocre, there are a lot of mediocre judges and people and lawyers. They are entitled to a little representation, aren't they, and a little chance? We can't have all Brandeis's, Frankfurter's and Cardozo's."**

Roman Hruska
Library of Congress

Of Scientists and the Super Natural: During a 1998 speech on the House Floor, U.S. Representative James Traficant (D-OH) lambasted scientists. He said: **"A new report says only 7 percent of scientists believe in God. That is right. And the reason they gave was that scientists are 'super smart.' Unbelievable. Most of these absent-minded professors cannot find the toilet."**

James Traficant
Official Photograph

237

Miscellaneous

No Excuses: U.S. House Speaker Thomas Brackett Reed (R-ME) needed a member of Congress to come to the Capital for an important vote. One Representative was delayed in a train because of flooding on the railroad. The member telegraphed the Speaker: **"Washout on line. Can't come."** Reed responded in a return telegram: **"Buy another shirt and come on the next train."**

Thomas Brackett Reed
Library of Congress

Must Be a Sinner to Serve: U.S. Senator Eugene McCarthy (D-MN) once studied at a monastery. He observed: **"No man could be equipped for the Presidency if he has never been tempted by one of the cardinal sins."**

Eugene McCarthy
Official Photograph

Republican Humor: Humorist P. J. O'Rourke opined: **"The Republicans are the party that says government doesn't work and they get elected to prove it."**

P.J. O'Rourke
CATO Institute

Congressional Truant: In 1978, Alabama Governor George Wallace appointed Maryon Pitman Allen to succeed her late husband James Allen in the U.S. Senate. Mr. Allen had died from a heart attack. Mrs. Allen spent much of her time in a failed attempt to win the remainder of the unexpired term. In fact, she missed 155 of 356, or 43.5% roll-call votes while on the campaign trial. That is the highest percentage of missed votes in any U.S. Senator in history.

Maryon Pittman Allen
Official Photograph

Goal: To Be a Nicer Son of a Bitch: In 1974, some reform-minded House Democratic caucus members wanted to oust U.S. Representative Wayne Hayes (D-OH), the longtime House Administrative Committee Chairman. Hayes survived in part because of his fundraising prowess in his role as Chairman of the Democratic Congressional Campaigning Committee (DCCC). However, few colleagues liked Hayes because of his short temper and vindictive personality. After surviving an attempt to dislodge him, Hayes told the Democratic Caucus: **"Obviously from everything that has been said in the newspapers, and quite a few things said publicly, I am a 'son of a bitch.' I will try to be a nicer 'son of a bitch.'"**

Wayne Hayes
Official Photograph

So He's Clean: On the eve of his 1983 election as Governor of Louisiana, Edwin Edwards told reporters: **"The only way I can lose this election is if I'm caught in bed with either a dead girl or a live boy."** Edwards won the election.

Edwin Edwards
Official Photograph

The Politics of Inclusion: In describing how conservative Ed King defeated Massachusetts Governor Michael Dukakis in the 1978 Democratic Primary, King aide Angelo Berlandi told supporters: **"We created a hate campaign. We put all the hate groups in one pot and let it boil."**

Campaign Button for the Ed King Gubernatorial Campaign

To Put it Bluntly: In 1982, when running for the U.S. House of Representatives for the first time, Democrat Barbara Boxer of California used the slogan: **"Barbara Boxer gives a damn."**

Barbara Boxer
Official Photograph

239

Miscellaneous

Calling Out the Nuts: In an interview with Judy Woodruff at a forum sponsored by *The Atlantic*, U.S. Senator Orrin Hatch (R-UT) bemoaned: **"We don't need nuts in the United States Senate, we need fiscal conservatives, and we've got some nuts on the other side and every once in a while we may find some on our side."**

Orrin Hatch
Official Photograph

Representative's Legacy on the Diamond: The first Congressional Baseball game was organized in 1909 by U.S. Representative John K. Tener (R-PA), a former Major League Baseball player. The Congressional game is still played today between the Democrats and Republicans.

John K. Tener
Official Photograph

Beg, But Don't Touch: During a meeting in Pennsylvania a State Government Committee chairman, Chairman Daryl Metcalfe (R-PA), lashed out at his Democratic colleague, ranking member Mathew Bradford: **"Representative Bradford, look, I'm a heterosexual. I have a wife, I love my wife, I don't like men as you might but stop touching me all the time. Keep your hands to yourself. If you want to touch someone, you have people on your side of the aisle that might like it. I don't."** A stunned Bradford retorted: **"My intention was to just beg for your permission for about 30 seconds."** To that, Metcalfe responded: **"Then beg, don't touch."**

Daryl Metcalfe
Official Photograph

Football and Politics: New Orleans Saints Quarterback Drew Brees is the grandson of U.S. Representative Jack Hightower (D-TX 1975-1985).

Drew Brees
Official NFL Photograph

240

Miscellaneous

Milk Cow Disease: In 2010, Ashley B. Carson, the Executive Director of The Older Women's League (OWL), wrote a column in *The Huffington Post* challenging former U.S. Senator Alan Simpson (R-WY), who was serving as the Co-Chairman of the Simpson-Bowles Commission on the Debt and Deficit. Carson challenged Simpson's assertion that Social Security is adding to the Federal Deficit. In response, Simpson sent Carson an email stating: **"I've made plenty of smart cracks about people on Social Security who milk it to the last degree. You know 'em too...We've reached a point now where it's like a milk cow with 310 million tits!"** Simpson later apologized for making the comment.

Alan Simpson
Official Photograph

Congressional Idiocy: American Author Mark Twain averred in a 1891 draft manuscript: **"Suppose you were an idiot and suppose you were a member of Congress. But I repeat myself."**

Mark Twain
Photograph by Mathew Brady

Sir Charles Speaks His Mind: Campaigning for Democrat Doug Jones over Republican Roy Moore in a 2017 U.S. Senate election, Alabama native Charles Barkley told a crowd in Birmingham: **"At some point, we've got to stop looking like idiots to the Nation."**

Charles Barkley
Gallery 2 Images

Spoken Like a True Autocrat: When a Republican member of the Georgia House of Representatives asked State House Speaker Tom Murphy (D-GA 1973-2002) a question about House Rules, Murphy responded: **"I'm not sure about the rules of the House, but this is how we do things here."**

Thomas Murphy
Photograph by Sethlywood1993

Miscellaneous

God is Ineligible to Vote in Alabama: After Alabama U.S. Senate candidate Roy Moore lost to Democrat Doug Jones in a 2017 special election, he refused to immediately concede the election, prompting former Arkansas Governor Mike Huckabee to tweet: **"Roy Moore won't concede; says will wait on God to speak," God wasn't registered to vote in Alabama but the [people] who voted did speak and it wasn't close enough for recount. In elections everyone does NOT get a trophy. I know first hand but it's best to exit with class."**

Mike Huckabee
Photograph by Gage Skidmore

Interesting Idea: In 2003, conservative televangelists Pat Robertson, interviewed Joel Mowbtay, author of *Dangerous Diplomacy: How the State Department Endangers America's Security* on his television show, the 700 Club. Robertson began the conversation by averring: **"I read your book. When you get through, you say, 'If I could just get a nuclear device inside Foggy Bottom, I think that's the answer,' and you say, 'We've got to blow that thing."**

Pat Robertson
Paparazzo Presents

New, New Yorker: On the day Robert F. Kennedy was elected to the U.S. Senate from New York, he did not meet the residency requirements to vote in the state.

Robert F. Kennedy
Lyndon Baines Johnson Library and Museum

Tick Tick Tick Tick: In 1983, Democrat Louisiana Gubernatorial candidate Edwin Edwards said of his Republican opponent David Treen: **"He's so slow it takes him an hour and a half to watch *60 Minutes*."**

David Treen
Official Photograph

242

Miscellaneous

Costly Error: Hubert Humphrey is the only Vice President to be honored on a U.S. Postage stamp. In 1991, the U.S. Postal Service was forced to spend $580,000 to destroy 300 million of these stamps because the stamp sheets say that he became Vice President in 1964. In actuality, Humphrey was elected in 1964, and assumed the office in 1965.

Hubert Humphrey Postage Stamp

Talk of Hemorrhoids by a Political Candidate: Failed 2017 U.S. Senate Candidate Roy Moore opened a press conference with this odd antidote: **"a seasoned old judge"** told him **"you need to have eyeglasses so it shows people that you study a lot and read a lot." "The next thing is you have to have graying hair or thinning hair. You have to have that to show your age. "Then you have to have one other thing. You have to have hemorrhoids. I said, 'Judge, I don't understand that. I don't have hemorrhoids.' 'Well, you have to have hemorrhoids.' I said, 'Why?' He said, 'It gives you a concerned look.'"**

Roy Moore
Official Photograph

The Low of the Low: Political Analyst Michael Baronet explained his lifetime trajectory in a speech at Grand Valley State University in Grand Rapids, Michigan: **"I have gone from one profession to another in my speckled career. Each one, which had tended to pay less and have a lower level of intellectual honesty and integrity than the one before. So I started off with law. Then I moved slightly down to political consulting. Then a real dropping in intellectual honesty and integrity, going down to journalism. And there's only one thing left, which in Academia. "**

Michael Barone
Photograph by Gage Skidmore

Every Municipality Gets a Visit: In 2006, losing Massachusetts Republican Lieutenant Governor nominee Reed Hillman visited all 351 municipalities in Massachusetts.

Reed Hillman
Official Photograph

Miscellaneous

White House Chef is Not a Man: The picture below of White House chef Martha Mulvey appeared in *The Evening Independent* of St. Petersburg, Florida in 1923. The caption oddly reads: **"The White House Chef is Not a Man!"**

The White House chef is not a man. Mrs. Martha Mulvey came to the White House during President Taft's administration. She not only prepares the daily meals for the chief executive and his family, but she also plans all the state dinners.

Martha Mulvey
Photograph printed in *The St. Petersburg Times*,
Copyright Harris & Ewing

Using the Holy Bible to Explain Tax Deductions and Fertilizer: In the 1982 case of *Schenk v. Commissioner of Internal Revenue*, Fifth Circuit Judge Irving Loeb Goldberg wrote: **"To every thing there is a season, and a time to every purpose under the heaven: A time to be born, and a time to die; a time to plant, and a time to pluck up that which is planted, a time to purchase fertilizer, and a time to take a deduction for that which is purchased."**

Judge Irving Loeb Goldberg
Texas Law Library, The University of Texas at Austin

Tammany Hall Stooge: John P. O'Brien was elected Mayor of New York City in 1932. He was the handpicked candidate of Tammany Hall (The Democratic Political Machine). O'Brien was not his own man. The day following his inauguration as Mayor, a reporter asked him who he would appoint as the next Police Chief. Referring to the Tammany Hall bosses, O'Brien responded: **"I don't know, they haven't told me yet."**

John P. O' Brien
Official Photograph

Miscellaneous

The Koch Rule: New York City Mayor Ed Koch did not require his supporters to support him on every issue. When running for re-election in 1989, Koch opined: **"If you agree with me on nine out of twelve issues, vote for me. If you agree with me on twelve out of twelve issues, see a psychiatrist."**

Ed Koch
Official Photograph

Author gets Unexpected Big Check: In 2018, the book *Fire and Fury* by Michael Wolf, which chronicles the administration of Donald Trump, became a best seller. However, not knowing there are two books with the same name, many readers accidentally purchased a book written in 2008 by University of Toronto Law Professor Randall Hansen about the allied bombing in WWII. A happy Hansen saw his book reach best-seller status. A bemused Hansen told *The Guardian:* **"It amused me. Part of me thought: can people really be that dumb to be confusing these books?"** Hansen reveled **"There was one tweet, he came forward and said, 'I bought this book by accident and there's no way I'm reading it,' in kind of this accusatory tone. I thought, well, it's not quite my fault, mate."**

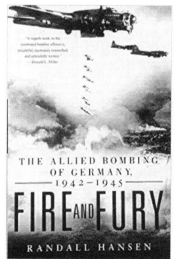

Fire and Fury by Randall Hansen

The Emperor Has Clothes: The Office of Mayor in Boston is almost omnipotent in that the city has a strong Mayor system, and a weak City Council. In 1967, when Kevin White was about to assume the office, his predecessor John Collins told him: **"It's Not Mayor, It's Emperor."**

John Collins
Boston Redevelopment Authority

The Politics of Kissing: In 1968, Norma B. Handloff, the Mayor of Newark, Delaware, told a luncheon gathering at a Temple University Club: **"Politicians are the greatest kissers in the world, and they don't kiss babies. Democrats kiss more than Republicans. They even kiss people they've met for the first time. Of course, I don't know what that proves."**

International Kissing Symbol

Miscellaneous

A Horse-whipping Senator: During a debate on legislation to combat Aids in 1991, U.S. Senator Jesse Helms (R-NC) said: **"I'm so old-fashioned, I believe in horse-whipping."** (Horse-whipping is the act of whipping a horse to control it.)

Jesse Helms
Official Photograph

That's Politics: At the funeral of former Massachusetts State Treasurer and Receiver General Robert Q. Crane, Businessman Jack Connors told the audience that he asked Crane which candidate he should support in a race, Crane responded: **"That's the easiest question anyone's ever asked me. We're going to be with the winner. We're going to support everyone, and remind the winner that 'We've been with you from the very beginning."**

Robert Q. Crane
Official Photograph

That Works: When U.S. Senator Alan Simpson (R-WY) was asked his **"church preference,"** he deadpanned: **"red brick."**

Alan Simpson
Official Photograph

Hard Not to Take Seriously: In a 1950 address before a Republican crowd in Wheeling, WV, U.S. Senator Joseph McCarthy (R-WI) gained the nation's attention by waving a piece of paper and claiming to have **"57 cases of individuals who appear to be either card-carrying members or certainly loyal to the Communist Party, but nevertheless are still helping to shape our foreign policy.** After the address, McCarthy told assembled news reporters: **"Look, you guys. That was a political speech to a bunch of Republicans. Don't take it seriously."**

Joseph McCarthy
Library of Congress

Miscellaneous

A Candidate With a Coonskin Cap: Memphis, TN political boss Ed Crump was a vociferous opponent of U.S. Senate Candidate Estes Kefauver. Crump wrote an editorial lampooning him by comparing Kefauver to a pet coon. Kefauver then sported a coonskin hat, telling supporters: **"I may be a coon, but I ain't Mr. Crump's pet coon."** From that point forward, Kefauver wore a coonskin cap when addressing a crowd.

Estes Kefauver Sporting his Signature Coonskin Cap on the cover of *Time Magazine*.

Not Elegant, But it Get the Point Across: According to a *New York Times* report, U.S. Senator Joe Manchin (D-WV) is no fan of the Senate, telling colleagues: **"This place sucks."**

Joe Manchin
Official Photograph

It's All Relative: U.S. Representative Stephen Lynch (D-MA) is sometimes referred to as the most conservative member of the Massachusetts Congressional delegation. Lynch takes that claim with a grain of salt. Lynch told the *Boston Globe*: **"Calling me the least liberal member from Massachusetts is like calling me the slowest Kenyan in the Boston Marathon. It's all relative."**

Stephen Lynch
Official Photograph

Teaching the "Say Hey Kid:" As a pupil at Fairfield Industrial High School in Birmingham, Alabama, future major league baseball Hall of Famer Willie Mays was a student of Angelina Rice, the mother of future U.S. Secretary of State Condoleezza Rice.

Willie Mays
Library of Congress

Congressional Fashion Critic: During Donald Trump's 2017 State of the Union Address, some female Democratic lawmakers wore white clothing in protest of the President. U.S. Representative Kevin Cramer (R-ND), a stalwart supporter of Trump observed of this action: **"It is a syndrome. There is no question, there is a disease associated with the notion that a bunch of women would wear bad-looking white pantsuits in solidarity with Hillary Clinton to celebrate her loss. You cannot get that weird."**

Kevin Cramer
Official Photograph

Democrats Commit Many More Mass Murders? In a 2018 radio interview, U.S. Representative Claudia Tenney (R-NY) observed: **"It's interesting that so many of these people that commit the mass murders end up being Democrats."**

Claudia Tenney
Official Photograph

Not a Workaholic: U.S. Senator Eugene McCarthy (D-MN) was known in the halls of Congress as a lackadaisical member of Congress, who would spend time reading poetry in his office, often missing votes and committee hearings. His colleagues and their staff members mocked his office as **"Sleepy Hollow."**

Eugene McCarthy
Official Photograph

Republican Supports a Democrat: In a rare display of bipartisan support, U.S. Senator Richard Burr (R-NC) sports a bumper sticker for the reelection of his Democratic colleague Joe Manchin of West Virginia on the back of his Volkswagen.

Richard Burr
Official Photograph

Miscellaneous

Seventeenth Century Values: Meldrim Thompson Jr. served as Governor of New Hampshire from 1973-1979. He was ultra conservative, advocating that the State National Guard receive nuclear weapons. When he was accused of propounding 18th century beliefs, Thompson responded: **"My beliefs are rooted in the values of the 17th century, and I'm proud of it."**

Meldrim Thomson Jr.
Official Photograph

Republican Gangsta Rap Enthusiast: U.S. Senator Marco Rubio (R-FL) told *GQ Magazine* that the rapper Pit Bull's songs are **"all party songs. There's no message for him, compared to like an Eminem. But look, there's always been a role for that in American music. There's always been a party person, but he's a young guy. You know, maybe as he gets older, he'll reflect in his music more as time goes on. I mean he's not Tupac. He's not gonna be writing poetry."**

Marco Rubio
Official Photograph

A Leg Up in Politics: In 2012, U.S. Representative Louise Slaughter (D-NY) suffered a shattered leg as the result of a fall she suffered during her re-election campaign. Making light of the circumstances, Slaughter joked that her new campaigning slogan would be: **"Vote Louise. She has a leg up."**

Louise Slaughter
Official Photograph

Political Porn: Adult film actress Melody "Mimi Miyagi" Domanyo: ran for the Republican Gubernatorial nomination in Nevada in 2006. She came in fifth place, garnering just 1.17% of the vote. Her slogan was: **"I'm bare and honest at all times."** She pledged to deal with gang violence **"so they don't do it anymore."**

Melody "Mimi Miyagi" Domanyo for Governor Campaign Poster

Chapter XXIII

This Date in American Political History

This Date
In American Political History

January

January 1, 1863 – President Abraham Lincoln signs **The Emancipation Proclamation**. The edict orders that all slaves "are, and henceforward shall be free."

January 2, 1939 – At age 31, Harold Stassen is sworn in as Governor of Minnesota, making him the youngest governor in Minnesota History.

January 3, 1992 – President George H. W. Bush and Russian President Boris Yeltsin sign **Start ll**, the **Strategic Arms Reduction Treaty** designed to eradicate heavy intercontinental ballistic missiles (ICBMS) and all other multiple-warhead (MIRVed) ICBMS.

January 4, 1995 – For the first time in 40 years, the Republican Party takes the reigns of power in both the U.S. House of Representatives and the U.S. Senate.

January 5, 1972 – President Richard M. Nixon and NASA Administrator James C. Fletcher announce the development of the Space Shuttle Program.

January 6, 1853 – President-Elect Franklin Pierce, his wife and their 11-year-old son are involved in an accident when their railroad car derails after it rolls over an embankment. Pierce and his wife survive but their son Benjamin ("Bennie") is crushed to death.

January 7, 1980 – President Jimmy Carter signs **The Chrysler Corporation Loan Guarantee Act**, which allowed Chrysler to avoid bankruptcy.

January 8, 2002 – President George W. Bush signs **The No Child Left Behind Act**, which enacts standards-based education reform.

January 9, 1951 -- The United Nations headquarters opens in New York City.

January 10, 1776 – Thomas Paine publishes *Common Sense* which gave *causes belli* for the colonies to succeed from Great Brittan.

January 11, 1964 – The report "Smoking and Health: Report of the Advisory Committee to the Surgeon General of the United States," was published. The report concluded definitively that there is a link between cancer and chronic bronchitis with cigarette smoking. At the time, General Luther Leonidas, M.D. was the U.S. Surgeon

January 12, 1932 – Arkansas voters make Hattie Caraway the first woman popularly elected to the United State Senate.

January 13, 1966 –U.S. Housing and Urban Development Secretary Robert C. Weaver is sworn in as the first African-American member of a President's cabinet.

January 14, 1963 – The Connecticut Colony Council adopts **The Fundamental Orders**. This written Constitution established a framework for the government of Connecticut.

January 15, 1973 – Frank Sturgis, Eugenio Martinez, Bernard Barker, and James McCord plead guilty to charges of conspiracy, burglary and wiretapping, stemming from the Watergate affair.

January 16, 1883 – President Chester A. Arthur signs into law **The Pendleton Civil Service Reform Act**, which requires the hiring and promotion of federal employees to be based on merit rather than on political connections. In addition, the law makes it a crime to raise political money on federal property.

January 17, 1961 – In his farewell address to the American people, President Dwight D. Eisenhower warns of the proliferation of a "Military-Industrial-Complex."

January 18, 1919 – The Paris Peace Conference opens at the Château of Versailles, near Paris, France. Representatives from more than 30 countries meet to negotiate a treaty to end WWI.

January 19, 1981 – The U.S. and Iranian governments agree to **The Algiers Accords**. The U.S. agrees not to interfere in Iran's internal affairs and Iran agrees to release the 52 Americans it is holding hostage.

January 20, 1981 – After 444 days in captivity, 52 American hostages are set free by Iranian students.

January 21, 1920 – The Paris Peace Conference came to an end. The Conference had begun a year earlier, on January 18, 1919. The Conference was called to negotiate the end of WWI.

January 22, 1973 – The U.S. Supreme Court hands down the landmark decision in *Roe v. Wade.* The court holds that states cannot regulate abortion during the first trimester. In the second trimester the states can regulate abortion "in ways that are reasonably related to maternal health." In the third trimester, the state can proscribe abortion "except where it is necessary in appropriate medical judgment for the preservation of the life or health of the mother."

January 23, 1845 – The U.S. Congress sets the Tuesday after the First Monday in November to be the day when Presidential elections are held.

January 24, 2003 – The **Homeland Security Department** is inaugurated as a cabinet department. The first Secretary of the Department is former Pennsylvania Governor Tom Ridge.

January 25, 1963 – President John F. Kennedy holds the first live television Press Conference by an incumbent U.S. President.

January 26, 1998 – President Bill Clinton, at the end of an event promoting his childcare initiative in the Roosevelt Room, exclaims: "I did not have sexual relations with that woman, Miss Lewinsky."

January 27, 1973 – **The Paris Agreement on Ending the War and Restoring Peace in Vietnam** is signed by representatives of the United States, North Vietnam, South Vietnam and the Provisional Revolutionary Government.

January 28, 1916 – President Woodrow Wilson nominates Louis Brandies to become the first Jewish U.S. Supreme Court Justice in American history.

January 29, 2002 – President George W. Bush declares that "Iraq, Iran and North Korea" constitute an "axis of evil."

January 30, 1835 – Richard Lawrence, who is mentally ill and believes he is King Richard III of England, attempts to assassinate President Andrew Jackson at a funeral. Lawrence believes that Jackson was keeping money from him and had killed his father. The shot misfires. This is the first known attempt to assassinate a U.S. President.

January 31, 1865 – General Robert E. Lee is appointed Commander-in-Chief of the forces for the Confederate States of America.

February

February 1, 1790 – The U.S. Supreme Court convenes for the fist time at the Merchants Exchange Building in what is then the nation's capital, New York City.

February 2, 1848 – The **Treaty of Guadalupe Hidalgo** is signed by representatives from the U.S. and Mexico, ending the Mexican-American War. The document requires Mexico to abrogate 55% of its territory in exchange for fifteen million dollars in compensation for damage to Mexican property from the war.

February 3, 1913 – The Sixteenth Amendment to the U.S. Constitution is ratified, sanctioning a federal income tax.

February 4, 2004 – The Supreme Judicial Court of Massachusetts rules that a state ban on Gay Marriage is unconstitutional.

February 5, 2003 – U.S. Secretary of State Colin Powell makes the case to the United Nations Security Council that Iraqi President Saddam Hussein has biological weapons and is trying to acquire nuclear weapons.

February 6, 1889 – **The Treaty of Paris**, ending the Spanish-American War, is ratified by the U.S. Senate. Under the treaty, the U.S. is awarded Cuba, the Philippines, Puerto Rico, and Guam.

February 7, 1861 – Alabama, Florida, Georgia, Louisiana, Mississippi, South Carolina, and Texas accept a provisional constitution for the Confederate States of America and inaugurate Montgomery, Alabama as the capital.

February 8, 1978 – U.S. Senate proceedings are broadcast live on radio for the first time.

February 9, 1825 – With no candidate garnering a majority of electoral votes, under terms of the Twelfth Amendment to the U.S. Constitution, the U.S. House of Representatives selects John Quincy Adams as President.

February 10, 1989 – Democrat Ron Brown is elected as the first African-American chairman of a major U.S political party.

February 11, 2006 – Vice President Dick Cheney shoots attorney Harry Whittington by accident during a hunting escapade in South Texas. Whittington suffers a "silent" heart attack but survives.

February 12, 1999 – President Bill Clinton is acquitted by the U.S. Senate on charges of perjury to a grand jury and obstruction of justice.

February 13, 1635 – Boston Latin is founded, becoming the first U.S. public school in the colonies.

February 14, 1899 – The U.S. Congress approves the use of voting machines for use in federal elections.

February 15, 1898 – The warship *U.S.S. Maine* explodes, causing the deaths of 260 men. This leads to the Spanish-American War. Though conventional belief was that the Spanish blew up the ship, in 1950 the U.S. Navy ruled that a faulty boiler had sunk the *U.S.S. Maine*.

February 16, 1741 – Benjamin Franklin debuts: *The General Magazine and Historical Chronicle for all the British Plantations in America.*

February 17, 1819 – The U.S. Congress passes the **Missouri Compromise**, which admits Missouri to the Union as a slave state and Maine as a free state.

February 18, 1856 – Former President Millard Fillmore captures the Presidential nomination of the Nativist American Party, a.k.a. the Know Nothing Party.

February 19, 1942 – President Franklin D. Roosevelt signs **Executive Order 9066** sanctioning the internment of Japanese Americans.

February 20, 1996 – Former Reagan Communications Advisor Patrick Buchanan Stuns the Republican establishment by winning the New Hampshire Republican Presidential Primary.

February 21, 1965 – Civil Rights leader Malcolm X is assassinated in Manhattan's Audubon Ballroom by three members of the Nation of Islam.

February 22, 1924 – President Calvin Coolidge delivers the first Presidential radio address from the White House.

February 23, 2008 – Democratic Presidential candidate Hillary Clinton excoriates rival Barack Obama for mailings his campaign put out criticizing her views on NAFTA and health insurance reform. At a campaign stop in Cincinnati, Ohio, Clinton exclaims "Shame on you, Barack Obama!"

February 24, 1868 – President Andrew Johnson is impeached by the U.S. House of Representatives for violating **The Tenure of Office Act** of 1867 by suspending Secretary of War Edwin Stanton.

February 25, 1870 – Mississippi Republican Hiram Revels becomes the first African-American to serve in the U.S. Senate. The Mississippi State Senate voted for him to serve the remainder of Senator Albert G. Brown's term. Brown had resigned the U.S. Senate seat at the beginning of the Civil War in 1861.

February 26, 1939 – First Lady Eleanor Roosevelt resigns from the *Daughters of the American Revolution* after the organization would not allow African-American opera singer Marian Anderson to sing to an integrated crowd at Constitution Hall in Washington, D.C. Mrs. Roosevelt obtains permission for her to sing in front of the Lincoln Memorial.

February 27, 1951 – The Twenty Second Amendment to the U.S. Constitution is ratified, limiting U.S. presidents to two terms in office.

February 28, 1946 – Ho Chi Minh, the Prime Minister of the Democratic Republic of Vietnam, writes a letter to President Harry S. Truman, requesting assistance in North Vietnam's fight for independence.

February 29, 1956 – President Dwight D. Eisenhower announces his intention to run for re-election.

March

March 1, 1781 – **The Articles of Confederation and Perpetual Union** is ratified by the Second Continental Congress.

March 2, 1877 – After a protracted electoral process, the U.S. Congress declares Rutherford B. Hayes the winner of the 1876 Presidential election over New York Governor Samuel Tilden.

March 3, 1849 – The U.S. Department of Interior is created.

March 4, 1987 – In a televised address, President Ronald Reagan states: "A few months ago I told the American people I did not trade arms for hostages. My heart and my best intentions still tell me that's true, but the facts and the evidence tell me it is not."

March 5, 1933 – President Franklin D. Roosevelt orders a four-day bank holiday.

March 6, 1820 – President James Monroe signs the **Missouri Compromise**, which admits Maine into the union as a free state and Missouri as a slave state.

March 7, 1801 – Massachusetts enacts the first state voter registration law.

March 8, 1983 – President Ronald Reagan calls the Soviet Union an "Evil Empire" while addressing the Annual Convention of the *National Association of Evangelicals.*

March 9, 1976 – Former Georgia Governor Jimmy Carter wins the Florida Democratic Presidential primary, beating Alabama Governor George C. Wallace, and becoming the candidate of the South.

March 10, 1848 – U.S. Senate ratifies **The Treaty of Guadalupe Hidalgo**, ending the Mexican War.

March 11, 1930 – President William Howard Taft becomes the first President to be buried at Arlington National Cemetery.

March 12, 1968 – U.S. Senator and Presidential candidate Eugene McCarthy (D-MN) scores a surprisingly strong showing in the New Hampshire Democratic Primary. He garnered 42.4% of the vote, just 7 points shy of the 49% mustered by President Lyndon B. Johnson.

March 13, 1868 – The U.S. Senate trial of President Andrew Johnson commences.

March 14, 1900 – The U.S. moves to the Gold Standard.

March 15, 1965 – Addressing a joint session of the U.S. Congress on Civil Rights, President Lyndon B. Johnson declares: "We Shall Overcome."

March 16, 1802 – The U.S. Congress approved legislation establishing the United States Military Academy at West Point.

March 17, 2008 – New York Governor Elliot Spitzer resigns his office after *The New York Times* reveals that he had utilized an illegal prostitution ring called the Emperors Club.

March 18, 1963 - In the case of *Gideon v. Wainwright*, the U.S Supreme Court rules that the Sixth Amendment to the U.S. Constitution mandates state courts to provide counsel in criminal cases for defendants who cannot afford one.

March 19, 1979 – Congress begins broadcasting live on C-SPAN. The first speaker is U.S. Representative Al Gore (D-TN.)

March 20, 2003 – Troops from the United States, the United Kingdom, Australia, and Poland invade Iraq.

March 21, 2000 – U.S. Representative Bobby Rush (D-IL), running for re-election, defeats his primary challenger, State Senator Barack Obama, by thirty-one points.

March 22, 1933 – President Franklin D. Roosevelt signs **The Beer and Wine Revenue Act**. This measure taxes alcoholic beverages and allows states to regulate these beverages.

March 23, 1983 – President Ronald Reagan proposes the **Strategic Defense Initiative (SDI)** to protect the U.S. against ballistic missiles.

March 24, 1999 – NATO begins a 78-day bombing campaign of Serbia, which successfully leads to Serbian President Slobodan Milosevic withdrawing his forces from Kosovo.

March 25, 1980 – In his bid for re-election, President Jimmy Carter loses the Democratic Presidential Primary in New York State to Challenger U.S. Senator Edward M. Kennedy (D-MA).

March 26, 1979 – Egyptian President Anwar el-Sadat and Israeli Prime Minister Menachem Begin sign the Camp David Accords, which ends a state of war between the two nations. President Jimmy Carter negotiated The Accords.

March 27, 2002 – President George W. Bush signs **The Campaign Reform Act of 2002**, regulating campaign spending and outlawing "soft money," contributions by unions and corporations to political parties.

March 28, 2007 – *The National Organization for Women* endorses Hillary Clinton for President.

March 29, 1975 – President Gerald R. Ford signs **Proclamation 4360**, which ends draft registration requirements for American males between 18 – 25 years old. (President Jimmy Carter later restored the draft registration)

March 30, 1981 – President Ronald Reagan is shot leaving the Washington Hilton Hotel after speaking to an AFL-CIO convention. Reagan suffered a punctured lung and was treated at George Washington University Hospital. The shooter is John Hinckley Jr., who was enamored with actor Jodie Foster. Hinckley thought if he shot a President, he would be a national figure with name-recognition tantamount to Foster.

March 31, 1968 – President Lyndon B. Johnson shocks the nation by announcing: "I shall not seek, and I will not accept the nomination of my party for another term as your President."

April

April 1, 1789 – The U.S. House of Representatives elects U.S. Representative Frederick Muhlenberg of Pennsylvania as its first Speaker of the House.

April 2, 1917 – President Woodrow Wilson asks the U.S. Congress for a declaration of war against Germany. Congress approves the declaration four days later.

April 3, 1948 – President Harry S. Truman signs the **European Recovery Program,** a.k.a. **The Marshall Plan.** The Plan provides $13.3 billion in aid to sixteen European countries between 1948 and 1952.

April 4, 1968 – *Southern Christian Leadership Conference* President Martin Luther King Jr. is shot and killed at the Lorrain Motel in Memphis, Tennessee. Escaped prisoner James Earl Ray admitted to the shooting and was convicted of the crime. He later declares his innocence.

April 5, 1792 – President George Washington vetoes **"The Apportionment Bill"** of 1792. This is the first presidential veto in U.S. history. The legislation would have fixed the size of the United States House of Representatives based on the United States Census of 1790. Washington believed the bill was unconstitutional.

April 6, 1896 – Former President Benjamin Harrison gets married for the second time. He marries Mary Scott Lord Dimmick, who was the niece of Harrison's first wife, the late Caroline Lavinia Scott Harrison. Dimmick is twenty-five years younger than Mr. Harrison. Harrison's children do not approve of the marriage and boycott the wedding.

April 7, 1965 – At an address at Johns Hopkins University, President Lyndon B. Johnson delivers his **"Peace Without Conquest"** speech, in which he declares his desire for "unconditional discussions." He proposes $1 billion in aid for a development project along the Mekong River.

April 8, 1912 – The Seventeenth Amendment to the U.S. Constitution, which allows for the direct election of U.S. Senators, is ratified. Prior to this amendment, state legislatures performed this function.

April 9, 1867 – The U.S. Senate ratifies **The Alaska Treaty of Cessation**, which provides for the purchase of Alaska from Russia.

April 10, 1869 – The U.S. Congress votes to increase the number of justices on the U.S. Supreme Court from 7 to 9.

April 11, 1951 – President Harry S. Truman announces that he has relieved General Douglas Macarthur of his position as Allied Commander of United Nations forces in the Far East. Macarthur and Truman had clashed when Macarthur threatened to attack China during the Korean War.

April 12, 1945 – President Franklin D. Roosevelt dies in office of a cerebral hemorrhage.

April 13, 1943 – The Thomas Jefferson Memorial is dedicated in Washington, D.C. on the 200th anniversary of Jefferson's birth.

April 14, 1912 – At the beginning of a baseball game between the Washington Senators and the Philadelphia Athletics on April 14, 1910 at Griffith Stadium, umpire Billy Evans hands a baseball to President William Howard Taft and asks him to throw it over home plate. The president does, and since then it has become a tradition for Presidents to throw out the first pitch on Opening Day.

April 15, 1865 – President Abraham Lincoln dies nine hours after being shot by Actor John Wilkes Booth while attending a showing of the play *American Cousin* at Ford's Theater in Washington, D.C.

April 16, 1947 – At an unveiling of his portrait in the South Carolina House of Representatives, Financier Bernard Baruch coins the term "Cold War: describing the rivalry between the United States and the Soviet Union. Baruch was a native South Carolinian. In describing the rivalry between the United States and the Soviet Union, Baruch referred to the rivalry as **"The Cold War."**

April 17, 1961 – Acting on a CIA plan approved by President John F. Kennedy, 400 armed Cuban exiles land at the Bay of Pigs on the coast of Cuba in a failed attempt to topple Cuban President Fidel Castro.

April 18, 1978 – The U.S. Senate votes to cede the Panama Canal to Panama on December 31, 1999.

April 19, 1933 – President Franklin D. Roosevelt announces the U.S. will leave the Gold Standard.

April 20, 1979 – While President Jimmy Carter is on a fishing trip in Plains, Georgia, a rabbit swims toward his boat. Carter swats at the rabbit with his canoe paddle, scaring it away.

April 21, 1789 – John Adams is sworn in as the nation's first Vice President at *Federal Hall* in Manhattan.

April 22, 1864 – The U.S. Congress authorizes the motto: "**In God We Trust**" on all newly minted U.S. coins.

April 23, 2004 - President George W. Bush lifts most sanctions against Libya in response to Libya's denunciation of terrorism and its actions to dismantle its Weapons of Mass Destruction.

April 24, 2007 – U.S. Representative Dennis Kucinich (D-OH) introduces **House Resolution 333**, a resolution impeaching Vice President Dick Cheney for fabricating the threat of Iraq having and potentially using Weapons of Mass Destruction and links between al Qaeda and Iraq, and threatening aggressive action toward Iran. The resolution has twelve co-sponsors.

April 25, 1945 - The United Nations Conference on International Organizations commences in San Francisco, California. The convention, which consists of 50 nations, drafts the United Nations Charter.

April 26, 1984 – President Ronald Reagan becomes the first U.S. President to visit China since full diplomatic relations were restored.

April 27, 1981 – The Gerald R. Ford Presidential Museum is dedicated in Grand Rapids, Michigan.

April 28, 1980 – U.S. Secretary of State Cyrus Vance resigns his post as a protest of the Carter Administration's military plan to rescue American hostages held in Iran.

April 29, 1861 – The Maryland House of Delegates votes not to secede from the Union.

April 30, 1789 – George Washington becomes the first President of the United States under the U.S. Constitution.

May

May 1, 2003 – Aboard the *U.S.S. Abraham Lincoln,* President George W. Bush declares: "Major Combat operations in Iraq have ended."

May 2, 1968 – A movement to draft California Governor Ronald Reagan for the Republican Presidential nomination begins.

May 3, 1802 – Washington, D.C. becomes a city.

May 4, 1970 – Four Kent State students die and nine are wounded from a confrontation with National Guardsman at a protest of the U.S. incursion into Cambodia.

May 5, 1827 – Future President Andrew Johnson marries Eliza McCardle.

May 6, 1960 – President Dwight D. Eisenhower signs the **Civil Rights Act of 1960,** providing federal oversight of local voter registration facilities.

May 7, 1968 – Alabama Governor Lurleen Brigham Wallace dies of cancer. She is the first female governor who dies in office.

May 8, 1861 – Richmond, Virginia becomes the capital of the Confederate States of America.

May 9, 1974 – The impeachment hearings against President Richard M. Nixon are gaveled into session by the U.S. House Judiciary Committee.

May 10, 1974 – House Republican Conference Chairman John B. Anderson (R-IL) calls on President Richard M. Nixon to resign. He says Nixon "has a deplorable lack of understanding" of the type of behavior the Presidency requires.

May 11, 1956 – Former President Harry S. Truman begins a four-week trip to Europe.

May 12, 2002 – Former President Jimmy Carter becomes the first former (or incumbent) U.S. President to visit Cuba under the regime of President Fidel Castro, which took the reigns of power in 1959.

May 13, 1884 – The U.S. Congress votes to repeal the **1862 Ironclad Test Oath**, which requires all civil servants (excluding members of Congress) and military personnel to affirm that they had never previously engaged in criminal or disloyal conduct.

May 14, 1975 – President Gerald R. Ford orders U.S. forces to retake the *S.S. Mayaguez,* an American merchant ship which the Khmer Rouge of Cambodia seized in international waters. The vessel is recovered and the 39 crewmembers are saved. Forty-one Americans die in the rescue attempt. Their names are the last on the Vietnam War Memorial in Washington, D.C.

May 15, 1972 – Democratic Presidential Candidate George Wallace is shot four times by Arthur Bremer at a campaign stop in Laurel, Maryland leaving Wallace paralyzed.

May 16, 1824 – Vice President Levi Morton who served under President Benjamin Harrison is born. **May 16, 1920** – Vice President Levi Morton dies.

May 17, 1954 – In the case of *Brown v. Board of Topeka,* the Supreme Court rules that "Separate but Equal is inheritably unequal" and disallows school segregation.

May 18, 1876 – The *Greenback Party*, which advocates the use of paper money, nominates its first presidential candidate, industrialist Peter Cooper.

May 19, 1921 – President Warren G. Harding signs **The Emergency Quota Act**, which limits to three percent the amount of persons living in the U.S. from any foreign nation, using 1910 census figures.

May 20, 1993 – President Bill Clinton signs the **National Voter Registration Act,** a.k.a. B mandating that states provide voter-registration services at disability centers, libraries, registration centers, schools, and through mail-in registration.

May 21, 1960 – The fourth and final presidential debate is held between U.S. Senator John F. Kennedy (D-MA) and Vice President Richard M. Nixon.

May 22, 1964 – At a commencement speech at the University of Michigan at Ann Arbor, President Lyndon B. Johnson announces a series of domestic programs which he coins "The Great Society."

May 23, 2006 – Former President Jimmy Carter and Vice President Walter Mondale become the longest living former U.S. President and Vice President in history, surpassing John Adams and Thomas Jefferson's record of 25 years, 122 days.

May 24, 2001 –U.S. Senator James Jeffords (R-VT) announces that he is leaving the Republican Party to become an Independent who will caucus with the Democrats. His switch is important because it gives the Democrats a one-vote majority in the Senate.

May 25, 1787 – The Constitutional Convention commences in Philadelphia, Pennsylvania. The meeting is advertised as a vehicle to amend the *Articles of Confederation and Perpetual Union*, but the result is that the delegates scrap the Articles and supplant them with the *Constitution of the United States*.

May 26, 1972 – President Richard M. Nixon and Leonid Brezhnev, the General Secretary of the Communist Party of the Soviet Union, sign **The Treaty on the Limitation of Anti-Ballistic Missile Systems** (ABM), mandating each country have only two ABM deployment areas.

May 27, 1997 – The U.S. Supreme Court unanimously rules that Paula Jones's sexual harassment lawsuit against President Bill Clinton can proceed while the President is still in office.

May 28, 1968 – U.S. Senator Eugene McCarthy (D-MN) upsets U.S. Senator Robert F. Kennedy (D-NY) in the Oregon Democratic Presidential primary 44.7% to 38.8%. This is the first time a Kennedy is defeated in an election.

May 29, 1968 – President Lyndon B. Johnson signs **The Consumer Credit Protection Act** into law. The measure requires creditors to state the cost of borrowing in terms the American people can understand.

May 30, 1806 – Future President Andrew Jackson shoots duelist Charles Dickinson in a duel after Dickinson insults Jackson's wife, Rachael Donelson.

May 31, 1989 – Speaker of the U.S. House of Representatives Jim Wright (D–TX) resigns the speakership amid eighty-nine charges of breaking congressional strictures. The investigation was begun by U.S. Representative Newt Gingrich (R-GA), himself a future Speaker.

June

June 1, 2006 – Dennis Hastert (R-IL), Speaker of the U.S. House of Representatives, becomes the longest serving Republican speaker in history. Hastert became Speaker on January 6, 1999.

June 2, 1924 – President Calvin Coolidge signs **The Indian Citizenship Act** into law, endowing citizenship to all Native Americans.

June 3, 1884 – The Republican National Convention opens in Chicago, Illinois. The presidential nomination is awarded to former Speaker of the U.S. House of Representatives and U.S. Secretary of State James G. Blaine. This is the last time a sitting Republican President (who was Chester A. Arthur) at the time is denied his party's presidential nomination.

June 4, 1912 – Massachusetts becomes first U.S. state to enact a minimum wage. The provision only applied to women and children.

June 5, 1968 – Presidential candidate Robert F. Kennedy is shot at the Ambassador hotel in Los Angeles, California by Arab Nationalist Sirhan Sirhan. Kennedy dies the next morning.

June 6, 1989 – U.S. House Majority Leader Tom Foley (D-WA) is elected Speaker of the U.S. House of Representatives, succeeding Jim Wright, who was forced to resign amid charges of ethics improprieties.

June 7, 2001 – President George W. Bush signs **The Economic Growth and Tax Relief Reconciliation Act**, providing $1.35 trillion in tax cuts for Americans.

June 8, 2008 – A fire severely damages the Texas Governor's Mansion in Austin. The Mansion was vacant at the time of the blaze and was under renovation. Governor Rick Perry was in Stockholm, Sweden at the time of the fire.

June 9, 1980 – Democratic Presidential candidate Jimmy Carter wins the coveted endorsement of Chicago Mayor Richard J. Daley in the Democratic presidential primary.

June 10, 1924 – The Republican Party, at its national convention in Cleveland, Ohio, nominates Calvin Coolidge to serve a full term as President.

June 11, 2001 – President George W. Bush makes his first overseas trip as President, visiting Belgium, Poland, Slovenia, and Sweden.

June 12, 2006 – U.S. Senator Robert C. Byrd (D-WV) breaks the all time Senate membership record, serving 17,327 days in the U.S. Senate.

June 13, 1970 – President Richard M. Nixon announces the appointment of the *President's Commission on Campus Unrest*, a nine-member commission to investigate campus violence. The Chairman of the commission is former Pennsylvania Governor William W. Scranton.

June 14, 1943 – In the case of West *Virginia Board of Education v. Barnette,* the U.S. Supreme Court rules that the First Amendment to the U.S. Constitution protects students from being forced to recite the Pledge of Allegiance and salute the American flag. The decision is handed down on Flag Day.

June 15, 1961 John Tower was elected in a special election to fill U.S. Senate seat representing Texas that was recently held by Vice President Lyndon B. Johnson. Tower becomes the first Republican to represent a Southern state since Reconstruction.

June 16, 1897 – A treaty annexing the Republic of Hawaii to the U.S. is signed.

June 17, 1930 – President Herbert Hoover signed **The Hawley-Smoot Tariff Act**, which raised tariffs on over 20,000 items in an effort to raise government revenue during the Great Depression.

June 18, 1873 – In the case of the *United States v. Susan B. Anthony.* Anthony, a suffragette, is found guilty of "unlawful voting" for voting in the 1872 Presidential election. She is penalized with a $100 fine, which she does not pay.

June 19, 1964 – A plane carting U.S. Senator Birch Bayh (D-IN), U.S. Senator Edward Kennedy (D-MA), and Kennedy aid Edward Moss crashes in Western Massachusetts. Bayh pulls Kennedy from the wreckage. No passenger is seriously hurt from the crash.

June 20, 1911 – The *National Association for the Advancement of Colored People (*the NAACP) formally incorporates in New York City.

June 21, 1898 – Guam, which the U.S. seized from Spain in the Spanish-American War, becomes a U.S. territory.

June 22, 1944 – President Franklin D. Roosevelt signs **The Servicemen's Readjustment Act** of 1944, a.k.a. the G.I. Bill into law. The act provides education benefits and unemployment compensation for U.S. veterans returning from WWII.

June 23, 1947 – The U.S. Congress overrides President Harry S. Truman's veto of **The Labor–Management Relations Act**, a.k.a., **The Taft–Hartley Act**, interdicting closed shops, banning unions from donating to political campaigns, and allowing employees to decline to be part of the collective bargaining process. In addition, the U.S. Attorney General is given an 80-day injunction when h/she believes a strike, or potential strike, might imperil the national health or safety." Though Truman vetoed the legislation, he wound up using it twelve times.

June 24, 1961 – President John F. Kennedy orders Vice President Lyndon B. Johnson to take charge of an effort to unify the U.S. satellite programs.

June 25, 1962 – The U.S. Supreme Court hands down the landmark decision in *Engel v. Vitale,* ruling that government-directed prayer in public schools is a violation of the Establishment Clause ("Government shall make no law respecting an establishment of religion") of the First Amendment to the U.S. Constitution.

June 26, 2008 – The U.S. Supreme Court rules in the case of *District of Columbia v. Heller* that the handgun ban in the District of Columbia is unconstitutional and that the Second Amendment to the U.S. Constitution protects the right of the individual to carry a firearm, but that the Second Amendment is not absolute. "It is not a right to keep and carry any weapon whatsoever in any manner whatsoever and for whatever purpose."

June 27, 1993 – In retaliation for a plot to kill former President George H.W. Bush, President Bill Clinton orders the bombing of the Iraqi Intelligence Service (IIS) headquarters.

June 28, 2007 – President George W. Bush nominates Admiral Michael Mullen to become the Chairman of the Joint Chiefs of Staff.

June 29, 1928 – At their national convention in Houston, Texas, the Democrats make New York Governor Al Smith the first Roman Catholic presidential nominee of a major U.S. political party in U.S. history.

June 30, 1982 – President Ronald Reagan issues *Executive Order 1236*, which establishes the President's Private Sector Survey on Cost Control in the Federal Government.

July

July 1, 1967 – The America Samoan Constitution takes effect, allowing for self-governing rule.

July 2, 1964 – President Lyndon B. Johnson signs **"The Civil Rights Act of 1964**." The statute forbids racial discrimination in public places.

July 3, 1952 – The U.S. Congress and President Harry S. Truman approve the Constitution for the Commonwealth of Puerto Rico.

July 4, 1826 - Presidents John Adams and Thomas Jefferson die on the 50th anniversary of the adoption of *The Declaration of Independence.*

July 5, 1960 – U.S. Senate Majority Leader Lyndon B. Johnson (D-TX) announces his candidacy for the Democratic nomination for President.

July 6, 2004 – Democratic Presidential nominee-apparent John Kerry announces his choice of former rival and U.S. Senator John Edwards (D-NC) as his Vice Presidential Running mate.

July 7, 1898 – President William McKinley signs **The Newlands Resolution**, which annexes Hawaii to the United States.

July 8, 1975 – President Gerald R. Ford announces that he will seek the Republican nomination for President in 1976.

July 9, 1924 – Former U.S. ambassador to the U.K. John William Davis is nominated on a record 103rd ballot as the Democratic Party's nominee for President.

July 10, 1850 – Vice President Millard Fillmore assumes the Presidency upon the death of President Zackary Taylor.

July 11, 1921 – William Howard Taft becomes the first and only former U.S. President to serve on the U.S. Supreme Court. He was nominated by President Warren G. Harding and confirmed by the U.S. Senate as Chief Justice of the United States.

July 12, 1984 – Democratic Presidential nominee-apparent Walter Mondale announces his choice of U.S. Representative Geraldine Ferraro (D-NY) to be his Vice Presidential running mate. She becomes the first woman nominated on a national ticket by a major political party.

July 13, 1985 – President Ronald Reagan undergoes surgery to remove polyps from his colon. Under a provision of the Twenty-Fifth Amendment to the U.S. Constitution, Vice President George H.W. Bush becomes acting President.

July 14, 2008 – *The New York Times* releases an op-ed entitled: "My Plan for Iraq" by Democratic Presidential candidate Barack Obama. Obama calls for a "phased redeployment of combat troops."

July 15, 1870 – Georgia becomes the last former Confederate state to re-join the Union.

July 16, 1996 – Arkansas Governor Jim Guy Tucker resigns after being convicted for fraud in the Whitewater Investigation. The charges are unrelated to Bill and Hilary Clinton. Arkansas law forbids convicted felons from serving as governor.

July 17, 2004 – While vacationing in Nantucket, Massachusetts, John Kerry, the presumptive Democratic Presidential nominee, is photographed windsurfing. The Republicans exploit this photograph in advertisements to caricature Kerry as a flip-flopper.

July 18, 1970 – Mary Jo Kopechne, a former staffer for New York Senator and Democratic Presidential candidate Robert F. Kennedy, dies in a car, which plunges off the Dike Bridge into a pond. The driver is Senator Edward Kennedy (D-MA). Kennedy swims to safety. He does not call authorities to tell them of the incident until the next day. He is punished for leaving the scene of the accident with a two-month jail sentence, which is suspended.

July 19, 1984 – At the Democratic National Convention, Presidential nominee Walter Mondale declares: "Mr. Reagan will raise taxes, and so will I. He won't tell you. I just did."

July 20, 1948 – President Harry S. Truman signs a proclamation calling for a peacetime draft and calling for 10 million men to register for military service within the next two months.

July 21, 1930 – The **U.S. Veterans Administration** is established.

July 22, 1955 – Vice President Richard M. Nixon becomes the first Vice President to preside over a Presidential Cabinet meeting, filling in for President Dwight D. Eisenhower who was recuperating from a heart attack.

July 23, 1987 – President Ronald Reagan announces the appointment of a 13-member Commission on the Human Immunodeficiency Virus Epidemic.

July 24, 2002 – The U.S. House of Representatives votes to expel U.S. Representative James Traficant (D-OH) after an Ohio jury finds him guilty on ten charges, including bribery, racketeering, fraud, and forcing congressional aides to work on his houseboat and farm without pay.

July 25, 2000 – President Bill Clinton, Israeli Prime Minister Ehud Barak, and Palestinian Authority Chairman Yasser Arafat emerge from a Camp David Summit without an agreement in the long-standing Israeli-Palestinian conflict.

July 26, 1952 – Illinois Governor Adlai Stevenson secures the nomination of the Democratic Party for President on the third ballot at the Democratic Convention held in Chicago.

July 27, 1953 – The **Korean War Armistice Agreement** is signed.

July 28, 1965 – President Lyndon B. Johnson orders the troop levels in Vietnam increased from 75,000 to 125,000.

July 29, 1989 – George W. Bush, who is serving as the Managing Partner for the Texas Rangers baseball team, agrees to trade young Sammy Sosa to the Chicago White Sox for veteran Designated hitter Harold Baines. Sosa goes on to be one of the greatest hitters in baseball history.

July 30, 1965 – President Lyndon B. Johnson signs **The Social Security Act of 1965**. The act established "Medicare," which provides health insurance for Americans 65 and older, and "Medicaid" which provides health insurance for the poor.

July 31, 1790 – The first U.S. patent is issued by President George Washington to Samuel Hopkins of Vermont. The patent covers a process for making potash and pearl ash.

August

August 1, 1923 – President Warren G. Harding dies of a stroke and is succeeded by Vice President Calvin Coolidge.

August 2, 1776 – Fifty-six delegates to the Second Continental Convention sign the **U.S. Declaration of Independence.**

August 3, 1972 – The U.S. Senate ratifies **The Anti-Ballistic Missile Treaty**, prohibiting the U.S. and Russia from deploying nationwide defenses against strategic ballistic missiles.

August 4, 1987– The Federal Communications Commission annuls **The Fairness Doctrine**, which mandated radio and TV stations to present controversial issues and to provide equitable coverage to different sides of the issue.

August 5, 1912 – The newly formed Progressive Party, a.k.a. the Bull Moose Party, nominates former Republican President Theodore Roosevelt for President.

August 6, 1965 – President Johnson signs **The National Voting Rights Act**, which disallows voter discrimination. The act bans practices in Southern states aimed at disenfranchising African-American voters, such as requiring them to pass a literary test.

August 7, 1964 – The U.S. Congress passes **The Gulf of Tonkin Resolution** giving President Lyndon B. Johnson *carte blanche* to use force in Vietnam.

August 8, 1925 – About 40,000 Ku Klux Klan members march in Washington, D.C. to protest civil rights protections for minority groups.

August 9, 1974 – Gerald Ford succeeds Richard M. Nixon to the Presidency. Nixon, the subject of the Watergate Scandal, announced his resignation the previous night.

August 10, 1846 – President James K. Polk signs legislation establishing **The Smithsonian Institution.**

August 11, 1852 – The anti-slavery Free Soil Party nominates New Hampshire Senator John P. Hale for President.

August 12, 2004 – New Jersey Governor James McGreevey announces he is " . . . a gay American" and that he cheated on his wife with a man.

August 13, 2000 – Democratic Presidential nominee Al Gore announces his selection of Connecticut Senator Joseph Lieberman as his running mate. Lieberman becomes the first Jewish American to be placed on a national ticket by a major political party.

August 14, 1945 – Japan unconditionally surrenders to the U.S., marking the end of WWII.

August 15, 1971 – President Richard M. Nixon imposes 90-days of Wage and Price Controls, and announces that the U.S. would stop redeeming gold for currency.

August 16, 1929 – By a vote of 85-1 the U.S. Senate ratifies **The Kellogg-Briand Pact**, "providing for the renunciation of war as an instrument of national policy." U.S. Secretary of State Frank Kellogg and French Foreign Minister Aristide Brand drafted the pact. Kellogg won a Noble Peace prize for his role in the treaty.

August 17, 1988 – At its National Convention in New Orleans, Louisiana, the Republican Party unanimously nominates Vice President George H. W. Bush as its presidential nominee.

August 18, 1914 – President Woodrow Wilson issues **"The Proclamation of Neutrality"** intended to avoid U.S. involvement in WWI.

August 19, 1976 – President Gerald R. Ford beats back a challenge from former California Governor Ronald Reagan to win the Republican Presidential nomination in Kansas City, Missouri.

August 20, 1974 – President Gerald R. Ford nominates New York Governor Nelson Rockefeller to become Vice President. Ford had vacated the Vice Presidency when he succeeded Richard M. Nixon to the Presidency.

August 21, 1945 – President Harry S. Truman ends **The Lend-Lease Program**, which supplied material to the Allied Powers during WWII.

August 22, 1984 – The Republican National Convention in Dallas, Texas nominates President Ronald Reagan for a second term as President.

August 23, 2008 – Democratic Presidential nominee Barack Obama text messages supporters, announcing his choice of U.S. Senator Joe Biden (D-DE) as his Vice Presidential running mate.

August 24, 1954 – President Dwight D. Eisenhower signs **The Communist Control Act**, banning the Communist party in the U.S.

August 25, 2008 – Pop star Madonna plays a video at the opening of "The Sticky Sweet Tour," juxtaposing images of Zimbabwe's president Robert Mugabe, Adolph Hitler, and presumptive U.S. Republican Presidential nominee John McCain.

August 26, 1968 – The tumultuous Democratic National Convention opens in Chicago, Illinois.

August 27, 1928 – Representatives from 15 nations, including the U.S., sign **The Kellogg-Briand Treaty** "providing for the renunciation of war as an instrument of national policy." The U.S. Senate later ratifies the pact.

August 28, 1963 – Martin Luther King Jr. delivers his *I Have a Dream* speech in front of the Lincoln memorial at the March on Washington for Jobs and Freedom.

August 29, 1961 – The Twenty-Third Amendment to the U.S. Constitution is ratified, allowing the District of Columbia residents to choose Electors for President and Vice President.

August 30, 1844 – The Abolitionist Liberty Party nominates abolitionist publisher and activist James Birney for President.

August 31, 1935 – President Franklin D. Roosevelt signs **The Neutrality Act,** banning the shipment of war materials, and barring U.S. citizens from traveling on belligerent vessels.

September

September 1, 2008 – The Republican National Convention opens in Minneapolis, Minnesota.

September 2, 1901 – During an oration at the Minnesota State Fair, Vice President Theodore Roosevelt first uses the African proverb which becomes synonymous with his own Presidency, which began twelve days later: "Speak Softly and Carry a Big Stick."

September 3, 1783 – **The Treaty of Paris is signed** by Great Brittan and the U.S., ending the American Revolutionary War and giving the U.S. colonies their independence.

September 4, 1957 – Arkansas Governor Orval Fabus orders the National Guard to stop African-American students from entering Little Rock Central High School.

September 5, 1774 – Peyton Randolph becomes the first President of the Continental Congress.

September 6, 1901 – Anarchist Leon Frank Czolgosz shoots President William McKinley at the Pan-American exposition in Buffalo, New York. McKinley dies eight days later.

September 7, 1977 – President Jimmy Carter and Panamanian president Omar Torrijos Herrera sign **The Panama Canal Treaty and Neutrality Treaty,** giving Panama full control of the canal on December 31,1999.

September 8, 1974 – President Gerald Ford issues **Proclamation 4311**, granting his Predecessor, Richard M. Nixon, a "full, free, and absolute pardon" for crimes he committed or may have committed as President.

September 9, 1957 – President Dwight D. Eisenhower signs the **Civil Rights Act of 1957**, making the U.S. Justice Department a guarantor of the right to vote and establishing a six-member commission to investigate charges that Americans are being disenfranchised from voting.

September 10, 1608 – English colonist John Smith is elected President of the governing council of Jamestown, Virginia.

September 11, 2001 – Nineteen al-Qaeda hijackers attack the Pentagon and World Trade Center. One plane, on the way to Washington, D.C. crashed in Shanksville, Pennsylvania. A total of 2,974 people perish in the attacks.

September 12, 1960 – In an Address to the *Greater Houston Ministerial Association* in Houston, Texas, Democratic Presidential nominee John F. Kennedy declares: "I am not the Catholic candidate for President. I am the Democratic Party's candidate for President who happens also to be a Catholic."

September 13, 1971 – Following four days of rioting at the *Attica Correctional Facility*, New York Governor Nelson Rockefeller orders 1,000 state troopers and national guardsmen to invade the prison. More than 40 people die.

September 14, 1901 – President William McKinley dies of wounds suffered from being shot by Anarchist Leon Frank Czolgosz at the Pan-American exposition in Buffalo, New York.

September 15, 1789 – President George Washington signs legislation establishing the U.S. Department of State.

September 16, 1940 – President Franklin D. Roosevelt signs the **Selective Training and Service Act of 1940**, which establishes a peacetime military draft.

September 17, 1787 – The U.S. Constitution is signed by 38 of the 41 delegates to the Constitutional Convention in Philadelphia.

September 18, 1850 – President Millard Fillmore signs **The Fugitive Slave Act**, which mandates that all slaves be returned to their masters.

September 19, 1796 – President George Washington's farewell address is published in *The Daily American Advertiser* and other American newspapers. In the address, Washington announces that he will not stand for re-election, calls for a constructionist view of the U.S. Constitution, condemns the proliferation of political parties, and admonishes the country to stay clear of "permanent alliances."

September 20, 1881 – President Chester A. Arthur takes the oath of office following the death of President James Garfield.

September 21, 2001 – President George W. Bush addresses a joint session of the U.S. Congress for the first time following the September 11 hijackings.

September 22, 1922 – President Warren G. Harding signs **The Cable Act,** which allows American women to keep their citizenship if they marry a foreigner.

September 23, 1950 – The U.S. Congress overrides the veto of President Harry S. Truman regarding **The Internal Security Act**, which requires American Communist organizations to register with the federal government.

September 24, 1955 – President Dwight D. Eisenhower survives a moderate heart attack while in Denver, Colorado.

September 25, 1981 – Sandra Day O'Connor is sworn in as first female U.S. Supreme Court Justice in U.S. history.

September 26, 1960 – Seventy Million Americans watch the first televised presidential debate between Massachusetts Senator John F. Kennedy and U.S. Vice President Richard M. Nixon.

September 27, 1964 – The *Warren Commission* rules that Lee Harvey Oswald was the loan gunman who shot and killed President John F. Kennedy in Dallas, Texas.

September 28, 1779 – Samuel Huntington is elected President of the Continental Congress.

September 29, 1965 – President Lyndon B. Johnson signs into law **The National Foundation on the Arts and Humanities Act**, which establishes the National Endowment for the Arts and the National Endowment for the Humanities.

September 30, 1968 – In a Salt Lake City speech, Vice President and Democratic Presidential nominee Hubert Humphrey breaks from the Johnson Administration by supporting a unilateral bombing halt by the U.S. in the Vietnam War "as an acceptable risk for peace."

October

October 1, 1986 – President Ronald Reagan signs **The Goldwater-Nichols Department of Defense Reorganization Act of 1986** into law. The measure reconstructs the military high command.

October 2, 1967 – Former U.S. Solicitor General Thurgood Marshall becomes the first African-American to serve on the U.S. Supreme Court.

October 3, 2008 – President George W. Bush signs **The Emergency Economic Stabilization Act of 2008**, allowing the Treasury Secretary to purchase as much as $700 billion in troubled assets.

October 4, 2002 – U.S. Senator Robert Byrd (D-WV) warns against a U.S. attack on Iraq, calling it: "Blind and improvident."

October 5, 1977 – President Jimmy Carter signs **The International Covenant on Civil and Political Rights.** However, The U.S. Senate does not ratify it until 1992.

October 6, 1976 – During the Second Presidential debate in San Francisco, California, between President Gerald R. Ford and former Georgia Governor Jimmy Carter, Ford makes a colossal gaff by stating that: "there is no Soviet domination of Eastern Europe and there never will be under a Ford Administration."

October 7, 2001 – The U.S. invasion of Afghanistan, a.k.a. *Operation Enduring Freedom*, begins.

October 8, 1974 – President Gerald R. Ford addressed a Joint Session of the U.S. Congress on his plan to "Whip Inflation Now."

October 9, 1953 – After his father's death from Pancreatic Cancer, future President Jimmy Carter leaves the Navy to take over the family farm in Plains, Georgia.

October 10, 1973 – Vice President Spiro Agnew resigns his post after pleading *nolo contendere* to charges of tax evasion and money laundering.

October 11, 2002 – U.S. Senate approves **The Authorization for Use of Military Force Against Iraq Resolution of 2002**. The House passed the Resolution hours earlier.

October 12, 2000 – al-Qaeda suicide bombers drive a small boat near the U.S. Navy Destroyer, *U.S.S. Cole* and detonate explosive. Seventeen American service members are killed and 39 injured. The Coal is out of commission for about six years.

October 13, 1978 – President Jimmy Carter signs the **Civil Service Reform Act of 1978**, reforming the federal government's civil service system. The duties of the U.S. Civil Service Commission are dispersed through three different agencies.

October 14, 1979 – **The National March on Washington for Lesbian and Gay Rights** is held in Washington, D.C. About 100,000 supporters of homosexual rights participate.

October 15, 1992 – Almost seventy million viewers watch the Presidential debate between President George H. W. Bush, Arkansas Governor Bill Clinton, and billionaire industrialist, H. Ross Perot.

October 16, 1901 – Booker T. Washington, author of *Up From Slavery,* becomes the first African-American invited to the White House by the President, who is Theodore Roosevelt.

October 17, 1974 – President Gerald R. Ford defends his decision to pardon former President Richard M. Nixon before the *Judiciary Subcommittee on Criminal Justice* in the U.S. House of Representatives.

October 18, 2007 – At a press conference, President George W. Bush warns: "If you're interested in avoiding World War III, it seems like you ought to be interested in preventing them (Iran) from having the knowledge necessary to make a nuclear weapon."

October 19, 1960 – President Dwight D. Eisenhower places a total embargo on U.S. exports to Cuba. The embargo survives to this day.

October 20, 1965 – The U.S. Supreme Court hands down its decision in *Griswold v. Connecticut.* The court rules that a law forbidding a Connecticut statue outlawing the use of contraceptives violates "the right to marital privacy." This is the first case in which the court recognized a right to privacy in the U.S. Constitution.

October 21, 1994 – President Bill Clinton launches the first official White House web site.

October 22, 1979 – President Jimmy Carter grants exiled Mohammad Rezā Shāh Pahlavi, the Shah of Iran, permission to receive medical treatment in the U.S. This inflames the Iranians, precipitating the Iranian Hostage Crisis.

October 23, 1983 – Two trucks with bombs drive into U.S. Marine headquarters in Beirut, Lebanon, where French and U.S. forces are stationed as part of a multinational peacekeeping force. 241 American military personnel died. This is the deadliest one-day death toll for the U.S. military since the battle of Iwo Jima in 1945. The group *Islamic Jihad* takes responsibility for the bombing.

October 24, 1978 – President Jimmy Carter signs **The Airline Deregulation Act**, limiting government controls over aviation.

October 25, 1983 – Along with Caribbean and Jamaican allies, President Ronald Reagan orders an invasion of Grenada, ousting the government of the chairman of the Revolutionary Military Council of Grenada, Hudson Austin, who rules over a Marxist regime with the support of Cuban President Fidel Castro.

October 26, 1972 – National Security Advisor Henry Kissinger says peace (in Vietnam) is "within a matter of weeks or less." It took about two more months to achieve peace.

October 27, 2005 – Speaker of the U.S. House of Representatives Dennis Hastert (R-IL) becomes the first speaker in history to author a blog. The blog was called: *"Speakers Journal."*

October 28, 1919 – The U.S. Congress overrides President Woodrow Wilson's veto of **The *Volstead Act*,** which enforces the Eighteenth Amendment to the U.S. Constitution, prohibiting the manufacture, sale, and transport of alcohol.

October 29, 2007 – U.S. Senator Judd Greg (R-NH) announces his endorsement of former Massachusetts Governor Mitt Romney for the Republican Presidential nomination.

October 30, 1912 – Vice President John Sherman dies a week before his re-election bid. President William Howard Taft chooses Columbia University President Nicholas Butler to fill the void.

October 31, 1998 – President Bill Clinton signs **The Iraq Liberation Act of 1998**, making it U.S. policy to support "regime change" in Iraq. The act funds Iraqi opposition groups.

November

November 1, 1800 – President John Adams becomes the first President to reside in the White House.

November 2, 1983 – President Ronald Reagan signs into law an act making the third Monday of every January Martin Luther King Jr. Day.

November 3, 1964 – President Lyndon B. Johnson defeats challenger U.S. Senator Barry Goldwater (R-AZ) in a landslide victory. Johnson mustered 61.1% of the vote, Goldwater garnered 38.5%. The only state Goldwater wins outside of the South is Arizona.

November 4, 1980– Banker Frank White upsets Bill Clinton in his bid for re-election as Arkansas Governor, making Clinton the youngest ex-governor in American history.

November 5, 1912 – Woodrow Wilson becomes the first Democrat to win a presidential election since Grover Cleveland in 1892.

November 6, 1984 – President Ronald Reagan is re-elected President with a record 525 out of 538 electoral votes. His challenger, former Vice President Walter Mondale, wins only his home state of Minnesota and the District of Columbia.

November 7, 1916 –Jeannette Rankin becomes the first woman elected to the United States House of Representatives by winning the at-large seat in Montana.

November 8, 1988 – Vice President George H.W. Bush beats Massachusetts Governor Michael Dukakis in the Presidential election. Bush became the first incumbent Vice President to win the presidency since Martin Van Buren in 1836.

November 9, 1906 – President Theodore Roosevelt begins a trip to Panama to inspect work on the Panama Canal. He becomes the first sitting President to leave the United States.

November 10, 1775 - The Continental Congress agrees to a resolution written by John Adams creating the Continental Marines. Today, this is celebrated as the birthday of the U.S. Marine Corps.

November 11, 1620 – **The Mayflower Compact** is signed by 41 Mayflower voyagers, establishing the governing structure of Plymouth Colony. The signers agree to follow the contract and: "mutually in the presence of God and one of another, Covenant and Combine ourselves together into a Civil Body Politic, for our better ordering and preservation."

November 12, 1979 - President Jimmy Carter signs **Executive Order 12170**, stopping oil imports from Iran and freezing Iranian assets in the US. This action comes eight days after Iranian students takes 63 U.S. embassy employees hostage.

November 13, 2008 – Vice President Dick Cheney welcomes Vice-President elect Joseph Biden to the Vice President's residence at the Naval Observatory in Washington, D.C.

November 14, 1935 – President Franklin D. Roosevelt signs **Proclamation 2148** providing for the "establishment of the Commonwealth of the Philippines."

November 15, 1777 – The Continental Congress approves The Articles of Confederation and Perpetual Union.

November 16, 2008 – Barack Obama resigns his Illinois U.S. Senate seat to prepare for his transition to the presidency.

November 17, 1933 – The United States officially recognizes the Soviet Union. William C. Bullitt becomes the U.S. ambassador to the Soviet Union.

November 18, 1949 – Vice President Alben Barkley (a widower) marries Elizabeth Jane Rucker Hadley. Barkley is the only Vice President to marry while in office.

November 19, 1863 – President Abraham Lincoln delivers the *Gettysburg Address* at the dedication of the Soldiers' National Cemetery in Gettysburg, Pennsylvania.

November 20. 1789 – New Jersey becomes the first state to ratify The Bill of Rights to the U.S. Constitution.

November 21, 1922 – Rebecca Ann Latimer Felton of Georgia becomes the first woman to serve in the U.S. Senate.

November 22, 1963 – President John F. Kennedy is shot and killed by Lee Harvey Oswald while riding in an open car in Dallas, Texas. Vice President Lyndon B. Johnson succeeds Kennedy. The Government-sponsored Warren Commission later concludes that Lee Harvey Oswald was the loan gunman.

November 23, 1921 – President Warren G. Harding signs **The Willis Campbell Act** forbidding doctors from prescribing beer or liquor for medicinal purposes.

November 24, 2008 – President-elect Barack Obama nominates New York Federal Reserve Board President Timothy Geithner for Treasury Secretary.

November 25, 1986 – It is divulged by U.S. Attorney General Edwin Meese that the proceeds of secret arms sales to Iran were funding the Nicaraguan Contras, a guerrilla organization working to oust the ruling socialist government of the Sandinista National Liberation Front. This activity is in direct violation of **The Boland Amendment,** which interdicts military support for the purpose of overthrowing the Government of Nicaragua.

November 26, 1789 – President George Washington declares this a day a national Thanksgiving for the *U.S. Constitution*. Today we know it simply as "Thanksgiving."

November 27, 1973 – The U.S. Senate votes to confirm Gerald R. Ford to become Vice President. The post was left vacant by the resignation of Spiro Agnew.

November 28, 2005 – U.S. Representative Randy "Duke" Cunningham (R-CA) pleads guilty to taking more than $2 million in bribes and resigns his congressional seat.

November 29, 1952 – President–Elect Dwight D. Eisenhower fulfills his campaign promise by going to Korea to review and analyze the ongoing Korean War.

November 30, 1993 – President Bill Clinton signs **The Brady Handgun Violence Prevention Act,** requiring gun buyers to undergo a five-day background check before being able to purchasing a handgun.

December

December 1, 1955 – Montgomery Fair Department Store Employee Rosa Parks refuses to give up her seat on a public bus to a white passenger, an event that leads to the Montgomery Bus Boycott.

December 2, 1823 – **Th**e **Monroe Doctrine,** written by U.S. Secretary of State John Quincy Adams, is established. It declares that the American citizens are: " . . . not to be considered as subjects for future colonization by any European powers."

December 3, 1991 – White House Chief of Staff John Sununu announces he will resign office after allegations of using military aircraft for personal and political trips.

December 4, 1978 – San Francisco Board of Supervisors President Diane Feinstein becomes mayor after the assassination of Mayor George Moscone. Mayor Mascone was murdered at City Hall by Dan White, a former member of the San Francisco Board of Supervisors.

December 5, 1933 – The Twenty-First Amendment to the U.S. Constitution is ratified, ending the prohibition of alcohol.

December 6, 1973 – Gerald R. Ford is sworn in as Vice President of the United States.

December 7, 1787 – Delaware becomes the first state to join the Union.

December 8, 1987 – President Ronald Reagan and Soviet Union General Secretary Mikhail Gorbachev sign **The Treaty Between the United States of America and the Union of Soviet Socialist Republics on the Elimination of Their Intermediate-Range and Shorter-Range Missiles**. The document calls for the obliteration of nuclear and conventional ground-launched ballistic and cruise missiles with intermediate ranges.

December 9, 1872 – After the removal from office of Louisiana Governor Henry Clay Warmoth, Lieutenant Governor Pinckney Benton Stewart Pinchback is sworn in to succeed him. Pinchback becomes the first African-American Governor in U.S. history.

December 10, 1869 – Wyoming becomes the first state to grant women the right to vote. Technically, New Jersey had granted unmarried women the right to vote in 1776 if they owned property. However, this right was rescinded in 1807.

December 11, 1971 – The Libertarian party of the United States is founded at the house of Colorado businessman David Nolan.

December 12, 1992 – Bill Clinton resigns as Governor of Arkansas. Lieutenant Governor Jim Guy Tucker succeeds him.

December 13, 2000 – Vice President Al Gore concedes the 2000 presidential election to Texas Governor George W. Bush.

December 14, 1946 – The U.N. General Assembly agrees to locate the U.N. headquarters in New York City.

December 15, 1791 – The Bill of Rights is ratified.

December 16, 1988 – A Federal jury convicts perennial presidential candidate Lyndon H. LaRouche Jr. of mail fraud, conspiracy to commit mail fraud, and tax evasion.

December 17, 2004 – President George W. Bush signs **The Intelligence Reform and Terrorism Prevention Act of 2004** which reforms American intelligence services and establishes a Director of National Intelligence, a National Counterterrorism Center, and the Privacy and Civil Liberties Oversight Board.

December 18, 1915 – President Woodrow Wilson marries Edith Bolling Galt. His first wife, Ellen Wilson died in 1914.

December 19, 1998 – The House of Representatives impeaches President Bill Clinton for "perjury" and "Obstruction of Justice" for his actions in the Monica Lewinsky episode.

December 20, 1989 – President George H. W. Bush launches *Operation Just Cause*, an invasion of Panama with the intent of capturing Manuel Noriega, the chief executive officer of Panama. Noriega is later convicted in the U.S. on federal charges of cocaine trafficking, racketeering, and money laundering in Miami, Florida.

December 21, 1620 – The Pilgrims land in Plymouth, Massachusetts.

December 22, 1961 – Massachusetts Governor Foster Furcolo appoints former Gloucester Mayor Benjamin A. Smith ll to fill the U.S. Senate seat vacated by President-elect John F. Kennedy.

December 23, 1913 – President Woodrow Wilson signs **The Federal Reserve Act** into law.

December 24, 1992 – President George H.W. Bush grants pardons to six Iran-Contra figures, including: Former Secretary of Defense Casper Weinberger, former Assistant Secretary of State for Inter-American Affairs Elliott Abrams, former National Security Adviser Robert McFarlane; and former CIA employees Duane Clarridge, Alan Fiers, and Clair George.

December 25, 1868 – President Andrew Johnson awards pardons to all who fought for the South during the U.S. Civil War.

December 26, 1862 – President Abraham Lincoln orders the largest mass execution in American history, the execution of 39 of the 303 Santee Sioux Indians. All were convicted of murder and rape by military tribunal.

December 27, 1968 – The United States agrees to sell Phantom jets to Israel.

December 28, 1973 – President Richard M. Nixon signs **The Endangered Species Act** into law.

December 29, 1846 – James K. Polk becomes the first U.S. President to have gas lighting in the White House.

December 30, 1905 – Former Idaho Governor Frank Steunenberg is assassinated when a bomb goes off outside of his front gate. Mine worker Albert Edward Horsley, aka Harry Orchard, was later convicted of the crime. He was sentenced to death, but his punishment was commuted to life imprisonment.

December 31, 2007 – The massive fifteen-year infrastructure project in Boston known as the "Big Dig" finally ends. Originally budgeted at $2.8 billion, the project cost taxpayers more than $24.3 billion, the most costly highway project in U.S. history.

Glossary of Political Terminology

Actual Malice: A precedent established in the Supreme Court case of *New York Times Co. v. Sullivan*, The court ruled that to establish libel against a public official, knowing falsity or reckless disregard for the truth must be proven.

Advisory Referendum: A measure that appears on the ballot which in non-binding. It is mostly used to engage popular opinion.

American Exceptionalism: Belief that America is superior to all other nations.

Anarchy: Absence of any governing authority.

Appellate Jurisdiction: The power of a Court to review lower Court decisions, and accept, modify or even overturn the decision of a lower level court.

Arkansas Project: An effort funded by newspaper publisher Richard Mellon Scaife to find damaging information on Bill Clinton.

Articles of Confederation and Perpetual Union: Written by the Continental Congress. This was the Constitution of the first thirteen colonies. This governing authority was written in 1776. Because of criticism from Federalists believing that the federal government lacked necessary power, it was eventually supplanted with the *U.S. Constitution*.

Australian Ballot: System employed in the United States in which all ballots are marked in secret.

Authoritarianism: System of government in which the state has much power over the individual.

Bicameralism: Two separate legislative chambers. At the federal level, the Congress is divided into the Senate and House of Representatives. The legislative branch in every state except Nebraska is also comprised of two chambers.

Bill of Attainder: The punishment of an individual without a trial. Article 1 Section 9 of the *U.S. Constitution* disallows this practice at the state and federal levels.

Blanket Primary: Primary in which the electorate can vote for members of different parties for different offices. For example, a voter could select a Republican candidate for Governor and a Democrat for State Senator. The leading vote-getter for each party goes on to compete in the general election.

Black Budget: Appropriations earmarked "secret" (usually military projects). They are kept hidden for national security purposes.

Blowback: A term coined by the CIA referring to the future negative unintended consequences of U.S. foreign policy, including covert operations. Many point to the Iran Hostage Crises in 1979 as being blowback by the Iranians for the U.S. support of the overthrow of Prime Minister Mohammad Mosaddeq in 1953.

Blue Dog Democrat: The modern term for a Conservative Democrat. Most come from more conservative parts of the country, including the South and the West, where the national Democratic Party is often looked upon as too liberal. The term was coined by U.S. Representative Peter Geren (D-TX 1989-1997) who said that Conservative Democrats were being choked blue by extreme Democrats and Republicans. Most Blue Dog Democrats are particularly interested in balancing the federal budget.

Boll weevils: A term referring to Conservative Democrats from the mid to late twentieth-century. A pre-curser to what is now known as a "Blue Dog Democrat."

Boondoggle: A project funded by the government with little redeeming value.

Budget Deficit: When annual government expenditures exceed annual government receipts.

Budget Surplus: When government receipts exceed government expenditures.

Bullet Vote: A voter has the option to select multiple candidates for an office, but chooses just one.

Bureaucracy: Commonly refers to the structure and regulation needed in a large organization such as a corporation or government entity to accomplish tasks.

Bush Doctrine: The U.S. will not distinguish between terrorists themselves and those who harbor the terrorists and will use force if necessary to "take out" regimes which represent a potential threat to the U.S.

Carter Doctrine: Offered in response to the Soviet Union's invasion of Afghanistan in 1980. President Jimmy Carter asserted that the U.S. would intervene militarily if necessary anywhere in the Persian Gulf to defend U.S. national interests.

Ceteris Paribus: Other things being equal.

Checks and Balances: A system in which different branches of government have oversight over the others, so none becomes omnipotent.

Clerk of the U.S. House of Representatives: The House's chief record-keeper. The Clerk is elected every two years.

Clinton Doctrine: The U.S. will intervene abroad to defend its values, including human rights.

Closed Primary: Primary election in which only members of one party are afforded the right to participate.

Cloture: Ending a filibuster. It needs the approval of 60 U.S. Senators.

CNN Effect: The belief that the images Americans see on their TV sets has a direct affect on how they view the foreign policies of their government. The term originates from the Somalia Crisis in the early-mid 1990's, when viewers saw the malnourished Somalis on TV. They then pressured their government to send troops to stop the suffering. Later, when they saw Somali's dragging a dead U.S. soldier through the streets, they demanded withdrawal.

Coattail Effect: The ability of a popular politician at the top of the ballot, such as a Governor or Senator, to bring voters to the polls who will also vote for other candidates of his/her political party further down the ballot. These other candidates could include members of the U.S. Congress, state legislators, and municipal officials.

Command Economy: System where the government rather than market forces centrally plans economic activity.

Commander-in-Chief Clause: Article 2, Section 2, Clause 1 of the *U.S. Constitution* says the President shall be: "Commander in Chief of the Army and Navy of the United States and the militia of the several states."

Common Law: The governing system based upon judicial precedence.

Common Victualler License: A license granted by a public entity allowing one to serve alcoholic beverages.

Communism: a system of government in which the entire population owns most property, and private property is extremely limited. Ex: North Korea, Vietnam, and Cuba.

Concurrent Resolution: A measure passed by both houses of the U.S. Congress that does not have the power of law and does not need the signature of the president.

Confederation: An alliance of groups.

Congress of the Confederation or the United States in Congress Assembled: The precursor to the United State Congress. It was the governing body of the United States from March 1, 1781 to March 4, 1789.

Congressional Delegate: A non-voting representative to the U.S. House of Representatives from American Samoa, Commonwealth of the Northern Mariana Islands, Guam, the United States Virgin Islands and the District of Columbia. They are elected to two-year terms. A Congressional Delegate has all privileges afforded other members, such as speaking privileges, drafting legislation, and committee voting. However, the Delegates are not afforded the right to vote on legislation.

Congressionalist: One who believes the U.S. Congress should have wide-ranging power.

Constitutional Republic: A system of government where the citizenry elect officials who must govern in a way that comports with a governing Constitution. The United States of America is an example.

Continuing Resolution: A Joint Resolution passed by Congress providing funding for government agencies at existing levels. This is a temporary measure to provide funding prior to the Congress and President working out an agreement for the full funding for the fiscal year.

Dean of the U.S. House of Representatives: Longest serving member of the House in consecutive terms. The Dean's only official duty is to swear in the Speaker of the House.

Declaration of Independence: Manuscript written by Thomas Jefferson in 1776 proclaiming independence of the U.S. from Great Britain.

Democratic Leadership Council (DLC): A now defunct non-profit corporation founded in 1985 to moderate the Democratic Party and expand its voter-base to include moderate voters. Former Chairman Bill Clinton used many of the themes of the DLC in his presidential campaign in 1992. Other former chairmen include then U.S. Senator Evan Bayh (D-IN), then U.S. Senator John Breaux (D-LA), and then U.S. Senator Sam Nunn (D-GA).

Democratic Peace Theory: Belief that liberal democracies do not go to war with each other because the majority of the population will never vote to go to war or elect people who would. Accordingly, if all nations were liberal democracies, there would be no war. Many Neo-Conservatives have adopted this premise.

De-politicized Citizenry: A system where the population is not actively engaged in the political decisions of their times.

Deputy President pro tempore: Any former President or Vice President who returns to serve in the U.S. Senate is entitled to this position, which includes an increase in salary.

DINO: Democrat-In-Name-Only

Direct Democracy: System where citizens participate in drafting and voting on laws. An example is a New England style town meeting.

Down Ballot: Candidates for offices, such as U.S. Congress, the state legislature, and municipal positions, whose office is not at the top of the ballot. The top might include candidates for President, Governor, Mayor, etc.

Dual Federalism: Doctrine espoused by U.S. Supreme Court Justice Roger Taney (1777-1864) which maintained that the state and federal governments should have separate but equal powers.

Earmark: Congressionally directed spending geared toward funding specific projects or programs such as constructing a new wing at a college, building a bicycle path, or preserving an historic landmark.

Electioneering: Actively working for a political candidate or ballot initiative.

Enumerated powers: Eighteen specific powers delegated to the United States Congress from Article 1 Section 8 of the *United States Constitution*.

Executive Agreement: An accord between the President and a foreign head of government that needs a simple up or down vote by both houses of Congress to win approval.

Ex post facto Law: A law passed "after the fact." Under the *U.S. Constitution*, no American can be penalized for violating a law before it becomes the law of the land.

Fascism: Authoritarian/nationalistic political ideology. Sometimes this is the amalgamation of religious and corporate interests.

Federalism: The delineation of powers between the federal and state governments.

Federalist Papers: Eighty-five articles written by John Jay, Alexander Hamilton, and James Madison and published in *The Independent Journal* and *The New York Packet*. They advocated for the ratification of the *U.S. Constitution*.

Filibuster: In the U.S. Senate, members are permitted to speak indefinitely on a subject to avoid a vote. Only with 60 votes can the Senate vote to invoke cloture, thus ending debate on voting. Then U.S. Senator Strom Thurmond (D-SC) holds the record for the longest filibuster. He spent 24 hours and 18 minutes filibustering the Civil Rights Act of 1957. There are also non-verbal tactical procedures within filibustering to delay a vote.

Free Rider: One who receives the benefits of government policy without incurring the costs.

Free Trade: Free flow of goods and services not subject to tariffs.

Functionary: A Government Official

Gerrymandering: The manipulation of the redistricting process at the state level to benefit the majority party and/or all incumbents. The term originated to describe Massachusetts Governor Elbridge Gerry's (1810-1812) successful attempt to maximize the numerical political advantage for his Democratic-Republican Party.

Great Society: An all-encompassing term for the social programs proposed by President Lyndon B. Johnson. Legislation was enacted in areas such as Health Care, Civil Rights, and Education Reform.

Gross Domestic Product: The market value of all goods and services produced in a country, usually annually.

Gross National Product: Measures of national income and output used to estimate the welfare of an economy through totaling the value of goods and services produced in an economy.

Half-Breeds: Moderate Republicans in the latter half of the nineteenth century who favored civil service reform.

Ideologue: A person with a certain grand design or philosophical mindset of how the world should be.

Impeachment: Article Two Section 4 of the *U.S. Constitution* states that "The President, Vice President, and all other civil Officers of the United States shall be removed from Office on Impeachment for, and Conviction of, Treason, Bribery, or other High Crimes and Misdemeanors." If a majority votes in the U.S. House of Representatives for impeachment, then the articles are sent to the Senate, where a two-thirds majority is required for conviction.

Imperialism: Encroachment of an empire on territory outside its borders.

Impoundment: The refusal of a sitting president to spend funds for something that the legislature has appropriated funds for.

Incrementalism: Achieving legislative goals step-by-step by passing a series of small legislation.

Incumbent: A current holder of an office.

Inflation: The rising prices of goods and services.

Infotainment: The amalgamation of news with entertainment.

Initiative: A vehicle for the citizens to propose legislation or constitutional amendments to be placed on the ballot for an up or down vote by the electorate. Accordingly, the usual legislative process is circumvented. Twenty-four states currently have some form of the initiative option.

Injunction: A Court order requiring a person or entity to do something or to refrain from doing a certain act or behavior.

Instant Runoff Voting: A voting system where voters rank all candidates. The candidate with the fewest first place votes is dropped and the voter's second choice replaces the first choice of those who placed him/her first. This process is repeated until two candidates remain.

Invisible Hand: A term coined by the Scottish Economist Adam Smith to describe his belief that there is a natural regulator in a free-market-system.

Isolationism: Belief that a country should be averse to all relations with other nations, including commercial, cultural, and military isolation.

Joint Resolution: A measure requiring approval of both chambers of Congress before going to the president for his/her subsequent approval or disapproval.

Judicial Review: Power of the Judicial branch of government to scrutinize for constitutional permissibility, actions by the Executive and Legislative branch. If the Justices rule the actions to be unconstitutional, they become null and void.

Jungle Primary: A primary election where candidates run for office on the same ballot. If no candidate musters a majority of the vote, there is a run-off between the two top finishers. This system is used in Louisiana.

Laissez-faire: A French word translated: "to allow to do, to leave alone." The term is used to mean that the government should not regulate the economy.

Lame duck: An incumbent elected official who has lost much of his/her influence because the official's term is nearing an end and they are not seeking re-election.

Layer-Cake Federalism: A system where the federal and state governments have clearly delineated and specific functions.

LBJ Rule: In 1959, the Texas legislature approved legislation allowing a politician to run for two political offices simultaneously. This benefited Lyndon B. Johnson in 1960 as he sought both re-election to the U.S. Senate and the Presidency. After failing to secure the Democratic presidential nomination, he ran for Vice President that year. He subsequently won both the Vice Presidency and re-election to the U.S. Senate. Other Texas officials, including U.S. Senators Lloyd Benson and Phil Gramm, and U.S. Representative Ron Paul, have used the law to seek higher office while running for re-election.

Legislative Referendum: The legislature refers a measure to the voters for their up or down vote.

Letters of Marque and Reprisal: Article 1, Section 8, Clause 11 of the *U.S. Constitution* gives the President the power to "grant Letters of Marque and Reprisal, and make rules concerning captures on land and water." It allows the president to search, seize, or destroy specified assets or personal belongings of a foreign party that has committed some offense under the laws of nations.

Libertarianism: A belief that government should be a limited-purpose entity devoted to protect a person's life, liberty, and property.

Line-Item Veto: Power of the executive to reject provisions in a piece of legislation without vetoing the legislation outright. At the federal level, the Line-Item Veto Act of 1996 was nullified in *Clinton v. City of New York*, 524 U.S. 417 (1998). The U.S. Supreme Court ruled that the Act violated the Presentment Clause of the *U.S. Constitution* because it impermissibly gave the President of the United States the power to unilaterally amend or repeal parts of statutes that had been duly passed by the United States Congress. At the state level, Forty-three state Governors have this privilege.

Lobbyist: Individual, representing a cause or organization, who tries to persuade government officials to support their point of view on issues.

Local Aid: Transfer of revenue from state to municipal governments to pay for local services.

Logrolling: When two members of a legislative body agree to support each other's legislation on separate issues.

Majority and Minority Leader: In both the U.S. House of Representatives and the U.S. Senate, these elected members serve as floor leader for their respective parties. When they are not there, a designee is selected. In the House, the Majority leader is second-in-command to the Speaker of the House.

Manifest Destiny: Originally referred to the belief that the U.S. was destined to expand from the Atlantic to the Pacific Ocean. Today it has come to mean that the U.S. must increase its territory.

Mayflower Compact: A document signed by 41 Mayflower voyagers on November 11, 1620 establishing the government structure of Plymouth Colony. The signers agreed to follow the contract and: "mutually in the presence of God and one of another, Covenant and Combine ourselves together into a Civil Body Politic, for our better ordering and preservation."

Micro Governing: Governing by focusing on specific small-bore issues.

Mixed Economy: An economic system that combines forces from multiple economic structures.

Moonbat: Term of derision for a liberal.

National Debt: The accumulative amount of annual deficits.

Nanny State: A pejorative phrase for a paternalistic government.

Neo-Conservatism: Former Cold War Liberal Democrats who became disillusioned with what they viewed as the Democratic Party's dovish foreign policy. Many supported then U.S. Senator Henry "Scoop" Jackson's (D-WA) bids for the Democratic Party's nomination in 1972 and 1976. After his loss, many gradually migrated to the Republican fold and supported President Ronald Reagan. Today, they are steadfast supporters of an activist foreign policy that promotes Democracy abroad. American intellectual Irving Kristol (1920-2009) is considered by many to be the Patron Saint of this ideology.

New Democrat: A Democrat who generally strives to bring the Democratic Party to the center of the political spectrum. The term New Democrat was popularized in 1992 when the Democratic Presidential Ticket of Bill Clinton and Al Gore came from this wing of the party. Most New Democrats are business oriented and favor fiscal austerity and free trade as a vehicle for economic expansion, rather than the more liberal view that government should redistribute the nation's wealth.

Nixon Doctrine: The U.S. will provide arms to allies, but will not do the actual fighting for them.

Nomination Papers: Papers that are required to be completed when an individual wants to run for public office.

Non-Interventionism: The doctrine that dictates that a country should avoid foreign entanglements with other nations while maintaining commercial and cultural intercourse. Thomas Jefferson said the U.S. should practice: "Peace, Commerce, and honest relations with all nations, entangled alliances with none."

Nonpartisan election: An election where candidates do not run as a member of a political party. Most municipal elections fall into this category.

Off-year election: Election held in the middle of a presidential term.

Oligarchy: Rule by the wealthy few.

Open Primary: Primary election in which members of all political parties are invited to participate.

Original Jurisdiction: Power of a court to hear a case for the first time.

Paleo-Conservative: Ideological descendants of a prominent philosophy in the Republican Party between WWI and WWII. They share a non-interventionist foreign policy, support for federalism, and oppose most government intervention in the economy. Many paleo-conservatives share a populist streak, opposing what they view as attempts by power elites and multi-national corporations to exert influence. In addition, many adherents to this ideology take a hard-line stance against affirmative action and illegal immigration. Examples include President Warren G. Harding (1921-1923), U.S. Senator Robert A. Taft (R-OH 1939-1953), and political commentator Patrick J. Buchanan.

Paleo-Liberal: An ideology that couples support for muscular foreign policy, including high defense spending, with an activist domestic policy, including a munificent social safety net. This belief was conventional liberal thinking during the first half of the Cold War. U.S. Senator Henry "Scoop" Jackson (D-WA 1953-1983) was a steadfast exponent of this ideology.

Partisan Election: Election in which candidates declare party affiliation.

Partisan: One who is a steadfast advocate of the interests of his/her political party or cause.

Patron: One who finances a political cause or politician.

Phone Mark: When a legislator does not get his/her earmark placed in legislation, a call is made to a government agency demanding funding. This is kept secret from the public, and is illegal in the U.S.

Plurality: Receiving more votes than any other candidate but not a majority.

Political Football: A topic which politicians debate, but without resolution. Politicians use the issue for their political advantage.

Political Parlance: Jargon related to politics.

Politicized Citizenry: A system where the population is actively engaged in the political decisions of their times.

Popular Referendum: A measure that appears on the ballot as a result of a voter petition drive. It affords the electorate an up or down vote on legislation passed by a legislative body.

Pork barrel spending: Government funding designed to benefit a special interest rather than benefit the public interest. It is often intended to benefit a constituent, a private company, or a campaign contributor of a politician.

POTUS: President of the United States.

President of the United States: The chief executive officer of the government who is both head of state and head of government. Presidential powers are derived from Article II of *The U.S. Constitution*.

President pro tempore *emeritus*: An honorific office awarded to any former President pro tempore of the U.S. Senate. While the office has no extra powers, its holder is awarded an increase in staff and salary.

President pro tempore of the Senate: Generally the most senior member of the majority party in the Senate holds this position. This person is the second-highest-ranking official of the United States Senate and is officially the presiding officer. Usually though, he or she delegates this duty to other members. Third in line of presidential succession, the office's powers are derived from Article I, Section 3 of the *U.S. Constitution*.

President-Elect: A winner of a presidential election who has yet to assume the office.

Presidentialist: An advocate of a strong federal executive branch.

Protectionism: The restriction of goods and services from abroad in order to protect domestic industries.

Reagan Doctrine: The U.S. will provide aid to forces fighting against communism, with the grand design of rolling it back.

Reconciliation: This process allows the U.S. Senate to consider any budget legislation without a filibuster.

Republicrat: A political pejorative used to define the common interests of the Republican and Democratic parties by those who think they are two sides of the same coin and have little differences.

Resident Commissioner of Puerto Rico: Non-voting representative to the U.S, Congress from the Commonwealth of Puerto Rico. The only representative elected to a four-year term. He or she has all privileges afforded other members, such as speaking privileges, drafting legislation, and committee voting, except voting on final approval of legislation.

Rider: A provision attached to unrelated legislation. Sometimes these are provisions that may be too controversial to pass on their own.

Rider's Choice: Belief that the decision to wear a motorcycle helmet while riding a motorcycle should be decided by the biker, not the government.

RINO: Republican-In-Name-Only.

Rockefeller Republican: A moderate-liberal block of Republicans who generally favor the policies of fiscal austerity and social liberalism championed by Nelson Rockefeller who served as New York Governor from 1959-1974 and as Vice President of the United States from 1974-1977.

Root-Canal-Economics: The concomitant raising of taxes and cutting government expenditures, usually to balance the budget.

Sedition: Attempts by citizens to topple their government.

Senatorial Courtesy: When the President nominates an individual to the position of Federal District Judge, Federal Marshall, or United States Attorney, it is customary for the President to consult first with the senior U.S. Senator of that state, but only if that senior Senator is a member of the President's political Party.

Separation of Powers: Division of powers among the three branches of government.

Shadow Senator: Voters in the District of Columbia elect two residents to serve in this position. They have no office in the U.S. Senate, and have no Senatorial authority. They do receive an office in the District of Columbia, courtesy of District taxpayers. The job of the Shadow Senator is to lobby members of the U.S. Government to support greater autonomy for the District, with the ultimate goal being outright statehood.

Shadow Representative: Voters in the District of Columbia elect one resident to serve in this position. The person elected to this position has no office or authority in the U.S. House of Representatives. Their job is to lobby members of the U.S. Government for autonomy for the District, with the ultimate goal being statehood for the District.

Social Conservative: One who believes the government should enforce a moral code for its population. Most are opposed to abortion rights, gay marriage, and most support school prayer.

Socialism: A social and economic structure where property and resources are owned by the government rather than by individuals or private companies.

Speaker of the House: Serves as Presiding officer of the U.S. House of Representatives. Under the Presidential Succession Act of 1947, he or she is second in line in presidential succession. Responsibilities include: Calling the House to order, Administering the oath of office to House Members, Presiding over debate, recognizing Members to speak on the floor, and preserving order; or delegating that power to another Member of Congress, setting the legislative agenda, and leading the appointment process for the chairs of the various committees and subcommittees in the House (including conference committees which negotiate final versions of legislation).

Speaker pro tempore: Presides over the U.S. House of Representatives in the absence of the Speaker of the House.

Special Election: An election held to fill a vacancy between elections.

Spending Gap: When all but essential government services are halted because the Federal Government cannot agree on a budget.

Spoils man: A politician who supports the appointment of public officials based on partisan political considerations.

Stalwart: Republicans in the latter half of the nineteenth century who opposed civil service reform. They supported the candidacy of Ulysses S. Grant for the Republican nomination in 1880 when he sought a third term for the presidency.

Standard-bearer: A Representative of a Political party or political movement.

Stare decisis: Latin for: "to stand by things decided." This term refers to the judicial theory that previous court decisions should be precedent and not changed.

287

State of Nature: The "natural condition of mankind" before governments are instituted. Seventeenth Century French philosopher Thomas Hobbes maintained that all human beings are in a state of war and their lives are: "solitary, poor, nasty, brutish, and short." English philosopher John Locke believed that reason which teaches "no one ought to harm another in his life, health, liberty or possessions" is the governor in this state.

Statute: A law usually written by a legislative branch of a government.

Supply-Side Economics: An economic doctrine popularized by President Ronald Reagan and his Economic Policy Advisor, Arthur Laffer. It asserts that when marginal tax rates are decreased, economic activity increases, resulting in an increase of government revenue.

Supreme Court of the United States: The highest court in the country. Its powers are derived from Article 3 of the *U.S. Constitution*. Members are nominated by the President and confirmed by the U.S. Senate. To receive confirmation they need a majority vote. The Court is composed of eight Associate Justices and one Chief Justice. The Court serves as arbiter of the *U.S. Constitution*.

Tariffs: Taxes on trade.

Third Party: A political party not associated with the two major ones. Examples include the Green Party, the Libertarian Party, and the Prohibition Party.

Ticket Splitting: When a voter chooses candidates of different parties for different offices. For example, the voter may choose a Democrat for President and a Republican for the U.S. Senate.

Timocracy: A system of government where government participation is limited to property owners. It can also refer to a government where rulers receive their position based on the place of honor they hold in a society.

Town Meeting: A form of direct democracy in which all registered voters in a municipality are invited to attend and vote on town laws and budgets.

Transaction Costs: The cost of doing business. An example would be the commission paid to a broker to purchase bonds.

Transfer Payment: Money from a government to an individual without the obligation of the individual to pay it back.

Unfunded Liability: A liability incurred this year that does not have to be paid until sometime in the future.

Unfunded Mandate: Regulations imposed on state and municipal governments without reimbursement from the federal government.

Unicameralism: A legislative branch composed of one chamber. Nebraska is the only state that has this system.

United States Congress: The legislative branch of the United States Government. Its powers are derived from Article 2 of the *U.S. Constitution*. It is composed of the U.S. House of Representatives and the U.S. Senate. House members represent a district of a state, while senators represent the entire state. Each state has two senators and at least one representative. The representatives are apportioned based on population of the state. The smallest state in population is Wyoming, which has only 1 representative. By contrast, California, the largest state, has fifty-three representatives.

Utopia: A perfect society. The term comes from the title of a book written by English Statesman Sir Thomas More.

Veto: This term is Latin for "I forbid." It is used to refer to the rejection of a proposal by the legislative branch by a Chief Executive.

Vice President of the United States: The occupant of this office is the President and presiding officer of the U.S. Senate. Most of the time this power is delegated to the President pro tempore and to other senators from the majority party. In addition, the Vice President has the power to cast the deciding vote should the Senate vote be tied. Finally, the Vice President certifies the official count of the Electoral College during Presidential elections.

***Virginia Declaration of Rights*:** Adopted unanimously by the Virginia Convention of Delegates on June 12, 1776, it was written by Virginia Statesman George Mason. The document affirms the Right to: "life, Liberty, and Property" and delineates restrictions on government power. Its influence is seen in the *Declaration of Independence* and in the *U.S. Constitution*.

War Powers Clause: Article 1, Section 8, Clause 11 of the *U.S. Constitution* grants Congress the power to: "Declare War."

Wedge Issue: An issue which divides supporters of a political cause, candidate, or political party. For example, both labor unions and environmentalists are traditionally part of the Democratic Party's base, yet they disagree over drilling for oil in the Arctic National Wildlife Refuge in Alaska.

Whip: A member of the congressional leadership. Both the majority and the minority party in the U.S. House of Representatives and in the U.S. Senate have one. Their paramount responsibility is to count the votes of members within their own caucus while trying to encourage members to toe the party line.

White Primary: System used in the South in the first half of the twentieth century in which non-white voters were excluded from participating in political primaries. This was ruled unconstitutional by the U.S. Supreme Court in 1944, in the case of *Smith v. Allwright.*

Wilmot Proviso: In 1846, President James K. Polk requested a $2 million appropriation to purchase land from Mexico. U.S. Representative David Wilmot (D-PA) proposed a rider to the legislation to prevent slavery in the new acquisition. It passed the U.S. House of Representatives but was tabled in the U.S. Senate. The rider finally passed in 1862. By that time, Wilmot was no longer in Congress.

Wingnut: Term of Derision for a conservative.

Winner-Take-All: The Candidate who garners the most votes wins the election.

Writ of *Certiorari:* Request of the court to review a case.

Writ of habeas corpus: Latin for "To present the body." This refers to the right of a defendant to appear before a judge and hear the charges against leveled against him/her.

Writ of *Mandamus*: A court order usually requiring a person or corporation to take some specific action.

Unitary State: A system where the Federal Government reigns supreme over the states, and where state power is only what is explicitly granted to them by the Federal Government.

***U.S. Constitution*:** The governing authority of the United States. The document was adopted on September 17, 1787 by the Constitutional Convention and Ratified on June 21, 1788. Thirty-nine Delegates signed it.

Yellow Dog Democrat: A loyal Democrat. This term originally referred to an Alabama Democrat in 1928 who voted for the Democratic party's Presidential nominee Al Smith, despite their misgivings over his Catholicism.

Index

Index

Index

Index

Index

Index

Index

Index

Index

Index

34606836R00172

Made in the USA
Columbia, SC
30 November 2018